day trips® series

day trips® from
the twin cities

second edition

getaway ideas for the local traveler

lisa meyers mcclintick

Globe
Pequot

Essex, Connecticut

Globe
Pequot

An imprint of Globe Pequot, the trade division of
The Rowman & Littlefield Publishing Group, Inc.
4501 Forbes Blvd., Ste. 200
Lanham, MD 20706
www.rowman.com

Distributed by NATIONAL BOOK NETWORK

Copyright © 2024 by the Rowman & Littlefield Publishing Group, Inc.

British Library Cataloguing in Publication Information available
ISSN 2324–8130
ISBN 978-1-4930-7581-2 (paper: alk paper)
ISBN 978-1-4930-7582-9 (electronic)

♾™ The paper used in this publication meets the minimum requirements of American National Standard for Information Sciences—Permanence of Paper for Printed Library Materials, ANSI/NISO Z39.48-1992.

contents

introduction x
using this guide xii

north

day trip 01

brainerd lakes' up-north escape 2
brainerd, mn. 2
nisswa, mn. 10

day trip 02

paul bunyan byway & family fun . . . 15
pequot lakes, mn 15
breezy point, mn 18
crosslake, mn. 19

day trip 03

lake mille lacs & ojibwe heritage. . . 22
onamia, mn 24
isle, mn. 27

day trip 04

cuyuna lakes & red-dirt adventures 28
crosby-ironton, mn. 28

day trip 05

northern rivers, rapids & forests . . . 35
hinckley, mn 37
sandstone, mn 39
moose lake, mn 40
cloquet-carlton, mn 42

day trip 06

**duluth's superior
    scenery & shipping** 44
skyline parkway 46

lincoln park. 47
canal park & downtown 49
east duluth, mn 56

northeast

day trip 01

ice age geology & scandinavians . . 60
taylors falls, mn 62
st. croix falls, wi 64
scandia, mn 66
lindstrom, mn 67

day trip 02

**the birkie, fat-tire races &
    giant fish**. 69
hayward, wi 71
cable, wi. 74

east

day trip 01

**shops, cycling & charm
    on the st. croix**. 77
stillwater, mn 77

day trip 02

**red cedar & chippewa
    river valleys** 84
menomonie, wi. 84
chippewa falls, wi. 88
eau claire, wi 91

southeast

day trip 01
wisconsin's great river road 97
stockholm, wi 99
pepin, wi 101
alma, wi 102
fountain city, wi 105

day trip 02
boots, pottery & riverboats 107
red wing, mn 107

day trip 03
eagles, toys & lake pepin 114
lake city, mn 114
wabasha, mn 117

day trip 04
the island city
    below the bluffs 121
winona, mn 121

day trip 05
caves, trails and root
    river floats 128
lanesboro, mn 128
preston 134

south

day trip 01
legacy of health & hospitality 137
rochester, mn 137

day trip 02
cannon river, colleges &
    jesse james 144
northfield, mn 144

day trip 03
I-35 river towns 151
faribault, mn 153
owatonna, mn 155

southwest

day trip 01
minnesota river valley orchards &
    sweets 158
jordan, mn 158
henderson, mn 161
st. peter, mn 162

day trip 02
waterfalls, bison & bike trails 165
mankato, mn 165

day trip 03
a taste of Germany 171
new ulm, mn 171

west

day trip 01
water skis & glacial lakes 178
spicer, mn 178
new london, mn 181

northwest

day trip 01
rocking in the granite city 184
st. cloud, mn 184

day trip 02
saints, scribes & lake wobegon . . . 191
st. joseph-collegeville, mn 191

day trip 03

land of vikings & lakes 198

alexandria, mn 198

day trip 04

lindbergh & the mississippi 203

little falls, mn. 203

appendix a: regional information. . 210

appendix b:

    festivals & celebrations 214

index 219

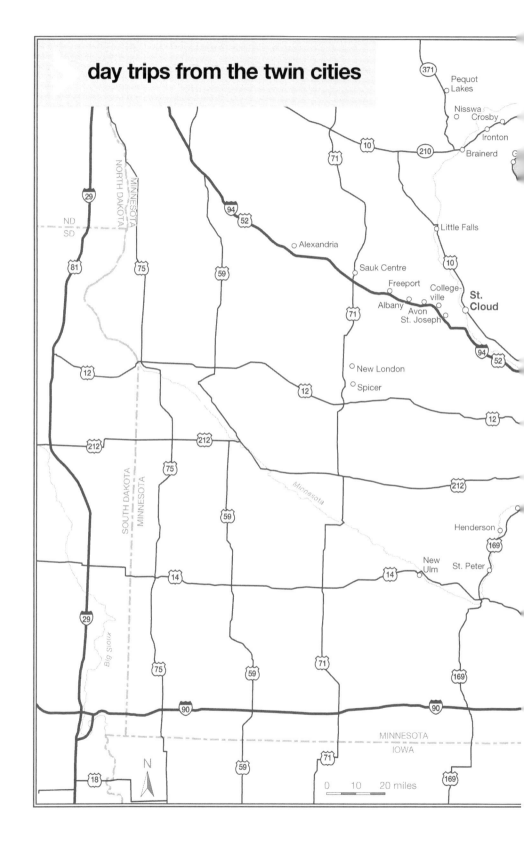

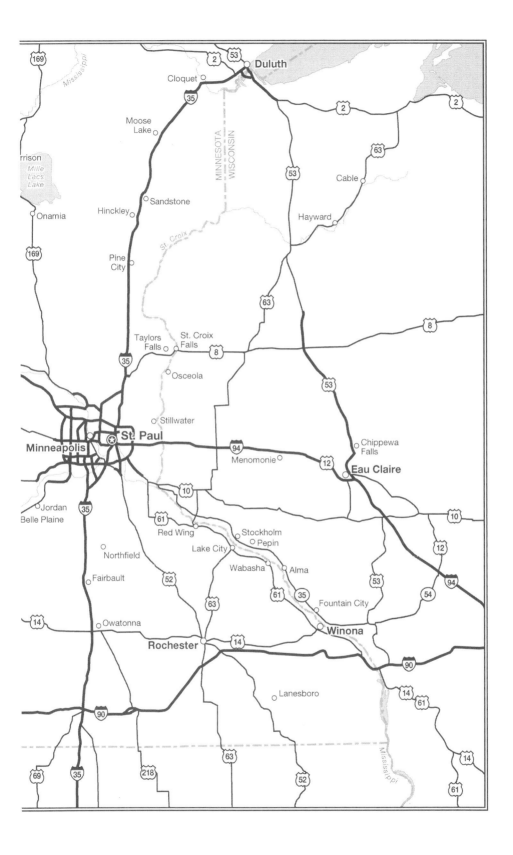

about the author

Award-winning writer and photographer Lisa Meyers McClintick has written hundreds of travel features for *USA Today*'s *Go Escape* publications, *Midwest Living,* Minneapolis *Star Tribune, AAA Living,* and more since 2000. She also wrote two editions of *The Dakotas Off the Beaten Path* (Globe Pequot Press, 2010 and 2015) and the first *Day Trips from the Twin Cities* in 2012.

She grew up in Prior Lake and worked at newspapers in central and southern Minnesota until she and her husband, Bob, put down roots in St. Cloud. They've explored most corners of the Upper Midwest with their son and fraternal twin daughters, always seeking great scenery, hands-on learning, active adventures, sweet bakeries, and great local food and drinks. As a lifelong nature lover and volunteer master naturalist, she's thrilled to live near 70-plus state parks, the mighty Mississippi, and more than 10,000 lakes.

You can reach her @minnelisa on Instagram, @lisamcclintick on X, or lisa-meyers-mcclintick at linkedin.com.

 # acknowledgments

Endless gratitude goes to my husband, Bob, who has been my partner and a fellow storyteller and editor since we fell in love at our college newspaper. You are my home—more than any address we've had.

Thanks, too, to our children, Jonathan, Katie, and Kylie, who gamely hit the road with me over the years and provided helpful input, and to my parents, Lyn and Rik, for planting the travel bug early, always offering encouragement, and sharing the great places they discover. To the rest of our extended family and friends—especially the Quartet—know that your support and enthusiasm take me farther than a full tank of gas.

Cheers to the Minnesota and Wisconsin communities who support creative visions, nurture talent, value the outdoors, and preserve historic sites that turn towns into memorable getaways. Thank you to Globe Pequot and editor Greta Schmitz for inviting me to tell their stories once again.

introduction

I've been lucky. For most of my life I've lived in Minnesota, with a few wonderful years in Hawaii and Germany that helped me appreciate what makes my home state stand out.

Within a 2- to 3-hour drive from the Twin Cities you can:

- Enjoy a coastal getaway along the world's largest freshwater lake and most-inland port city.

- Reach many of the state's 11,842 inland lakes, plus prime fishing lakes and rivers in Wisconsin.

- Follow the scenic beginnings of the Mississippi River, the world's fourth-longest river system when you include the Missouri River.

- Explore more than 30 state parks, as well as state and national forests and recreation areas with beaches, museums, and trails to paddle, hike, bike, ski, or snowshoe.

- Taste the delicious bounty from farms, orchards, wineries, cideries, and breweries that grow produce developed especially for this northern climate.

- Watch for wildlife and birds along one of the world's busiest migration routes.

The Twin Cities, which grew around the confluence of the Mississippi, Minnesota, and St. Croix Rivers, is also surrounded by many landscapes. To experience them, hit the road and listen for the hum of history. Picture oxcarts and wagons creaking and squeaking across western prairies. Hear the thunk of axes and crack of old-growth pines as lumberjacks took down the Northwoods and trains whistled and clattered across the land. Feel the heartbeat and rhythm in Dakota and Ojibwe drumming, singing, language and enduring cultures.

The more you explore, the more chapters of history click together. Rivers brought fur traders and explorers into a land of indigenous communities, followed by a flood of pioneers from New England, Scandinavia, Germany, and Ireland. My family's ancestors were among them, establishing villages in central Wisconsin and along the Minnesota River near New Ulm.

Then came the lumber barons and titans of industry with railroads, shipping, and mining. They had ambitious visions, leaving their mark with opulent commercial buildings and prosperous neighborhoods.

In the last decade since the first *Day Trips* guidebook came out, more cities are embracing their rivers and lakefronts, bike trails are extending, artists are contributing public sculptures and vibrant murals, and there's a fresh sense of connection as more small businesses, such as breweries and coffee shops, open with their own character and vibe.

I humbly offer four challenges for you in your travels:

1. Don't put off plans and wait for the perfect day or most idyllic weather to go exploring. Just go. Each season has its own soundtrack and scenery that provide a fresh experience in even the most familiar destinations. The bare trees of March in Mississippi River Bluff Country provide the clearest views for watching bald eagles soar across the water. Spring rains make waterfalls thunder and fire up the annual spring peeper chorus. November storms churn Lake Superior waves and attract freshwater surfers. Shoulder seasons let you avoid crowds and have the coziest cafes mostly to yourself.

2. Ditch your vehicle. Trade it for another mode of transportation. Borrow a canoe or kayak. Grab a seat on a scenic train ride or paddleboat. Give zip-lining a try—or floating above the St. Croix River Valley in a hot air balloon.

3. Taste each season by seeking out a new-to-you farm, creamery, orchard, or farm-to-table eatery. They'll make the best of the freshest, most-local ingredients.

4. Finally, write a wish list on the inside cover of this guide. Figure out what you enjoy the most and start exploring!

using this guide

Day Trips from the Twin Cities is organized by general direction from Minneapolis and St. Paul: north, northeast, east, southeast, south, southwest, west, and northwest. It doesn't include every worthy destination, but instead highlights 25 trips that appeal to many travelers: families on a budget, adventurers, couples seeking romance and relaxation, friends looking for fun, and history buffs. Given the geography of Minnesota and some parts of western Wisconsin, most destinations feature lakes or rivers. Each day trip can be reached from downtown Minneapolis or St. Paul within 30 minutes to 3 hours. The more popular and distant areas, such as Brainerd Lakes or Duluth, are best enjoyed over a weekend or a week, but they're included due to their popularity, the fact that a super-packed day trip might be all you can manage budget-wise or schedule-wise, and because a scenic drive for some travelers can be as rewarding as the destination.

hours & prices

Peak season in the Upper Midwest generally runs from Memorial Day through Labor Day. Because opening times and prices fluctuate with the ebb and flow of tourists (and even the economy), it's best to check for up-to-date hours, admission, and prices before your trip. That's especially true if you are traveling during the shoulder seasons of spring and fall, which can be a good time to score deals on lodging. Many destinations thrive when the snow flies, but a few shut down for the cold season or for a month or two after the holidays.

pricing key

The price codes for accommodations and restaurants are represented as a scale of one to three dollar signs ($). You can assume that all establishments listed accept major credit cards unless otherwise noted. For details, contact the locations directly.

restaurants

The price code reflects the average price of dinner entrées for two (excluding cocktails, wine, appetizers, desserts, tax, and tip). You should usually expect to pay less for lunch and/or breakfast, when applicable.

$	$10 to $20
$$	$20 to $40
$$$	more than $40

accommodations

Consider this a gauge of the average cost per night of a double-occupancy room during the peak price period (not including tax or extras). Please also note that in some areas a two-night stay (or more) is required during peak season. Prices may spike during festivals and special events as well. Always check online or call to find out if any discounts are available.

$ less than $100
$$ $100 to $175
$$$ more than $175

travel tips

General hours of operation: Please verify hours before you go. It's also possible that places listed in this guidebook may go out of business or be sold to new owners with a different vision.

Seasonal lodging deals: In general, traveling Sunday to Wednesday in any season is more affordable than over weekends, and shoulder seasons typically offer the best discounts, with the exception of holidays and long weekends, such as Presidents' Day. If you want summer discounts, travel or schedule in early June or for the last two weeks of August. Winter, too, can offer affordable escapes, except at places that thrive on skiing, snowmobiling, and ice fishing.

Dress in layers: Summer in the Midwest does not always mean hot and sunny, and there's a reason for the phrase "Cooler by the lake." Plan a few rainy-day options and bring warm layers of clothing just in case. For fall foliage trips, color usually peaks in northern Minnesota by the last week of September and early to mid-October for central and southern Minnesota. It varies from year to year based on weather, but you can check with the Minnesota Department of Natural Resources or with visitor centers for fall color updates.

Sales tax: Minnesota sales tax is 6.875 percent as of this guide's publication, but it can rise to up to 2 percent more in some cities. Clothing and most groceries are exempt from sales tax. Wisconsin state sales taxes are generally 5 percent, with possible increases from additional county or city sale taxes.

Lodging tax: Hotels rarely include tax or gratuities in their published rates. These can raise a hotel rate by more than 12 percent.

Selected lodging & restaurants: Most destinations offer chain hotels and restaurants, which are generally not included in the these chapters, as they operate on standards that are similar across the country. The lodging and restaurant options highlighted are typically local to the area.

Fueling up: If you are near the Wisconsin border and need to fuel up, Minnesota's gas prices often run a nickel or dime cheaper per gallon due to different state taxes. Apps such as GasBuddy can help pinpoint the best deals.

Electric charging stations: If you need to find electric vehicle (EV) charging stations, you can download apps such as Plug Share or ChargePoint or check for locations on the US Department of Energy's Alternative Fuels Data Center website: afdc.energy.gov.

travel tips

carry a road map

While GPS will be reliable for most locations in this book, it's wise to have a paper map as backup, especially for remote areas. Most visitor guides have maps included, or you can grab a map at state tourism visitor centers.

follow the speed limits

- While speed limits are up to 70 miles per hour on rural interstates, they drop down to 55–60 mph as you near city limits.

- Law enforcement doubles the fines for speeding if you're caught in a construction zone. Check online with apps such as MN 511 to be prepared for detours, slowdowns, and lower speed limits. Reroute if necessary and always stay buckled up.

beware of deer

- Thousands of accidents are caused each year by deer crossing the roads. The collisions mostly cause vehicle damage, but they can be fatal, especially for motorcyclists.

- Watch carefully along roadways, especially ones marked with deer crossing signs, those in wooded areas, or roads that have forest on one side and crops on the other. Be especially vigilant in late May to early June when fawns are out and in the peak collision months of October and November when crop harvests, deer hunting, and rutting season have more deer on the move.

- If you see a deer, don't swerve! Losing control of a vehicle often leads to more damage than the collision would. Apply brakes immediately and honk your horn.

winter driving

- For winter trips, watch for fog, mist, drifting snow, ice, and the more nebulous and difficult-to-see black ice that forms from car exhaust at major intersections.

- Give yourself extra time to travel and allow more space between your vehicle and others in winter.

- Do not crowd snowplow crews clearing highways.

- Keep jumper cables in your trunk or ask resorts about battery plug-ins during winter's coldest months.

- Keep your windshield fluid reservoir filled during the slushy winter meltdown.

- Maintain good tlre pressure and treads that also help during sleet storms or early-summer downpours.

- Watch weather forecasts and check road conditions before heading out at 511mn.org or 511wi.gov or by downloading the apps, which also can be helpful during construction season.

highway designations

Major state and federal highways will be listed in this book in terms of their numbered designations, with a few secondary references used most often by residents. US 61, for example, is also part of the North Shore Scenic Byway along Lake Superior or the Great River Road south of Red Wing. "CR" refers to a county road.

where to get more information

Day Trips attempts to cover a variety of bases and interests, but if you're looking for additional material, you'll find links to local tourism bureaus in most introductory paragraphs and in the appendix. Check community social media sites, tap their websites and blogs, and pick up printed brochures or read digital copies online. Here are the best one-stop resources:

minnesota

Explore Minnesota Office of Tourism
121 Seventh Place East
Suite 360
St. Paul, MN 55101
(651) 556-8465, (888) VISITMN [847–4866] exploreminnesota.com

Minnesota Department of Natural Resources
500 Lafayette Rd.

St. Paul, MN 55155-4040

(651) 296-6157, (888) 646-6367

dnr.state.mn.us

Minnesota Grown Program

625 Robert St. North

St. Paul, MN 55155-2538

(651) 201-6140

minnesotagrown.com

Minnesota Historical Society

345 W. Kellogg Blvd.

St. Paul, MN 55102-1906

(651) 259-3000

mnhs.org

wisconsin

Wisconsin Department of Tourism

201 W. Washington Ave.

PO Box 8690

Madison, WI 53708-8690

(800) 432-8747, (608) 266-2161

travelwisconsin.com

Wisconsin Department of Natural Resources

101 S. Webster St.

PO Box 7921

Madison, WI 53707-7921

(888) 936-7463, (608) 266-2621

dnr.wi.gov

Wisconsin Historical Society

816 State St.

Madison, WI 53706

(608) 264-6535

wisconsinhistory.org

north

day trip 01

>>> **brainerd lakes' up-north escape:**
brainerd, mn; nisswa, mn

When Minnesotans say they're going "Up North," chances are good they're heading toward Brainerd Lakes and beyond. With close to 400 lakes and hundreds of lodging options, this area has been a beloved getaway for more than a century. Families can seek a resort and lake to fit their style—from a place that's small and intimate for pad-dling, pontoon rides, and potlucks to sprawling legendary resorts with pools, waterskiing, wakeboarding, trophy fishing, kids' camps. and more activities than you can fit into a full week at the lake.

brainerd, mn

The City of Brainerd straddles the Mississippi River and blends into Baxter, which has the MN 371 retail corridor. Together they serve as the hub for an area population that reaches close to 90,000 with full-time residents, seasonal residents, and vacationers. The most popular destinations perch along the shores of 9,947-acre Gull Lake and seven others in a chain linked by the Gull River. It buzzes with water sports, pontoon and pleasure cruis-ers, and early-morning anglers hoping to hook a walleye or other trophy fish.

That said, there is plenty to do away from the lakes as well. Nostalgic Paul Bunyan Land has been making supersized family memories for generations. Ask any adult who experienced the childhood shock of seeing its iconic 26-foot-tall lumberjack, who not only talks but greets everyone by name. Families can also bike the 115-mile Paul Bunyan State

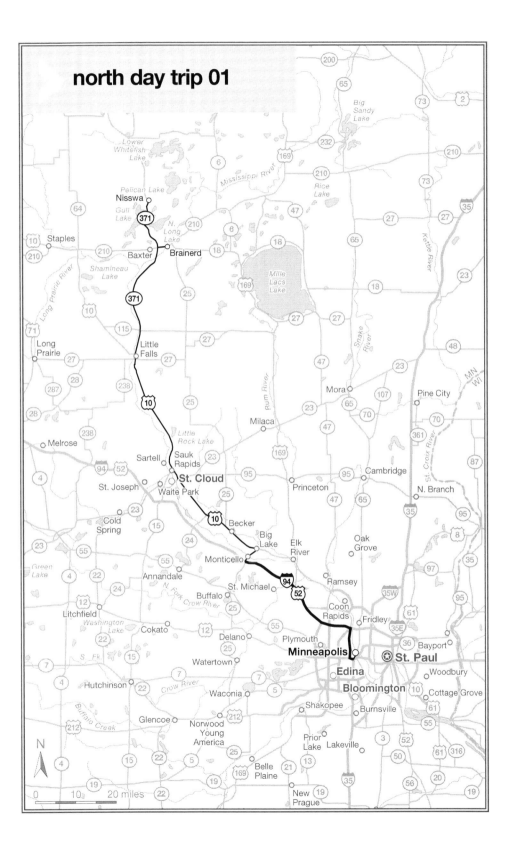

Trail, feed a giraffe and ride a camel at Safari North Wildlife Park, zip above the pines, splash through indoor water parks, putt through pirate-themed minigolf, or feel the rib-cage rumble of full-throttle motorsports at the famed Brainerd International Raceway.

You can find dining throughout the area, as well as restaurants, bakeries, breweries, distilleries, boutiques, and bike shops in downtown Brainerd and along MN 371.

The area may be quieter in the winter, but it's never boring as Brainerd rolls out snow-mobiling, dogsled rides, skating, hockey rinks, skiing, and the world's largest ice-fishing contest—a sight to behold, with 10,000 ice holes drilled into Hole in the Day Bay.

getting there

Take I-94 to MN 25, exiting at Monticello. Head east just over 3 miles, crossing the Mississippi River and connecting with US 10 as you reach Big Lake. Follow US 10 north for 60 miles until the highway splits. Stay right to follow MN 371 to Brainerd-Baxter.

Word of advice: Leave early for summer weekend getaways or pack your patience. Cabin traffic can be heavy as Twin Citians vacationers and cabin owners flood north on Friday and home again on Sunday.

where to go

Brainerd International Raceway and Resort. 5523 Birchdale Rd.; (866) 444-4455; birmn.com. Brainerd revs and rumbles into a racing frenzy every August when it hosts the Lucas Oil NHRA Nationals. More than 110,000 people pack the raceway for the legendary race that stretches across four days. It's often cited as one of the favorite stops for race teams and fans alike because of on-site camping at what's affectionately called "The Zoo." The more-than-40-year-old BIR hosts races throughout the summer, such as muscle car races, bracket drag racing, snowmobile watercross races, the MotoAmerica Superbike Racing, and street-car showdown.

Raceway lodging options include 164 sites in the Pleasureland RV VIP Campground and 12 deluxe condos that face the infield and grandstands. There are 200 acres for open camping as well.

Racing fans can also get behind the wheel and on the track at BIR's Performance Driving School. Instructors give professional racing lessons or teach you how to handle your own car better to prevent accidents.

Brainerd Lakes Area Welcome Center. 7393 MN 371 South; (800) 450-2838; explorebrainerdlakes.com. With a visitor center floor that literally maps out the area's lakes, this is an ideal place to start your trip. Sandwiched between north- and southbound lanes of the highway, it stays well stocked with brochures and an impressive gift shop. Don't forget to take a photo with the almost 12-foot-tall Paul Bunyan statue out front. You can find additional welcome centers in Pequot Lakes and Crosslake.

Brainerd Zip Line Tour. 9898 CR 77 SW, Nisswa; (218) 656-1111. If you're craving an eagle's-eye view of the area, this zip line tour runs during Mount Ski Gull's offseason and offers 15-mile views of state forest and Gull Lake. Rates start at $85 per person.

Crow Wing State Park. 3124 State Park Rd.; (218) 825-3075; dnr.state.mn.us. Head west of the Brainerd Lakes Visitor Center to reach this park that preserves a chapel and former fur trader's house from Old Crow Wing, a town that boomed along the Mississippi River before railroads routed people to Brainerd. You'll find a camper cabin, 59 campsites, scenic stretches to paddle, riverside trails, and a southern entry point for the paved Paul Bunyan State Trail. Bike into Brainerd, or pick your own distance on the 115-mile trail stretching to Bemidji.

Gull Lake Cruises. 11000 Craguns Dr. (at Cragun's Resort); (833) 232-0317; gulllake cruises.com. Public cruises offer a chance to get on Gull Lake (the largest on the Gull Chain of Lakes), see lakeshore homes and resorts, and enjoy the themed trips with brunch, lunch, dinner, desserts, sunsets, and live music.

Gull Lake Recreational Area. 10867 E. Gull Lake Dr.; (218) 829-3334; recreation.gov. Tucked away in the woods, this campground run by the US Army Corps of Engineers includes a public beach, fishing pier, boat launch, picnic area and grills, and the popular East Gull Lake Trail, which is paved for 7 miles. Most people don't realize it's also on the National Register of Historic Places—not for the 1912 dam but for the 12 complete burial mounds and several partial ones that date back to the Woodland Culture and an ancient village along the lake. The campground is open May through early October.

Northern Pacific Center. 1511 Northern Pacific Rd.; (218) 270-8113; northernpacific center.com. Find fun apparel, home decor, upcycling, and gifts in The Shoppes at Northern Pacific Center. An assortment of local boutiques such as the Frugal Farmhouse, the Vintage Fern, and Pickin Sistas can be found in Building No. 2 of the historic railroad complex. You can also grab a comfy couch for coffee flights, lemonade flights, and tea at Loco Express Coffeehouse and Boutique or satisfy your sweet tooth with flavored popcorn, ice cream, candy, and toys at Goody's Gourmet Treats.

Northland Kart Kountry. 17568 MN 371; (218) 454-1602; northlandkartkountry.com. Get behind the wheel of Indy Viper, Bullit or Can Am go-karts to race around multiple tracks. Other options include off-road vehicles, water wars, batting cages, a bungee bounce, climb-ing wall, minigolf, and more for kids or adults who want to let loose and feel like one for a few hours. Prices start at $8 per go-kart ride.

Paul Bunyan Land and This Old Farm. 17553 MN 18; (218) 764-2524; paulbunyanland .com. If there could be one icon for generations of Brainerd-bound vacationers, award that title to this talking Paul Bunyan who greets kids by name as they head into this amusement park. The nostalgia continues with a Tilt-A-Whirl, Ferris wheel, and other fair favorites. Paul

bring on winter fun

While biking, golfing, and boating rule the summer, don't overlook the exhilaration of winter fun. Stop at the Brainerd Lakes Area Welcome Center or check online for more details on trails and equipment rental.

Snowmobiling

About 1,200 miles of trails radiate through the Brainerd area. For distance and a smooth ride, head across Gull Lake and catch the Paul Bunyan Trail near Nisswa. It's a 50-mile cruise to Walker and Leech Lake or about a 6-hour round trip with lunch stop. Find more-challenging loop trails through the Pillsbury State Forest. Cragun's Resort rents the state's largest fleet of snowmobiles plus full winter gear if needed.

__Note:__ Anyone born after 1976 is required to take an online safety certification course before operating snowmobiles. Find details at dnr.state.mn.us.

Cross-country Skiing

You'll find more than 200 miles of Nordic ski trails throughout the area. Northland Arboretum features 12 kilometers of groomed trails through jack pine and birch trees, with 5 kilometers lit for nighttime skiing. 14250 Conservation Dr., Baxter; (218) 829-8770; northlandarb.org.

Other popular options include 20 kilometers of trails through Grand View Lodge's Pines Golf Course; 10 kilometers of trails at Crow Wing State Park; and Pine Beach cross-country ski trails, a network of 0.5- to 3.5-mile loops that cross the Legacy and Classic golf courses, circle Cragun's and Kavanaugh's resort properties, and stretch into Pillsbury State Forest.

You'll need a Minnesota Ski Pass to help fund grooming for trails through state parks or forests. It costs $10/day or $25/season. Buy one online at dnr.state.mn .us or by phone at (888) 665-4236.

Downhill Skiing

Ski Gull offers 12 runs, a terrain park, and a tubing hill on the west side of Gull Lake. It's an ideal place to learn, with gentle terrain and lessons from the staff at this community-run nonprofit organization. Open weekends and holidays through-out the winter. Lift tickets start at $20 for youths 6–17; $26 for adults on weekday afternoons. 9898 CR 77, Nisswa; (218) 963-4353; skigull.com.

Bunyan sat for decades near the main intersection of MN 371 and MN 210 until the attraction moved 8 miles east of Brainerd and joined with This Old Farm. You can spend half the day with carnival rides and a petting zoo and the other half wandering more than three dozen historic buildings at Pioneer Village, with schoolrooms, a set piece from the movie *Iron Will*, classic cars and gas pumps, and a logging camp. Open Friday through Tuesday Memorial Day weekend through Labor Day. The 32 campsites are open spring through fall. Haunted Hidden Hollows also opens in the fall. Admission with unlimited rides starts at $19.

Paul Bunyan State Trail. Brainerd to Bemidji; paulbunyantrail.com. This 119-mile trail provides a bikers' and snowmobilers' paradise, letting them zip between 14 towns along the easy grade of this former railway line through forest and along lakes. It's one of the country's oldest and longest Rails-to-Trails projects. Find parking and trail access spots at Crow Wing State Park, Brainerd, Merrifield, Nisswa, Pequot Lakes, Jenkins, Pine River, Backus, Hackensack, and Walker. Need a bike? Rent one in downtown Brainerd (Easy Rider; 415 Washington St.; 218-829-5516; easyriders.com) or Nisswa (Up North Bike Rentals; 5476 City Hall St.; 218-821-5399; upnorthbikerentals.com). If you want to try out just one section of trail, cruise the 7 miles from Nisswa to Pequot Lakes. Long-distance bicyclists can connect to the Heartland Trail as well, for an additional 49 miles.

Pirate's Cove. 5197 Birchdale Rd.; (218) 828-9002; piratescove.com. This souped-up, swashbuckling minigolf course is one of 25 in the nation and the only one in Minnesota. Its holes lead players through caves (watch out for water hazards!), across a pirate ship, over footbridges, under waterfalls, and past a battle scene where a cannon occasionally booms. Make sure to read the pirate facts and history scattered throughout the course, which is challenging—and entertaining—even for adults. Choose the Captain's Course, Blackbeard's Challenge, or a combo deal for all 36 holes. Open the last week in April through the third week in October. Minigolf prices start at $8.95 kids 4 to 12 and $9.95 (adults).

Safari North Wildlife Park. 8493 MN 371; (218) 454-1662; safarinorth.com. This nice-sized zoo just off MN 371, 2 miles north of the welcome center, offers the chance to feed giraffes, coax parakeets onto your head or hands, ride camels, gawk at alligators, and while away an afternoon with mammals, reptiles, and birds from the region, Africa, and other parts of the globe. A train runs through the 10-acre zoo for an extra fee. Open daily early May through early October; $20, adults; $16, ages 2–12.

where to eat

Bar Harbor Supper Club. 8164 Interlachen Rd.; (218) 963-2568; barharborsupperclub .com. If you want an upscale date night that includes live music and lakeside scenery, head to this supper club with its lighthouse-inspired tower on the Gull Lake Causeway. Originally a gambling hall and bar in 1937, it's now a place for dinners such as dry-aged filet mignon and crab-topped halibut, happy hours watching boats motor by, or dancing until dark. Open seasonally for dinner Wednesday to Sunday. $$$.

Dunmire's on the Lake. 19090 MN 371; (218) 454–069; dunmiresbar.com. This North Long Lake destination aims for an elegant night out with caviar appetizers, pork chops glazed with maple bacon jam, seafood pasta and lobster tails, plus more casual burgers and sandwiches. Leave room for tiramisu or carrot cake. $$.

Ernie's on Gull. 10424 Gull Point Rd., East Gull Lake; (218) 829-3918; erniesongull.com. This restaurant and full-service marina tucked along a Gull Lake peninsula welcomes diners arriving by car, boat, or snowmobile. Look for gourmet burgers such as one served on a French toast bun with bacon and maple syrup or a ground lamb patty with tzatziki and feta, walleye tacos with kohlrabi slaw, or seasonally influenced tenderloins and pastas. The location includes the seasonal **On Point Burger Co.** on the patio. $$.

Knotty Pine Bakery. 707 Laurel St.; (218) 454-2470; knottypinebakery.com. Start the day with ham-and-cheese biscuits, mini fruit pies, and festive sugar cookies before a photo session by the vibrant "You Betcha" mural around the corner or downtown shopping at Cat-Tale's Books and Gifts, Fancy Pants Chocolates, the Crossing Arts Alliance, and boutiques. $.

The Local 218. 723 Mill Ave; (218) 270-3195; local-218.com. Go casual with a variety of sandwich favorites, such as Philly cheesesteak and shrimp po'boys, or elevate to artfully plated Angus beef steaks, lobster tails, pistachio-crusted walleye, daily specials such as sushi, and desserts. Open for lunch and dinner Tuesday through Saturday plus Sunday for brunch. $$.

Notch 8. 1551 Northern Pacific Rd.; (218) 454-6688; notch8brainerd.com. This chow house and drinkery tucked into the historic Northern Pacific Center puts fun twists on casual favorites such as a barbecue burger made with brisket, short rib, and ground chuck; sushi nachos; wings with a flight of seven sauces; pizzas such as one topped with stout beer sausage, homemade Italian sausage, and wild mushrooms or one with dill pickles, cream cheese, ham and white wine cream sauce. Wash it down with local brews or finish sweetly with mini-doughnuts dipped in caramel, chocolate, and raspberry sauce. $–$$.

Zorbaz. 8105 Lost Lake Rd., Nisswa; (218) 963-4790; zorbaz.com. This popular up-north pizza chain sits along Gull Lake's causeway with a steady parade of boats puttering by. They have all the expected pizzas, along with a Greek chicken pizza, one inspired by a Reuben sandwich, and a Thai-spiced creation with bacon, onions, pineapple, and banana peppers. Cool down with one of 48 beer selections, grab a spot on the patio, join a beach volleyball game, or kick back to music provided by a DJ or band. $–$$.

where to stay

Arrowwood Lodge at Brainerd Lakes. 6967 Lake Forest Rd., Baxter; (218) 822-5634; arrowwoodbrainerdlodge.com. A Paul Bunyan–themed 30,000-square-foot water park with holographic slides, 102 rooms that sleep two to eight guests, log cabin decor, and free breakfast buffet make this an easy family getaway. Specialty suites include a cinema suite, kitchen suite, and kids' suite with bunks and 3-D murals. Check the website for offseason waterpark hours. $$.

Cragun's Resort. 11000 Craguns Dr.; (800) 272-4867; craguns.com. This venerable and sprawling resort encompasses more than 200 units along a generous stretch of Gull Lake. Besides its history and size, the depth of year-round activities, lakeside outdoor pool and sundeck, indoor pool and play area, and 54 golf holes at The Legacy courses make this resort stand out. Staff offer guided fishing, golf lessons, a summer kids' camp, and waterskiing sessions and organize welcome receptions and socials. You can also rent just about anything here: bikes, wakeboards, boats, snowmobiles, ice houses, skates, and more. Lodging choices include lakeview lodge rooms with fireplaces and balconies, vintage lakeside cabins, reunion houses, and new vacation homes along the golf course. $$–$$$.

Kavanaugh's Sylvan Lake Resort. 1685 Kavanaugh Dr., East Gull Lake; (218) 829-5226; kavanaughs.com. This resort's blend of more than 50 units, mostly lakeside condos and luxury cottages with patios and fireplaces, comes with amenities such as tennis or pickleball courts, basketball courts, playgrounds, and indoor and outdoor pools in addition to bike trails. Watch for a romantic skating rink and Nordic ski trails in the winter and easy access to 108 golf holes within 1 mile in the warm months. $$–$$$.

world's largest ice-fishing contest

Put this on your bucket list: Witness or join in the world's largest charitable ice-fishing contest. The Brainerd Jaycees drill more than 10,000 holes into Gull Lake's **Hole in the Day Bay.** *The pure spectacle of that many holes, more than $200,000 in prizes (including trucks and snowmobiles), and a festive atmosphere lure more than 10,000 anglers from across the country and beyond. The annual* **Brainerd Jaycees Ice-Fishing Extravaganza** *also draws about 2,000 spectators (icefishing.org). Dress smart and in layers. Boot- and hand-warmers help. The show goes on even with below-zero temperatures and wicked windchills.*

Madden's on Gull Lake. 11266 Pine Beach Peninsula Rd.; (218) 829-2811; maddens .com. As one of the area's largest and most legendary resorts—and nearing the century mark—Madden's also ranks among the top resorts in the Midwest according to travel magazines such as *Travel + Leisure* and *Condé Nast Traveler*. Its 287 seasonal units (historic hotel rooms, condos, villas, cabins and reunion houses) sprawl across Pine Beach Peninsula on 1,000 acres with enough to do that most guests stay put—especially if they're on the meal plan with seven eateries and restaurants. Golfers come for The Classic and three additional courses. Other activities including a summer Adventure Cove for kids, inflatable playgrounds on the water, lawn bowling, croquet, tennis, trail rides, paddleboarding, waterskiing and wakeboarding lessons, guided fishing, biking, and even seaplane certification. A saltwater pool was added to the main lodge's deck in 2023, and at Madden's spa, guests can get pedicures and manicures while gazing at the lake or settle in for massage and body treatments. The resort runs from the last weekend in April through late October. $$–$$$.

Three Bears Waterpark. 15739 Audubon Way; (218) 828-3232; brainerdhi.com. Holiday Inn Express and Suites in Baxter offers four passes to its indoor waterpark for hotel guests. Passes may also be available to the public Sunday through Thursday. Call for current hours and fees.

Train Bell Resort. 21489 Train Bell Rd., Merrifield; (218) 829-4941; trainbellresort.com. This smaller old-fashioned family resort has been chugging along for more than a century, specializing in lighthearted themed activities throughout the summer such as weekly dances, medallion hunts, minnow races, and a ride on their Train Bell Express. Cabins, condos, villas, and a reunion home sit between the North Long Lake Beach and Paul Bunyan Bike Trails. $$$.

nisswa, mn

Twenty miles north of Brainerd on MN 371, Nisswa's concentrated downtown rules as the area's top shopping destination. It's classy enough to keep big-city shoppers happy, but down-to-earth, too. Look for Paul Bunyan on the totem pole and turtles all over town. The turtles offer a nod to Nisswa's almost 50-year tradition of turtle races at 2 p.m. every Wednesday from mid-June through mid-August. You can bring your own turtle, pick one from a bucket, or just enjoy cheering them on for an old-fashioned afternoon.

getting there

Continue on MN 371 about 20 miles north of Brainerd-Baxter to reach Nisswa. Exit at CR 18 to head downtown.

where to go

Adventure to Go. 4871 CR 77; (218) 820-1301; adventuretogomn.com. Rent an inflatable paddleboard, kayak, or bike here or arrange a delivery to your vacation destination to explore the lakes and trails. Safety equipment included.

Glacial Waters Spa. 23521 Nokomis Ave.; (218) 963-8700; grandviewlodge.com. This stand-alone Arts and Crafts–style spa based at Grand View Lodge stays busy year-round with warm fireplaces that feel especially cozy during winter and a salt room added for halotherapy add-ons. Guests can take an 85-minute fragrant soak in a private room with a fireplace and view of surrounding woods, followed by an hour-long massage. A spa cabin allows groups of up to 10 friends to bring in food and drinks and get treatments without following the hushed-voice code of the main spa.

Nisswa Family Fun Waterpark. 4871 CR 77; (218) 820-3046; nisswaoutdoorwaterpark .com. Kids splash down a 465-foot-long body slide, a drop slide, and a family slide with a heated activity pool for cooling off on summer days.

Up North Bike Rentals. 5476 City Hall St.; (218) 821-5399; upnorthbikerentals.com. Rent a bike or surrey for a trip along the Paul Bunyan State Trail. Cruise to Pequot Lakes to the north or Merrifield to the south ($10/hour; $30/day).

where to shop

Here's a sampling of fun places in Nisswa's tightly packed, bustling downtown. Some are seasonal and have shorter winter hours. If you are visiting offseason, verify hours first.

The Chocolate Ox. 25452 Main St., Nisswa; (218) 963-4443; thechocolateox.com. Loaded with nostalgic candy and soda pop, gourmet chocolates, jelly beans, jawbreakers, licorice, and ice cream, don't expect to get in and out of this popular stop quickly. Sweet temptations are everywhere. $.

Lundrigans. 25521 Main St.; (218) 963-2647; lundrigansclothing.com. This store full of stylish, cabin-comfy men's and women's clothing has become an up-north fixture. You'll find everything from Woolrich flannels and Norwegian wool sweaters to breezy dresses for summers on the dock.

get help finding fish

*If you're new to fishing, want to learn new techniques, or simply don't know where to go with 400-plus lakes within a 30-mile radius, a fishing guide can help. You can find many guides available for hire. One of the best-known outfitters is **Walleye Dan Guide Service** (9287 Anderson Rd., 218-839-5598; walleyedan.com). Guides keep tabs on the local fishing scene as it changes throughout the four seasons and daily weather conditions. They also supply the boat, bait, equipment, and expertise for a tasty—or trophy—catch.*

Martin's Sports Shop. 25451 Main St.; (218) 963-2341; martinssportshop.com. Look for the alpine-themed building with flags and you'll find four seasons' worth of sports equipment, along with breathable, warm clothing and gear. Rent bikes, in-line skates, tennis rackets, water skis, wakeboards, snowshoes, and cross-country skis. Open daily.

Nisswa Totem Pole Boutique Marketplace. 25485 Main St.; (218) 961-0045; facebook .com/NisswaTotemPole. This longtime tourist stop still features a totem pole and mechanical rides out front, but the inside has been transformed into a marketplace with handcrafted local decor, gifts such as jewelry, and apparel with regional themes.

Turtle Town Books & Gifts 25491 Main St.; (218) 963-4891; turtletownnisswa.com. Stop in for a light lakeside novel, bestsellers, books on fishing techniques, guides to native flowers and trees, kids' books, and puzzles and games to play on rainy days.

Zaiser's. 25424 Main St.; (218) 963-2404; facebook.com/Zaisers. This red-door boutique blends style, sass, and kitchen savvy with sections of cookware and tools, funky shoes and boots, unique jewelry, bath products, toys, gags and magic tricks, and whimsical gifts such as staplers shaped like fish.

golfers' paradise

It may not be sunny and warm year-round, but Minnesota has long claimed more golfers and golf courses per capita than anywhere else in the United States. The Brainerd Lakes area boasts many of the best, earning endless adoration from national golf magazines, which have named it one of the best 50 golf destinations in the world. The sport's top legends designed several challenging courses here that frame the beauty of Northwoods forest, lakes, and wetlands.

Altogether, there are more than 20 courses within a 45-minute drive of Brainerd. Here are some of the best near Gull Lake:

The Classic at Madden's. *11672 CR 18 West, Brainerd; (218) 829-2811; maddens.com. This course elevated the game at Madden's, which also claims the area's first golf course, Pine Beach East, from the 1930s.*

Dutch Legacy. *11000 Craguns Dr., Brainerd; (218) 825-3700. This Audubon Signature Sanctuary course is one of two Legacy courses at Cragun's Resort. Bobby's Legacy features elevated tees and lake views ($125 for each).*

The Pines Golf Course. *23521 Nokomis Ave., Nisswa; (218) 963-8755; grandviewlodge.com. These 27 holes were carved through the forest ($104).*

where to eat

Big Axe Brewing. 25435 Main St.; (218) 961-2337; bigaxebrewing.com. After two years as a taproom, Big Axe expanded into dining in 2017. Bold wings, brisket, burgers, walleye, and even salads pair with brews such as amber or brown ale, strawberry/guava milkshake IPA, and Endless Summer Kolsch. You can also nosh on something lighter, such as their smoked trout dip with pita chips, and sip house-made cream soda and root beer. In summer you can dine on the patio alongside Samantha French's colorful and cooling mural of a woman underwater. $–$$.

Ganley's Restaurant. 25396 Main St.; (218) 963-2993; ganleysrestaurant.com. This family-owned business has been dishing up hearty breakfasts, classic dinner fare, and local favorites such as the walleye sandwich for more than three decades. You can also grab an ice cream or malt to go at the pickup window. Open for breakfast and lunch. $.

Main Street Alehouse. 25559 Main St.; (218) 961-6724; mainstreetnisswa.com. Go for the 30 tap beers and other spirits, or settle in for a meal that elevates with seasonal, creative sides and sauces. Try a burger made from chuck and short rib with peach chutney, Brie, and cardamom crème fraiche; a cheesesteak with wild mushrooms and house-made beet sauerkraut; or walleye with cherry-almond wild rice. $$.

Northwoods Pub at Grand View Lodge. 23521 Nokomis Ave.; (218) 963-8756; grand viewlodge.com. This casual pub shines during the summer, when you can sit on the shaded patio of Minnesota's most picturesque historic lodge while enjoying glimpses of Gull Lake through the trees. Food ranges from bison burgers and a Minnesota chopped salad with grilled chicken and wild rice to beer-battered walleye fillet with lemon caper remoulade sauce. If you are seeking something more gourmet and upscale, check out Grand View's Cru restaurant or Char steakhouse. $$.

Roundhouse Brewery. 23836 Smiley Rd.; (218) 963-2739; roundhousebrew.com. After outgrowing its Brainerd location, this local craft brewer moved to Nisswa with its Union Station event center, the Wreck Room axe-throwing, and the Dining Car with food such as potstickers and chicken lettuce wraps to smoked brisket and walleye sandwiches. Dogs are welcome on the patio, and you'll find a full line of beers to try, along with sodas and hard seltzers. $$.

Sherwood North. 8789 Interlachen Rd.; (218) 963-6261; sherwoodnorth.com. Enjoy a vintage up-north date night in this log restaurant built in the 1930s. Even the drive here, hugging the outskirts or shores of Gull Lake, can set the mood for an elegant meal with popovers, smoked seafood platter, steaks, and seafood. $$$.

Stonehouse Coffee & Roastery. 25346 S. Main St.; (218) 961-2326; stonehousecoffee .com. You can smell the coffee roasting, not just brewing, at this artsy breakfast hot spot.

The owners travel the globe to choose more than 20 varieties of beans. They also sell fresh-baked scones or muffins and their own pancake mix. $.

Zorbaz. 8105 Lost Lake Rd.; (218) 963-4790; zorbaz.com. This popular up-north pizza chain sits along Gull Lake's causeway with a steady parade of boats puttering by. They have all the expected pizzas, along with a Greek chicken pizza, one inspired by a Reuben sandwich, and a Thai-spiced creation with bacon, onions, pineapple, and banana peppers. Wash them down with one of 48 beers. If it's warm, grab a spot on the patio, join a beach volleyball game, or kick back to music provided by a DJ or band. $–$$.

where to stay

Good Ol' Days Resort. 26050 Oak Ln.; (218) 963-2478; goodoldaysresort.com. Luxury cottages overlook Lower Cullen Lake, while lodge rooms offer a more economical option. The lodge includes an open-hearth fireplace in the living room, a dining area, game room, and four-season porch. A 10-minute walk from Good Ol' Days on the Paul Bunyan Trail runs straight into downtown Nisswa. $$–$$$.

Grand View Lodge. 23521 Nokomis Ave.; (800) 432-3788; grandviewlodge.com. This imposing 1900s log lodge on a hillside above Gull Lake ranks among Minnesota's most picturesque resorts. The sprawling property offers more than 200 lodging options that include rooms in the historic lodge or a new 60-room boutique hotel, cabins along Gull Lake, golf course villas, luxury homes, and reunion houses. Guests dine at on-site restaurants, take pontoon cruises and fishing trips, go on horseback or sleigh rides, unwind at Glacial Waters Spa, soak in multiple hot tubs, and swim at indoor and outdoor pools on the south waterfront and at North Park, a new recreation facility. $$–$$$.

Quarterdeck Resort. 9820 Birch Bay Dr. SW; (218) 963-2482; quarterdeckresort.com. Lodge suites include kitchenettes, fireplaces, and balconies that overlook the west side of Gull Lake. Guests can also stay in lakeside cottages or new beach houses with multiple bedrooms and rent pontoons for scenic lake cruises. $$.

day trip 02

north

>>> **paul bunyan byway & family fun:**
pequot lakes, mn; breezy point resort,
mn; crosslake, mn

If you crave small towns and being farther from the hub of Brainerd-Baxter, keep driving north on MN 371 until you see the Pequot Lakes water tower, painted to look like Paul Bunyan's fishing bobber. You'll find another visitor center, more shops and restaurants, and another large-scale resort and recreational hub as you head east on CR 11 toward Breezy Point. Keep following the lower loop of the 54-mile Paul Bunyan Scenic Byway to Crosslake and back toward Pequot Lakes for more up-north scenery, views of the Whitefish Chain of Lakes, and a taste of Minnesota with friendly waves from pontoons and golf carts or at meat raffles and fish fries.

Small towns peak during summer, when they hum with festivals and weekly events that lure people off the lakes. (Keep an eye out for Elvis crooning at the Breezy Point Marina.) Autumn offers an ideal time for romantic escapes, man-cations, and girlfriend getaways—especially for golfers and anglers. Winter brings recreation from silent sports to snowmobiling and more festivals from Winterfest to Bobber Bocce on Ice—a hybrid of bocce ball and curling.

pequot lakes, mn

Paul Bunyan's fishing bobber doubles as the water tower in this town of 2,400 residents where you can also pose for photos downtown with Babe the Big Blue Ox. It's also a good rest stop for Paul Bunyan State Trail bicyclists or snowmobilers and the gateway to the Paul Bunyan Scenic Byway as it loops east toward the Whitefish Chain of Lakes.

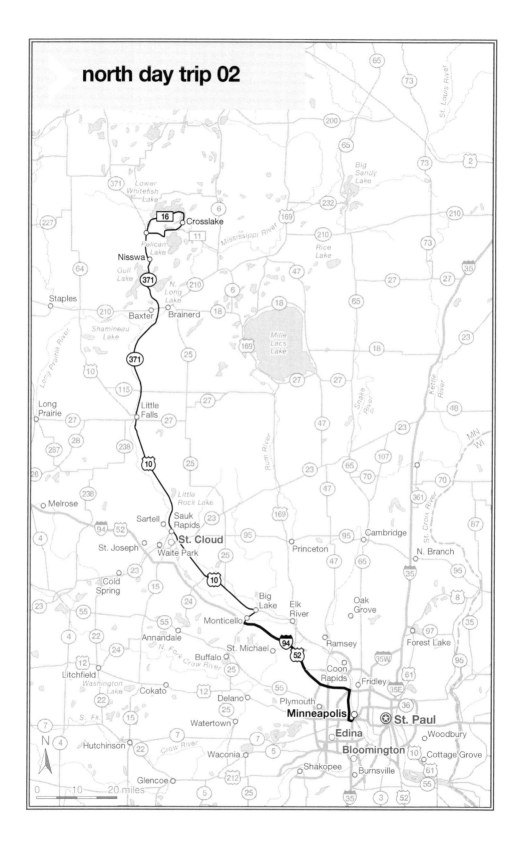

north day trip 02

Downtown is also popular for shopping, with clusters of shops such as Latte' Da Boutique, Leslie's, Fishy Gifts, and others selling Minnesota-themed apparel, games, books, gourmet snacks, craft supplies, and more.

The town's population doubles in early July for its Bean Hole Days, one of the state's most unique festivals. Crews slow-cook wood-fired iron pots of beans that are buried overnight and served the next day. A tasty town tradition since 1938, it's only one of many celebrations you can find here and throughout the area's small towns year-round.

If you visit in the fall, don't miss climbing the fire tower to get above the tree line and see the full spectacle of colors.

getting there

From the Twin Cities, follow I-94 west, exiting at Clearwater. Take MN 24 east to US 10. Follow US 10 north to Little Falls, where you catch MN 371. Follow it north to Pequot Lakes (about a 2.5-hour drive) and the Paul Bunyan Scenic Byway loop.

where to go

Paul Bunyan Scenic Byway. Starting at CR 11 and MN 371; paulbunyanscenicbyway.org. The legend of Paul Bunyan playfully comes to life with interpretive signs and kiosks along this 54-mile scenic drive. The first stop east of Pequot Lakes, Paul M. Thiede Fire Tower Park, lets you climb up the former fire tower to see fall colors blaze across the woods. Download podcasts from the website above to learn more about stops along the byway. The route heads east to Breezy Point, north to Crosslake and Manhattan Beach, then west to Pine River and south to Jenkins.

Pequot Lakes Welcome Center and Trailside Park. 31095 Government Dr.; (218) 568-8911; pequotlakes.com. Get oriented with brochures and maps, burn energy at the playground or on the Paul Bunyan State Trail, watch for Paul Bunyan's giant footprints, and catch a free Saturday-night summer band concert.

The Preserve at Grand View Lodge. 5506 Preserve Blvd.; (218) 568-4944; grandview .com. It's all about the views at The Preserve, with 11 of 18 golf holes beginning with elevated tees.

Whitefish Golf Club. 7883 CR 16; (218) 543-4900; whitefishgolf.com. This 18-hole golf course sits midway between Pequot Lakes and Crosslake, offering another scenic option for anyone preferring to swing a club than cast a fishing pole.

where to eat

A-Pine Family Restaurant. 33039 Old MN 371; (218) 568-8353; apinerestaurant.com. This longtime family restaurant serves up comfort-food breakfast, lunch, and dinner. Even better: Grandma Betty Jane's pies in dozens of flavors, from rhubarb custard to bumble berry and peaches and cream.

Lucky's Tavern. 31020 Government Dr.; (218) 568-4177. Go hungry or share plates so you don't miss appetizers like deep-fried Reuben balls and homemade pizza rolls or its much beloved Hungarian mushroom soup, along with Irish faves such as shepherd's pie and pot-pie, hot beef sandwiches, and meat loaf dinners. $.

MN Traders Co. 31038 Government Dr.; (218) 568-1071; mntradersco.com. This sleek and modern gathering space with a loft and swinging chairs invites people to linger for coffee drinks like the Nordic (expresso, local honey, lavender syrup, and oat milk), gourmet teas with herbs and spice, craft cocktails such as the hot honey peach margarita, or mimosa flights and local brews. Leave room for seasonal eats such as their waffle breakfast sandwich and flatbread pizzas, or split a loaded charcuterie board with friends. $$.

Norway Ridge Supper Club. 34757 CR 39; (218) 543-6136; norwayridge.com. Opened in 1948 as one of northern Minnesota's first supper clubs, Norway Ridge has served generations of diners sourdough-battered appetizers, smoked chicken and ribs, sunfish, walleye, and seafood in its pine-paneled dining room overlooking Kimble Lake. $$$.

Tasty Pizza North. 28921 Peterson Path; (218) 568-4404. This casual eatery, a spin-off of a Twin Cities pizza place dating back to 1963, keeps it old-school with thin, crisp crusts and classic toppings, vegetarian options, and the Tasty Hi-Five (sausage, Canadian bacon, pepperoni, hamburger, and Polish sausage). Meatballs on an Italian roll, spaghetti, and tacos round out the menu. $–$$.

breezy point, mn

East of Pequot Lakes, Breezy Point has about 2,400 residents and is best known as the home to Breezy Point Resort on the shores of Pelican Lake. With four seasons of recreation, a marina, an ice arena, and a conference center, it's big enough to be its own community and hosts several events open to everyone.

getting there

Follow CR 11 about five miles east to Breezy Point.

where to go

Breezy Belle Cruise. 9252 Breezy Point Dr.; (218) 562-7672; breezybelle.com. Take a 2-hour guided tour of Pelican Lake 5 miles east of Pequot Lakes. This 100-passenger paddlewheel boat gets churning every Wednesday and Sunday night during the summer. Reservations must be made at least a day in advance ($14–$23).

Deacon's Lodge Golf Course. 9348 Arnold Palmer Dr.; (218) 562-6262; breezypoint.com. Grand View's most prestigious course was designed by Arnold Palmer to wind through pines, lakes, and wetlands.

Whitebirch Golf Course. 7891 CR 11; (218) 562-7970; breezypoint.com. This championship course boasts more than 6,700 yards of fairways and undulating greens.

where to eat

Dockside Lounge. 9252 Breezy Point Dr.; (218) 562-7170; breezypointresort.com. Breezy Point has several dining options, but this one stands out for its lakeside location, live entertainment during the summer (including Chris Olson's Elvis tribute concerts), and a casual vibe that welcomes diners arriving by boat, snowmobile, bicycle, or vehicle.

where to stay

Breezy Point Resort. 9252 Breezy Point Dr.; (218) 562-7970; breezypointresort.com. This year-round resort with 250 units of hotel rooms, condos, villas, and reunion houses began as a small lakeside escape in 1921 and just keeps growing. Its property includes a marina (218-562-7164) and 14-acre Gooseberry Island for picnics and swimming. $$.

crosslake, mn

If you keep driving north on the Paul Bunyan Scenic Byway, you'll reach **Crosslake.** This town of 1,300 residents hugs the shore of Cross Lake, part of the Whitefish Chain of Lakes which links 13 bodies of water. It tends to be quieter than Gull Lake, Brainerd's resort hub, with smaller resorts and residences along its shores.

Fans of Minnesota's State Bird—the loon—look forward to seeing the bird on the lake and learning more about loons once the three-story National Loon Center is built near the US Army Corps of Engineers campground. The campground includes a public day-use area with a boat ramp, fishing piers, and picnic tables where the Pine River and Pine River dam connect to Cross Lake. It's a short stroll to the town's boutiques and shopping such as The Lake + Company and restaurants.

A bonus for families: Crosslake offers Big Fun Tuesdays from late June through early August. Join in with Paul Bunyan–themed games, including a pancake toss, gunnysack races, minnow races, and fish toss.

For more information, stop at the Crosslake Welcome Center at the corner of CR 3 and MN 66, or call (218) 692-4027.

getting there

Follow CR 11 north and east of Breezy Point for almost 6 miles. At the roundabout, take the third exit to follow CR 3 north about 3 miles to Crosslake. The route is labeled as the Paul Bunyan Scenic Byway.

where to go

Cross Lake Recreation Area. 35507 CR 66; (651) 290-5793; recreation.gov. You can stay at this popular campground with 123 campsites along Cross Lake or park in the day use area to use the boat ramp or enjoy fishing from the pier, swimming, using the playground, picnic areas and pollinator garden.

National Loon Center. (218) 692-5666; nationallooncenter.org. This nonprofit organization is dedicated to telling the story of Minnesota's state bird, known for its expert diving, devoted parenting, and primal calls that echo across the water. You can find a gift shop, The Nest, at 14303 Gould St. until the $18 million interactional, educational, and recreational center is built and ready to open. It's expected to debut in 2025 and continue the organization's longtime mission to keep lakes and fresh water healthy for loons and the entire ecosystem.

where to eat

14 Lakes Brewery. 36846 CR 66; (218) 692-4129; facebook.com/14lakesbrewery. Grab a brew, such as the Pig Lake Peanut Butter Porter, Clamshell Cream Ale, or a sour beer with blueberry, and then play a game of cornhole on the patio, join a loon trivia contest, or relax outside with your favorite pooch. $.

Lake Country Craft and Cones. 36084 CR 66; (218) 692-4411; lakecountrycrafts.com. You can find gifts and local crafts at this homey yellow shop, but it's best known for selling more Kemps ice cream than any other Minnesota ice cream cafe. They scoop close to three dozen flavors and always put a jelly bean in the bottom of the cone. Also available: coffee, shakes, and sandwiches. $.

Maucieri's Italian Bistro. 34650 CR 3; (218) 692-4800; maucieris.com. Look for their secret sauce (or "gravy") slathered on their meatballs, baked rigatoni, meatball sandwiches, pizza, or the Italian Stallion, a sandwich heaped with handmade Italian sausage and cheese. Open for dinner Sunday through Wednesday and lunch and dinner Thursday through Saturday. Closed Monday, October through February. $$.

Moonlite Bay Family Restaurant and Bar. 37627 CR 66; (218) 692-3575; moonlitebay .com. This former dance hall built in 1933 now ranks among the area's favorite stops with its wonderfully retro sign and the option to arrive by boat, car, or snowmobile. Grab a burger, pizza, wrap, or ribs and dine on the spacious patio overlooking Cross Lake's Moonlite Bay and watch for events like the Classic Boat Show and Cardboard Boat Races. $–$$.

where to stay

Black Pine Beach Resort. 10732 CR 16; (218) 543-4714; blackpinebeach.com. This classic family-run resort lets kids roam to the beach with inflatable toys on Pig Lake (part of the Whitefish Chain of Lakes), write a note to the Elf Himself at the Secret Garden, play games, go for a paddle, and try to catch fish for dinner. The 143 knotty-pine cabins range from two to six bedrooms and are available from May 1 to October 31. $$–$$$.

Boyd Lodge. 36539 Silver Peak Road; (800) 450-2693; boydlodge.com. Since 1934 this resort has welcomed guests like family with turtle races, scavenger hunts, root beer floats and movie nights, along with fishing and swimming. They offer loft cabins and modern cottages with up to four bedrooms, mostly along Rush Lake. Guests can boat from Rush Lake or cross a pond bridge to reach Lower Whitefish Lake with the resort's main beach and additional docks to access the Whitefish Chain of Lakes. $$–$$$.

Clamshell Beach Resort. 35197 S. Clamshell Dr.; (218) 851-5309; clamshellbeach. com. This longtime resort on the Whitefish Chain of Lakes has replaced historic cabins with upscale multistory cottages with three to four bedrooms. These modern units feature screened porches, spacious kitchens, log decor, and bedrooms with colorful woodland-themed quilts. The resort also has an outdoor pool, beach, and swimming dock. $$$.

day trip 03

north

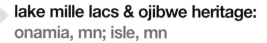

lake mille lacs & ojibwe heritage:
onamia, mn; isle, mn

Craving a unique getaway? You can find winter lodging that sleeps 10, has a kitchen, and stays warm, but it may be a little rustic. It's tough to get plumbing when you're sitting atop a frozen 132,000-acre Mille Lacs Lake.

Minnesota's second-largest lake becomes one of the world's most famous ice-fishing destinations each winter. About two dozen resorts plow hundreds of miles of ice roads and build villages with thousands of ice houses starting from around Christmas (or whenever ice is thick enough to be safe) through late February.

The lake's wide-open expanse—more than 200 square miles—is also popular with summer kite-surfers and winter kite-snowboarders, who harness the wind for a 14- to 18-mile trip shore to shore. Colorful kites fill the sky during the annual Mille Lakes Kite Crossing Festival, held in early March.

With a lake this large, it helps to have a fishing guide or advice from local resorts whether you're here in winter or on a hot summer day in search of walleye, northern pike, perch, muskellunge, tullibee, or smallmouth bass.

Mille Lacs is also known for launch fishing—using a larger boat with a crew that can comfortably accommodate and help a group to fish. It's an ideal and often more affordable option for first-time anglers or anyone without their own fishing gear and tackle.

While on or near the water, keep an eye out for Lake Mille Lacs National Wildlife Refuge. Composed of two rocky islands, Spirit and Hennepin, the refuge ranks as the smallest in the country at just over 0.5 acre and has protected one of four breeding colonies for terns since 1915. The Lake Mille Lacs Byway, which encircles the entire lake, has been designed as an

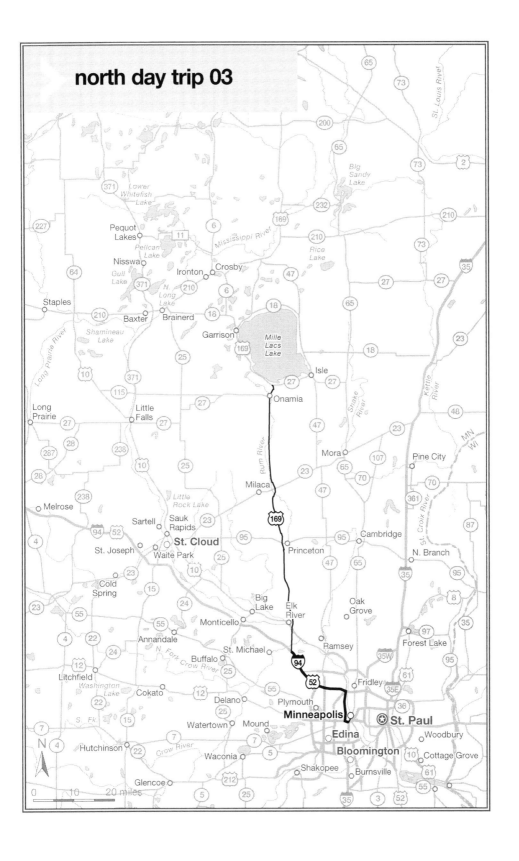

north day trip 03

Important Birding Area by the National Audubon Society, providing a home to 231 species of birds, including terns, bald eagles, waterfowl, and Bonaparte's gulls.

The area's abundant wildlife, woodland foraging, fishing, wild rice, and river routes have drawn people to the Mille Lacs area for at least 9,000 years, especially near the Rum River, an area preserved and protected by Mille Lacs Kathio State Park.

You can learn more about the area's indigenous heritage at the Minnesota Historical Society's Mille Lacs Indian Museum and Trading Post. Colorful exhibits, interactive videos, and craft demonstrations tell stories of their culture and long history living along Mille Lacs' 76 miles of shoreline, now dotted with the towns of Isle, Garrison, and Onamia. You can also find artwork at the Mille Lacs Band of Ojibwe's Grand Casino Mille Lacs. Even better: Visit the Mille Lacs Band's August powwow for a full appreciation of their vibrant and sacred traditions, with drumming, singing, dancing, and majestic regalia.

For more information on the area, go to Mille Lacs Area Tourism's website (millelacs .com) or call (320) 676-9972.

getting there

Follow US 169 about 86 miles north of Minneapolis until you reach Onamia. Head west along the southern shore of Lake Mille Lacs to reach Mille Lacs Kathio State Park, or head east on MN 27 to reach Isle.

onamia, mn

The town of Onamia (pop. 800) sits along the southern shore of Lake Mille Lacs where the Rum River flows out of it and widens into Ogechie Lake, Shakopee Lake, and Lake Onamia before flowing 154 miles south to the Mississippi River. The community is home to the Mille Lacs Band of Ojibwe's tribal headquarters and Mille Lacs Kathio State Park, which preserves evidence of ancestors who have lived here for thousands of years.

where to go

Black Brook Golf Course. 40005 85th Ave., Onamia; (320) 532-4574; izatys.com. The 6,867-yard 18-hole Black Brook course was designed around natural water and marsh hazards and was Minnesota's fifth golf course to have been certified by the National Audubon Sanctuary.

Grand Casino Mille Lacs. 777 Grand Ave., Onamia; (320) 532-7777; grandcasinomn com. The 66,000-square-foot casino run by the Mille Lacs Band of Ojibwe features video slot machines, EZ Play coinless slot machines, keno and poker machines, a 150-seat bingo hall, live poker, table games, and a high-limit gaming area. It's also a good venue to catch a national band or performer on tour.

Hairy Mosquito Trading Post. 21287 US 169, Milaca; (320) 983-5240; hairymosquito .com. Fifteen miles south of Onamia and right along the highway, this roadside stop offers an unexpected hub of artisans who sell their wares and often demonstrate their work. You'll find them polishing and cutting rocks, carving bone and wood, blowing glass, silversmithing, blacksmithing, and creating leather goods. You can also shop for antiques and barnwood, grab ice cream or gourmet cupcakes, catch a musician on the outdoor stage, or hit a special event, such as the Rock n' Gem Show, Primitive Arts Festival, and the Bloodsucker's Bash with all kinds of classic cars and bikes.

Mille Lacs Indian Museum and Trading Post. 43411 Oodena Dr., Onamia; (320) 532-3632; mnhs.org/millelacs. As the only state-run museum dedicated to Native American culture, the Mille Lacs Indian Museum features videos of powwow dances, intricate beadwork and basket weaving, and interactive displays to highlight Ojibwe culture, including the creation of the jingle dress. The trading post, a nod to a real one that once stood here, offers an expansive selection of beads, indigenous arts and crafts, books, and souvenirs. Special events and classes may include beading workshops, birchbark ornaments, or wild ricing demonstrations. Open daily Memorial Day through Labor Day. Check for offseason hours. $10 for adults; $8 for seniors, students age 5 and older, and active military.

Mille Lacs Kathio State Park. 15066 Kathio State Park Rd., Onamia; (320) 532-3523; dnr .state.mn.us. This park sprawls across 10,000 acres between the southwest corner of Mille Lacs Lake and the Rum River, which also widens to two inland lakes. This area has been home to ancient tribes and later the Mdewakanton Dakota and Mille Lacs Band of Ojibwe. This National Historic Landmark can be a good place to catch archaeologists in action at the Petaga Point archaeological site, but most visitors key on recreation: 70 camping sites, 5 camper cabins, horseback and hiking trails, a beach, snowmobiling and cross-country ski trails, and even a sledding hill near a heated chalet. Don't miss climbing the 100-foot-tall former fire tower—especially in the fall. Daily park admission: $7.

Mille Lacs Soo Line Trail. (320) 676-9972. dnr.state.mn.us. For an easy ride, grab this 11-mile paved section of the Soo Line State Trail. It connects Mille Lacs Kathio and Father Hennepin State Parks, the latter of which has a beach for cooling off. The trail parallels a gravel multiuse trail that's open to ATV and snowmobile riders. In the winter, crews groom the paved trail for cross-country skiing. In addition to accessing the trail at the state parks, you can also access the Soo Line at the Library/Depot on Roosevelt Road in Onamia or 1 block south of Main Street on Fifth Avenue in Isle.

Rolling Hills Arabians and Farm Tours. 18339 407th St.; (320) 362-4998; rollinghill-sarabiansandfarmtours.com. This farm offers families the chance to see and meet resident horses, alpacas, goats, deer, potbellied pigs, rabbits, and more. Introductory riding lessons and trail rides also can be arranged. Reservations required for all visits, with tours starting at $35 per carload.

where to stay

Eddy's. 41334 Shakopee Lake Rd.; (800) 657-4704; eddysresort.com. The Mille Lacs Band of Ojibwe purchased this vintage resort and renovated it with a modern but comfy retro vibe. It includes the Launch Bar and Grill with a view of the lake and tasty eats such as smoked brisket sandwich with bourbon bacon jam, beer cheese mac, and poutine with prime rib. $$.

Grand Casino Mille Lacs. 777 Grand Ave.; (800) 626-5825; grandcasinomn.com. You'll find close to 500 hotel rooms here, including many suites with sitting areas or a Jacuzzi. The hotel includes an indoor pool, spa, four-screen movie theater, and shopping. There also are RV sites, an electric car charging station, and complimentary outdoor pet boarding. Watch for intricate indigenous art throughout the lobby at this Mille Lacs Band of Ojibwe property. $.

Izatys Resort. 40005 85th Ave.; (320) 532-4574; izatys.com. This large lakeside resort (pronounced eye-ZAY-tees) is a favorite for families with kids, golfers, and wedding parties. You can choose standard rooms in Links Lodge Hotel or larger units with kitchens in the beach villas or townhomes. The property includes an outdoor and indoor pool, pickleball courts, the 18-hole Black Brook Golf Course, and dining at Club XIX with a Friday fish fry and pastas such as lobster linguine. $–$$.

where to eat

Bayview Bar and Grill. 39497 92nd Ave.; (320) 532-3936; bayviewbarandgrill.net. This spot along Lake Mille Lacs has offered drinks and meals for more than a century. These days, customers come by boat or car, snowmobile, or motorcycle. Grab a summer spot on the patio with a cold beer, or warm up indoors with burgers, pizza, roasted chicken, and appetizers. You can hear live music Saturday nights from 9 p.m. to 1 a.m. $–$$.

Cedarwood Family Restaurant. 515 Main St.; (320) 532-4414; facebook.com/cedar woodcafe2. Homey and affordable, this is the place for a warm bowl of soup, a plate of hash browns and kielbasa, a tuna melt, or barbecue ribs. $.

Happy's Drive-In. 11373 Stevens Rd.; (320) 532-3336. About 1 mile north of Onamia, this is a good stop for families, especially with its play areas for running off cooped-up-in-the-car energy. They serve old-fashioned roadside food. Think soups, sloppy joes, burgers, sand-wiches, and, of course, ice cream. $.

1991 Kitchen. 777 Grand Ave.; (320) 532-7777. Inside Grand Casino, this restaurant serves breakfast, lunch, and dinner that ranges from fancy (morning mimosas and walleye with eggs) to classic (prime rib or hot turkey dinner). $–$$.

isle, mn

With about 800 residents, this town hugs the southeastern shore of Lake Mille Lacs and dubs itself the "walleye capital of the world."

where to go

Father Hennepin State Park. 41296 Father Hennepin Park Rd.; (320) 676-8763; dnr .state.mn.us. This 320-acre park named for a French priest and the area's first recorded European explorer features the largest public beach along Mille Lacs Lake. You'll also find 103 campsites, 4.5 miles of hiking trails, 2.5 miles of cross-country ski trails, 2 boat ramps, and 2 fishing piers. Albino white-tailed deer are occasionally spotted by visitors here. Daily park admission: $7.

where to eat

Da Boathouse Restaurant and Bar. 43469 Vista Rd.; (320) 676-3999; macstwinbay.com. When you are starving for a big, hot meal after a long stretch of fishing or being on the trails, this casual eatery at Mac's Twin Bay marina and campground grills ham-turkey-bacon melts, serves hearty plates of a wild rice–Tater Tots hot dish and Swedish meatballs with mashed potatoes, plus an all-you-can-eat fish fry on Friday nights, as well as prime rib on Saturdays with soup and salad bar. $$.

Isle Bakery. 210 Second Ave. S; (320) 676-0222; isle-bakery.business.site. Walk into this downtown shop to inhale the yeasty scent of fresh bread for picnics and sugary glazes on fresh doughnuts and cookies, along with pies, brittle, and other seasonal treats. $.

where to stay

Appeldoorn's Sunset Bay Resort. 45401 Mille Lacs Pkwy., Isle; (320) 676-8834; appel doorns.com. More than a dozen cabins, plus four-unit homes and a reunion house with 10 bedrooms can be found here along the lake. Guests can rent Wave Runners, boats, pontoons, or snowmobiles, hire fishing guides, and rent ice houses. Pets allowed for an extra fee. $$.

McQuoid's Inn. 1325 MN 47, Isle; (320) 676-3535; mcquoidsinn.com. Guests in these remodeled hotel rooms aren't directly on the lake but can access it from the Thaines River, as it parallels and connects with Mille Lacs. There also are log condos, cabins, and camp-sites. Launch fishing (a larger group on a boat), private guides, and portable ice houses are available, as well as snowmobiles and gear for exploring 300 miles of groomed trails. $$.

day trip 04

north

cuyuna lakes & red-dirt adventures:
crosby-ironton, mn

crosby-ironton, mn

Say "Iron Range" to most Minnesotans and they think of Virginia, Hibbing, Chisholm, and other communities on the Mesabi Iron Range. But Minnesota claims two other iron ranges: the Vermilion Range in Ely and the Cuyuna Range by Crosby and Ironton, two modest mining communities that blur together where MN 210 and MN 6 intersect. While Cuyuna ranks as the smallest iron range, its once-industrial landscape has transformed into a red-dirt adventure hub serving up a potluck of fun. Think quiet places to paddle; scuba diving and swimming in lakes clear up to 40 feet deep; fishing for trout or bass; bicycling along paved trails; or trying the area's biggest draw—shredding some serious (and scenic) mountain bike trails.

The Cuyuna Range produced more than 100 million tons of iron ore in the early half of the 1900s. It was grinding and sometimes deadly work, as you'll learn at historical displays or the Milford Mine Memorial, which poignantly preserves the place where 41 men died when a shaft collapsed and instantly flooded in Minnesota's worst mining disaster.

When the mines closed half a century ago, Mother Nature began to take over. Open-pit mining left behind tall hills of excavated materials now cloaked in trees and sumac. The greenery alters and softens the rugged landscape that can feel like a mini–Boundary Waters on a quiet day in a kayak (if you can ignore the sight of a cell tower).

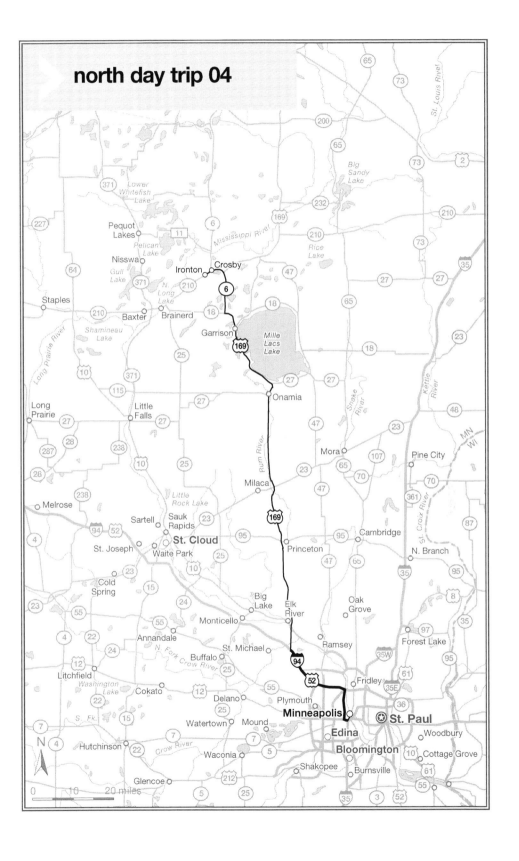

north day trip 04

The pits where machines chewed through red earth and rock became 17 mine lakes filled with spring water and rain, making them colder and clearer than nearby natural lakes— perfect for trout (which is stocked in the lakes) and peering into the mysterious depths. Glide across on a paddleboard and you might see skeletal branches of drowned trees not far from shore. They look like ghostly coral with small sunfish darting through the branches. Try a scuba diving lesson and you might see an old mine shaft, a loon taking a dive, abandoned vehicles—and a few fake skeletons just for fun.

What became Cuyuna Country State Recreation Area ranks among Minnesota's prettiest and most distinctive playgrounds. You can camp, glamp in cabins inspired by mining shacks, share a yurt with friends, and rent cottages or homes. You can bring your own gear or rent from area resorts and outfitters. Trails make it easy to pedal into downtown Crosby

hit the trails

Cuyuna Country State Recreation Area's park office is at 307 Third St., Ironton; (218) 772-3690; dnr.state.mn.us. Grab a good map and ask fellow bikers for their favorite features along 70 miles of rugged mountain bike trails for both beginners and advanced riders who come from across the country to explore this silver-level International Mountain Bike Association (IMBA) destination.

At least 30 miles of trails were designed and built to take full advantage of the terrain with features mountain bikers love the most, from narrow boardwalks that ribbon through aspen forest to rocky ledges overlooking mine lakes. If you're new to the sport, the Sagamore unit is an easier set of trails to get started on. Another option is traveling the Mahnomen unit in a clockwise direction, starting at the rally center.

For fun, try the aptly named Bobsled Trail that twists and speeds downhill, while the Ferrous Wheel Trail spins into a 360-degree thrill ride with large berms for banking sideways. The Sand Hog Trail's downhill design won an IMBA's Flow Country Trail Award. Also noteworthy: Check out views from Miner's Mountain Overlook or the Portsmouth Mine Overlook. Portsmouth Mine Lake drops 395 feet deep.

If you're not into "Shredding the Red" at Cuyuna, bicyclists can also choose from 100 miles of paved trails and gravel road cycling.

You can dive into any mine or natural lake to cool off and wash away the red-dirt dust after working up a sweat, but there's also an official beach and a boat landing that's handy for launching kayaks or standup paddleboards.

Beginning and experienced divers can join organized dives or take lessons in the mine lakes, which go as deep as 530 feet and have visibility of 30 to 60 feet.

and Ironton for cooling off with an iced coffee or freshly tapped beer—or feeding voracious appetites with seriously good eats.

For up-to-date trail information and travel tips, reach out to the Cuyuna Lakes Chamber of Commerce at 117 W. Main St. (inside the mid-Minnesota Federal Credit Union), Ironton; (218) 546-8131; cuyunalakes.com.

getting there

Follow US 169 north from the Twin Cities and around the western shore of Mille Lacs Lake to Garrison. At Garrison, take MN 18 north to MN 6 north. At Deerwood, MN 6 will merge with MN 210 and curve west around Serpent Lake before heading into downtown Crosby and Ironton.

For winter visits, watch for trail updates to find out when ski trails are groomed and when mountain bike trails are ready for fat-tire biking.

area outfitters and rentals:

- **Cuyuna Outfitters.** *10 Third Ave., Crosby; (218) 838-1932; cuyunaoutfitters .com. This is the first place to rent clear kayaks, which take full advantage of mine lake clarity. You can also get regular kayaks, paddleboards, inflatable rafts, canoes, and small campers.*
- **Cykel.** *324 Curtis Ave., Ironton; (218) 545-4545; cykelonline.com. Named for the Swedish word for "cycle," this shop 3 blocks from the recreation area's entrance rents hardtail, full-suspension, and fat-tire bikes and e-bikes. Ask about seasonal group rides every Thursday and Saturday evening. You can also rent tandem and single kayaks, fishing kayaks, and standup paddleboards, which they will deliver within a 10-mile radius. The shop also sells equipment, helps customers build custom bikes, performs safety checks, and services bikes.*
- **Minnesota School of Diving.** *712 Washington St., Brainerd; (218) 829-5953; mndiving.com. This Brainerd-based dive school has created more than 50 unique dive sites in the Cuyuna lakes and sponsors two to three fun dives, which include cookouts, each week in the summer. They also have dive maps if you want to go on your own.*
- **Red Raven Bike and Coffee Shop.** *2 Third Ave. SW; (218) 833-2788; redraven.bike. Rent hardtail or full-suspension bikes, kids' bikes, or e-bikes or get a tune-up before hitting the trails.*
- **Unbound Adventures,** *(218) 839-4708; unboundadventuresmn.com. To reserve kayaks (tandem or single) or mountain biking gear, you can do the process online and have equipment delivered.*

where to go

Crosby Memorial Park. 2 Second St. SW, Crosby. Kids in tow? Make a stop at one of the area's best beaches and most spacious community parks. The imaginative playground incorporates Vikings, dragons, farm animals, and ocean murals in between slides, forts, monkey bars, and tunnels. The park also includes camping spots, a picnic area, a skateboard park, and a 20-foot sea serpent statue named *Kahnah'bek*, Ojibwe for "serpent."

Cuyuna Meets the World Murals. Downtown Crosby, Deerwood, and Ironton. Between Summer 2018 and 2020, seven new murals added color and art to area downtowns while depicting the local culture, past and present. One mural shows the 1957 flight of the Man High II balloon from the Portsmouth Mine. Its operator reached 110,000 feet high during the 32-hour flight and was the first person to see the Earth's curvature from space. Data on the altitude's effect on the human body was later used by NASA.

Hallett Antique Mall. 10 Fourth St. SE, Aitkin. (218) 546-5444; facebook/com/people/ Hallett-Antique-Mall. Anyone who enjoyed the ever-changing assortment of goods from dozens of dealers in downtown Crosby can find even more space with its new location 19 miles away in Aitkin. Look for items such as Blue Mountain pottery, vintage knives, military artifacts, Red Wing crocks, wooden snowshoes, furniture, and other collectibles from dozens of dealers. At more than 11,500 square feet, it's considered the biggest antiques store in Central Minnesota.

Jack's 18. 25039 Tame Fish Rd., Deerwood; (218) 678-2885; ruttgers.com. Minnesota native Joel Goldstrand designed this 18-hole course around 2 lakes that come into play on half the holes. The signature 230-yard 18th hole requires a tee shot over Bass Lake. The course is part of Ruttger's resort, which also has Alec's Nine, a more leisurely executive course. Jack's 18 twilight rates begin at $43.

Milford Mine Memorial Park. 26351 Milford Lake Dr, Crosby; crowing.gov. This serene park just south of where MN 6 crosses the Mississippi River doubles as a poignant memorial to the dangers of mining. Its boardwalks and paths wind around the once-200-foot-deep Milford Mine, where a shaft collapsed on February 5, 1924. It instantly flooded multiple levels with water and mud that killed 41 miners. Only seven men made it to safety. Interpretive signs explain the disaster that left 38 women without husbands and 83 children without fathers.

where to eat

Cuyuna Brewing Company. 1 E. Main St., Crosby; (218) 866-0914; cuyunabrewing.com. Enjoy favorites like the Silver Dollar Lager and Yawkey Red Ale, or try something different, like a margarita seltzer or strawberry beer-mosa. Burritos California also joined the business, offering burritos and bowls, tacos, and quesadillas (218-330-5617). $$.

Heartland Kitchen. 131 W. Main St., Crosby; (218) 546-5746. Grab sweet rolls or cranberry wild rice bread to go, or take a seat for homey servings of hot meat sandwiches and several varieties of pie. On Sunday they serve turkey dinner and offer an all-day buffet with unique items such as lefse layered with apples and honey. Open 7 a.m. to 3:30 p.m. $.

The Hudson. 208 Curtis Ave., Ironton; (218) 772-0096; hudson218.com. This former Hudson auto dealership throws open its garage door on warm days when customers gather indoors or outside by the firepit for steaming expresso and breakfast wraps, sandwiches on wild rice bread, scotcharoos, and iced cocktails. $–$$.

Iron Range Eatery. 6 W. Main St.; Crosby; (218) 545-5444; ironrange.3cheersmn.com. Sit inside or out to enjoy from-scratch seasonally inspired thin-crust pizza, slow-braised short ribs with white cheddar au gratin, and a dill pickle–brined breaded chicken sandwich. $$.

MacDaddy's Donut Garage. 221 Fourth St.; (218) 772-0222; facebook.com/macdaddys donuts. For a shot of sugar, grab a cronut, caramel roll, apple fritter, or other bakery bestsellers. $.

North Country Café. 12 W. Main St., Crosby; (218) 545-9908; facebook.com/north countrycafe. Fuel up for the day with stuffed hash browns smothered in sausage gravy, peanut butter and banana waffles, or cinnamon roll French toast, or get there in time for lunchtime burgers and sandwiches. $$.

Red Raven Bike and Coffee Shop. 2 Third Ave. SW, Crosby; (218) 833-2788; redraven. bike. You know you're in a bike town when you can wheel in for a bike tune-up, rent a bike, or buy a bike—and then grab an iced coffee or chai, fruit smoothie, a breakfast burrito, or The Raven, their signature sandwich: egg, grilled turkey breast, spicy strawberry jam, and cheese on a croissant. $.

Ruby's On the Lake at Ruttger's Bay Lake Lodge. 25039 Tame Fish Lake Rd., Deerwood; (218) 678-2885; ruttgers.com. This century-old resort has more-casual options, but it feels like an event to dine in the 1920s lodge with 54-foot-tall poplar logs. Entrées range from citrus-glazed scallops wrapped with bacon to grilled mint lamp chops with pear salsa or a vegetarian Thai curry. Open for breakfast and dinner April through October. $$$.

Victual and Rave Cream Works. 124 Main St., Crosby; (218) 545-1000; shopvictual.com. This place has mastered superpremium ice cream that's lactose-free, with creative flavors such as baklava, lavender honey with sunflower seeds, pink squirrel, and a strawberry layered with goat cheese, balsamic, and black pepper. Gourmet tastes curate its other foods, such as small-batch crackers, charcuterie, regional artisanal cheeses, liqueurs for cocktails, and more to add flair to happy hour or a picnic to go. $–$$.

where to stay

Cuyuna Cove. 22642 MN 6, Crosby; (218) 389-4087; cuyunacove.com. These tiny custom-built cabins (215 square feet) feel like tree houses for grown-ups, with patios, a spa-inspired bathroom, a kitchenette, and big windows that overlook the woods on the outskirts of Crosby with easy access to trails and downtown dining. $$$.

Red Rider Resort. 23457 CR 31, Crosby; (218) 838-6858; redriderresort.com. Among the 8 camper cabins built on Manuel Lake are two built on stilts with a cable-walk bridge and screen porch tucked below for a tree-fort feel. Guests bring their own bedding for most cabins, which have single beds bunked over doubles. Two cabins have private bathrooms. There is also a shared shower, bathroom, and kitchen building. The resort also rents 10 tent and 4 RV sites. $–$$.

Ruttger's Bay Lake Lodge. 25039 Tame Fish Lake Rd., Deerwood; (800) 450-4545; ruttgers.com. This seasonal resort's roots go back to 1898. It has grown to be one of the largest in the Brainerd Lakes area with 200 units blending villas, condos, cottages, and lodge rooms, along with new five-bedroom vacation homes. Many of the cabins stretch along the large beach with giant water toys. There's also a summer kids' camp, two golf courses, three restaurants, a meal plan, a Fine Line Salon and Spa (218-678-2157) featuring Aveda products, pickleball courts, and all-trails e-bikes that can be rented for Cuyuna mountain bike trails. Open April to October. $$–$$$.

State Forest Campgrounds. (218) 772-3690; dnr.state.mn.us. Cuyuna Country State Recreation Area also manages Clint Converse Campground in Land O'Lakes State Forest and Greer Lake Campground in the Crow Wing Forest. Sites are first come, first served. $.

True North Basecamp. 835 First St. SW, Crosby; (218) 883-2267; truenorthbasecamp .com. This enclave of 6 steel-wrapped modern camping cabins fits the area's mining vibe. Each has full and bunk beds, heat, A/C, electricity, and a shared shower and restroom build-ing. Some feature bike-themed artwork. The handy cabin location puts guests near trails and a short pedal from downtown, while also feeling like a serene getaway with views of Armour No. 2 Mine Lake as it reflects the evening sunset. The property also rents 14 campsites, 4 camper sites and has a handful of cabin tents with 7.5-foot ceilings and mattresses for extra comfort. $–$$.

day trip 05

north

northern rivers, rapids & forests:
hinckley, mn; sandstone, mn; moose lake, mn; cloquet-carlton, mn

You don't have to drive all the way to Lake Superior to enjoy rugged scenery, wild rivers, and adrenaline-pumping adventure. That all starts roughly 90 minutes north of the Twin Cities with St. Croix State Park, the largest state park in Minnesota, covering more than 34,000 acres.

If that's not impressive enough, consider this: The south–north corridor from Hinckley to Carlton and east–west between I-35 and the Wisconsin border encompasses the St. Louis River, four state parks, three state forests, two rapids-rich rivers, and three state trails that stretch for hundreds of miles.

It's ideal for anyone who craves trading the urban or suburban jungle for camping, riding ATVs, bicycling, mountain biking, horseback riding, cross-country skiing, and zipping through wild woods on a snowmobile.

There also are two designated Minnesota scenic byways that get you off the interstate, traveling through tunnels of pine, above deep valleys, and over to Jay Cooke State Park, where a swinging bridge sways above raging rapids and ancient rocks.

If you choose quiet sports, keep your ears and eyes open for a glimpse of the black bears and wolves that make their home here.

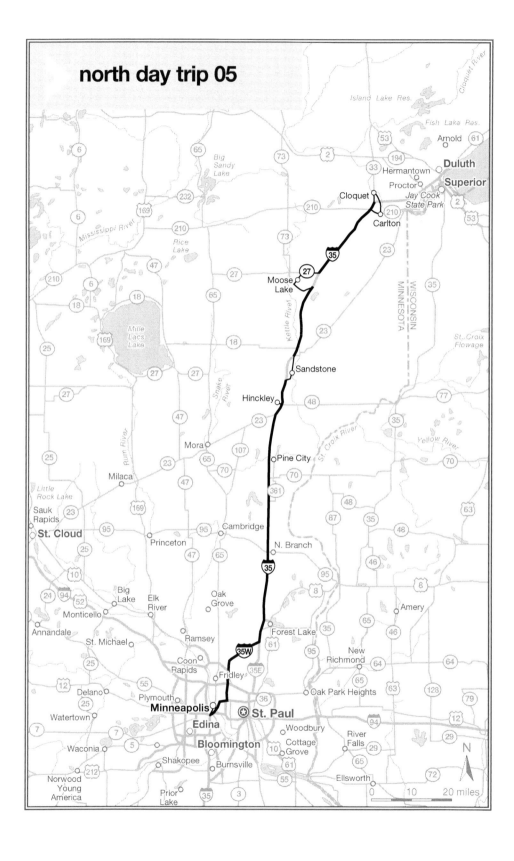

hinckley, mn

If there's a hub for this forested, river-rich corridor of the state, it's Hinckley. The midway point between the Twin Cities and Duluth offers restaurants and lodging, anchored by Grand Casino. For additional information, contact the Hinckley Convention and Visitors Bureau at (320) 384-0126; hinckleymn.com.

getting there

Take I-35 north of the Twin Cities about 90 minutes to reach Hinckley.

where to go

Antiques America. 113 Weber Ave.; (320) 384-7272; antiques-america.com. More than 40 dealers sell everything from World War II collectibles and tools to books, porcelain, toys, and furniture. Open daily.

Gandy Dancer Trail. (218) 460-7021; dnr.state.mn.us. Accessible about 18 miles east of Hinckley through St. Croix State Park, this ATV and off-road motorcycle trail starts in Danbury, Wisconsin, and runs about 31 miles, connecting with additional trails in the 42,000-acre St. Croix State Forest and 100 miles of trails in the 92,000-acre Nemadji State Forest. Off-road trucks and cars are allowed in some designated sections.

Grand Casino Hinckley. 300 Lady Luck Dr.; (320) 384-7427; grandcasinomn.com. Look for big-name performances and tribute concerts here (often country and western stars), along with slot machines, bingo, poker, blackjack, and pull-tabs. It's also home to the Grand Harmony Spa and Grand National Golf Course, where Joel Goldstrand designed 18 holes around the rolling terrain, trees, and ponds. The Mille Lacs Band of Ojibwe, which owns the Grand Casinos, also hosts a powwow each June.

Hinckley Fire Museum. 106 Old Hwy. 61 South; (320) 384-7338; hinckleyfiremuseum .com. Heart-wrenching tales from one of the country's deadliest wildfires unfold at this restored 1894 St. Paul and Duluth Railroad depot. A summerlong drought, sparks from trains and small fires, too many slash piles from logging, and oppressive heat with a cold front moving in ignited the perfect storm of fires on September 1, 1894. Flames rose more than a mile high and roared across the area, devastating six towns, burning 480 square acres, and killing more than 400 people. Additional exhibits feature Native Americans, the logging era, and trains. Open May to mid-October.

St. Croix Scenic Byway. If you love a scenic drive, check out a nearby stretch of a scenic byway that begins at Point Douglas near Hastings, where the St. Croix and Mississippi Rivers meet south of the Twin Cities, and winds its way 124 miles north along the Minnesota-Wisconsin border until it reaches Hinckley and St. Croix State Park.

state forest vs. state park

*The corridor between I-35 and the Wisconsin border has one of Minnesota's highest concentrations of state forests, state parks, state trails, and even national park land with what's along the St. Croix River. You can find scenic biking, quiet hikes, horseback rides, and rivers to paddle, but it's even more popular for off-road vehicles: ATVs, motorcycles, and vehicles and trucks that can handle rugged forest trails. You can get campsite and trail maps through the **Minnesota Department of Natural Resources**; (888) 646-6367; dnr.state.mn.us.*

State forest campsites cannot be reserved, so it's good to have a backup plan if your first choice is full. The same goes for National Park Service paddle-in sites along the St. Croix River. State forest campsites generally cost less and are less crowded than state parks, but they're also more rustic. You'll still have fire pits and picnic tables but expect vault toilets and water pumps instead of flush toilets, showers, and sinks.

Take cash to buy local firewood. Outside firewood is not allowed in order to control potential insect infestations, such as the emerald ash borer.

St. Croix State Park. 30065 St. Croix Park Rd.; (320) 280-7880; dnr.state.mn.us. Minnesota's largest state park lies about 15 miles east of Pine City and Hinckley. The St. Croix, a National Scenic and Wild River, and the Kettle, the state's first designated Wild and Scenic River, cross the park, which includes 211 campground sites, remote canoe-in and backpack sites, 5 historic cabins from the 1940s, and 2 guesthouses that sleep 15. Climb the 100-foot-tall fire tower on the park's west side to get a feel for the vastness of forest and admire peak fall colors. You can also take your pick of 127 miles of hiking trails that traverse the bluffs of the St. Croix and the rocky rapids of the Kettle. Additional trails are designated for mountain bikers, horseback riders, skiers, ATV riders, and snowmobilers, with extensions leading into neighboring state forests. If you like fishing, try one of the trout streams feeding into the St. Croix. Check at the park office for seasonal canoe and ski rentals.

Willard Munger Trail. Parking at the intersection of CR 61 and CR18; dnr.state.mn.us. This historic train route now is a 70-mile paved trail that starts a block north of the Hinckley Fire Museum. The trail runs to Duluth with a scenic trek through Jay Cooke State Park. A 37-mile segment memorializes the route the fire took from Hinckley to Barnum and how quick thinking by a train engineer helped rescue residents fleeing the flames.

where to eat

Tobies. 404 Fire Monument Rd.; (320) 384-6174; tobies.com. Many travelers consider it sacrilegious to bypass Hinckley—the halfway point to Duluth—without a stop at Tobies. The huge caramel and cinnamon rolls hog the spotlight, but this often-packed place serves meals 24 hours a day. You can order a pulled-pork eggs Benedict or cinnamon swirl French toast, grab a brisket burger, or splurge on steak and lobster. Look for live entertainment Friday and Saturday nights, with karaoke on Sundays. $$–$$$.

Whistle Stop Café. 305 S. Old Hwy. 61; (320) 384-6106; whistlestopcafehinckley.com. Start the day with a "4 am train wreck," a plate of hash browns with just about everything on top, or opt for a hot beef commercial, hamburger steak with gravy, Friday-night fish fry, and homemade pies. $.

Winds Steakhouse. 777 Lady Luck Dr., Grand Casino Hinckley; (320) 384-7777. The most upscale restaurant at Grand Casino Hinckley serves crab legs, steak tournedos, braised buffalo ribs, and pistachio-crusted walleye. Opens at 5 p.m. Wednesday through Sunday. $$$.

where to stay

Grand Casino Hinckley. 777 Lady Luck Dr.; (320) 384-7771; grandcasinomn.com. Of the roughly 1,000 hotel rooms in Hinckley, the casino owns most of them, including a popular RV park with chalets. The main hotel, which is attached to the casino, has 563 rooms. $$.

sandstone, mn

With a historic sandstone quarry and the scenic Kettle River rushing through Banning State Park, this community of 1,550 residents attracts high-adrenaline athletes, who tackle the rapids in summer and climb ice formations in winter.

getting there

Take I-35 about 11 miles north of Hinckley to Sandstone.

where to go

Banning State Park. 61101 Banning Park Rd.; (320) 245-2668; dnr.state.mn.us. The last state park along the St. Croix Scenic Byway draws gutsy adventurers for world-class whitewater kayaking on the roaring Kettle River each spring. They churn and shoot through the Blueberry Slide, Dragon's Tooth, and Hell's Gate rapids. Hikers can explore an old sandstone quarry and scenic trails along the river in this 6,000-acre park. In winter you may see ice-climbers scaling their way up frozen falls. $7 daily admission.

Osprey Wilds Environmental Learning Center. 54165 Audubon Dr.; (320) 245-2648; ospreywilds.org. This 535-acre refuge on Grindstone Lake includes 7 miles of hiking and skiing trails. While it's used as a conference center, the organization also offers several public programs with various speakers, youth and family weekends, and women's wellness weekends. Grindstone Lake, one of the deepest lake basins in the state, is stocked with trout.

Robinson Quarry Park. 710 Old Wagon Rd.; (320) 372-0756; sandstone.govoffice.com. You can access the Kettle River from this former quarry and hike to Wolf Creek Falls or Big Spring Falls, but it's best known for climbing opportunities. Climbers scale the steep rock walls in summer or return in the thick of winter, when it's a sought-after ice-climbing destination (facebook.com/SandstoneIcePark). The annual Ice Fest offers a chance to try the sport, meet with other enthusiasts, and build complementary skills such as winter camping.

where to stay

Getaway Kettle River. 77112 Long Lake Rd., Willow River; getaway.house/minneapolis. This newer national chain put 49 portable tiny cabins on 96 acres between Sandstone and Moose Lake. Each comes with a queen bed or two bunked queen beds with a window facing the woods. Small kitchens and bathrooms with a shower are included. Sites come with outdoor chairs, a picnic table, and a fire pit. $$–$$$.

Waldheim Resort. 9096 Waldheim Ln., Finlayson; (320) 321-9096; waldheimresort.com. West of Sandstone, this traditional resort has 5 two- to three-bedroom cabins on Pine Lake and 30 seasonal RV sites. $$.

Willow River Campground. (320) 216-3910; dnr.state.mn.us. This campground lies within General Andrews State Forest in between Sandstone and Moose Lake and includes a 35-site campground. Most sites are along Zalesky Lake, also known as the Willow River Flowage. There also are 40 miles of hiking trails and 37 for ATV and off-highway motorcycle riding. The 7,700-acre forest includes a state nursery that produces 5 million forest seedlings a year. $.

moose lake, mn

Carlton County was once the rim of Glacial Lake Duluth, making this the heart of agate country and home to the Agate and Geological Interpretive Center at Moose Lake State Park. The town hosts Agate Days each July and buries about 350 pounds of agates into 4 tons of rock spread across downtown. It's a good place to tap the expertise of Carlton County Gem and Mineral Club members.

getting there

Head north on I-35 again and drive about 30 miles from Sandstone to Moose Lake.

where to go

Moose Lake Chamber of Commerce. 4524 S. Arrowhead Ln.; (218) 485-4145; moose lakechamber.com. Use the website to register for a free agate hunting permit and maps of area quarries that allow rockhounding.

Moose Lake Depot & Fires of 1918 Museum. 900 Folz Blvd.; (218) 485-4234; moose lakeareahistory.com. Twenty-four years after the Great Hinckley Fire, another devastating fire killed 453 people. It destroyed the cities of Moose Lake,Cloquet, and other communities, ranking it among the nation's deadliest fires. The museum shares the details, with a 27-foot monument commemorating those who died. Open 10 a.m. to 4 p.m. Monday through Saturday and noon to 3 p.m. Sunday, late May through mid-October. Admission: $2, adults; $1, children.

Moose Lake State Park. 4252 CR 137; (218) 485-5420; dnr.state.mn.us. Rock hounds can browse impressive displays of Minnesota's official gemstone, Lake Superior agates, among the other polished treasures at the 4,500-square-foot Agate and Geological Interpretive Center. If you're inspired to seek your own agates, ask a staff member for a map to local gravel quarries. Moose Lake Park also has a lake, beach, boat rentals, and 55 campsites. Agate exhibits are open 9 a.m. to 4 p.m. Sun through Wed, 9 a.m. to 6 p.m. on Thurs, and 9 a.m. to 9 p.m. Fri and Sat, Memorial Day through Labor Day.

Soo Line South Trail. Downtown; dnr.state.mn.us. This 114-mile trail starts near Superior, Wisconsin, and runs southwest to Minnesota through Moose Lake and almost to Little Falls. The Soo Line South intersects the Willard Munger Trail in downtown Moose Lake. The Portage Trail connects both trails with Moose Lake State Park.

where to eat

Lazy Moose Grill. 300 Arrowhead Ln.; (218) 485-8712; lazygrills.com. Homemade buns for bacon cheeseburgers, from-scratch pies, and wild rice meat loaf are among the favorites at this restaurant that also has a gift shop. $.

Moose Lake Brewing Company. 244 Lakeshore Dr.; (218) 485-4585; mooselakebrewing .com. Enjoy a Moosehead lakeview with a summer brew such as Crazy Camper apricot cream ale. Other choices include Pulp Mill raspberry vanilla milkshake IPA, a black cherry seltzer, and a honey nut brown ale. $.

where to stay

Moose Lake City Campground. (218) 485-4761. This city campground includes a beach with lifeguards, a boat landing, tennis courts, and a playground. Open the Friday before the fishing opener through the last weekend in September. $.

cloquet-carlton, mn

The St. Louis River rumbles and churns its way through Cloquet and nearby Carlton before spilling into Lake Superior.

getting there

Follow I-35 about 24 miles to MN 210. Carlton is 3 miles to the east. Head on I-35 one more exit to reach Cloquet.

where to go

Black Bear Casino Resort. 1785 MN 210, Carlton; (888) 771-0777; blackbearcasino resort.com. You can't miss this towering property with 250 hotel rooms along I-35. Its casino blends slot machines, blackjack, bingo, table games, and a players' club. The resort also includes the Cobalt Nightclub and Cabaret, Otter Creek Event Center for concerts, a golf course, and a connecting trail for snowmobilers to reach the Wood City Riders Trail System (woodcityriders.com).

Jay Cooke State Park. 780 MN 210, Carlton; (218) 673-7000; dnr.state.mn.us. If you need a good thrill, walk across this park's iconic swinging suspension bridge at spring meltdown as water gushes beneath you and thunders between jagged wedges of graywacke rock. Ancient rocks make this an especially scenic and intriguing river, along with a portage trail used by voyageurs dodging the rapids some 300 years ago. The 8,800-acre park encompasses 50 miles of hiking trails, 32 miles of easy-to-difficult cross-country skiing, 13 miles of mountain biking, and 8 miles of paved trail leading into Carlton. Look for a profusion of wildflowers each spring, head to Oldenburg Point for sweeping views of the valley and fall colors, and keep an eye open for signs of wolves. There are 79 campsites here, along with 8 backpack sites and walk-in sites, and 5 camper cabins with electricity and heat. $7 daily permit.

Minnesota Whitewater Rafting. 3214 River Gate Ave., Cloquet; (218) 522-4446; minnesotawhitewater.com. Professional guides get groups onto the St. Louis River for whitewater rafting, float trips, or fishing.

Mont Du Lac Resort. 3125 S. Mont Du Lac Rd.; Superior, WI; (218) 626-3797; mdlresort .com. Only 10 miles east of Carlton and just over the Wisconsin border, this ski resort opens 11 runs that drop more than 300 feet and overlook the St. Louis River and Jay Cooke State Park. The terrain park rotates 20 features, and a tubing park has four runs with a carpet conveyor. Summer activities include disc golf, summer slides, mountain biking, and archery. The resort touts its annual Bowfest as the world's largest outdoor archery and music festival.

Rushing Rapids and Veterans Evergreen Scenic Byways. Take the 9-mile scenic Rushing Rapids Scenic Byway as it parallels the St. Louis River from Carlton to Jay Cooke State Park and ends at the intersection with MN 23. Turn south on the 50-mile Veterans

Evergreen Memorial Byway (a section of MN 23) for an alternative route back to I-35 and the Twin Cities.

R. W. Lindholm Service Station. Corner of MN 33 and Cloquet Ave., Cloquet. Frank Lloyd Wright designed this gas station, built in 1956. It features a copper roof, a jutting triangular canopy that points toward the St. Louis River, a second-floor waiting room, generous windows, and skylights. It cost $20,000 at a time when most service stations were being built for $5,000.

Swiftwater Adventures. 121 Vermilion St.; Carlton; (218) 451-3218; swiftwatermn.com. Professionals guide rafting through churning rapids on the St. Louis River.

where to eat

Gordy's Hi-Hat. 415 Sunnyside Dr.; Cloquet; (218) 879-6125; gordys-hihat.com. A beloved drive-in since 1960, this family business churns out hand-pattied burgers, homemade onion rings, hand-battered fish, fries, shakes, and frothy root beer. Vegetarian wild rice burgers and salads are also available. While the drive-in is open May through Sept, Gordy's Warming House next door serves steaming coffee drinks, ice cream, pie, soups, and sandwiches year-round with a bonus for dog-lovers: a fully enclosed dog park. $.

where to stay

Black Bear Casino Resort. 1785 MN 210, Carlton; (888) 771-0777; blackbearcasino resort.com. This 250-room hotel run by the Fond du Lac Band of Ojibwe includes a pool, the Seven Fires Steakhouse, a buffet and deli, plus easy access to the casino and event venues. $.

Cloquet/Duluth KOA Journey. 1381 Kampground Rd., Carlton; (218) 879-5726; koa .com. This is the place if you want a pool and hot tub, full hookups, and wireless access to go with your camping experience. You also can rent bikes here, join in family activities, or rent a rustic camping cabin. Open May to early October. $.

Oldenburg House. 604 Chestnut Ave.; Carlton; (218) 384-4835; oldenburghouse.com. For a homey stay, settle into one of three suites in this 1894 home where a gourmet breakfast is served in the morning and guests are only a few blocks from the Willard Munger State Trail. $$–$$$.

day trip 06

north

>>> **duluth's superior scenery & shipping:**
skyline parkway, lincoln park, canal park
& downtown, east duluth

After road-tripping almost 2.5 hours north on I-35 to Duluth, you finally crest Thompson Hill and get that first breathtaking view of the St. Louis River and Lake Superior. Duluth—with its bustling harbor and the world's most-inland port—knows how to make an impression.

You can easily spend a day, a weekend, or a week wandering Duluth's popular Canal Park with its shops and galleries, museums and freshwater aquarium, and scenic lake walk. But there's much more to Duluth beyond its waterfront. There's a thriving arts scene, stellar made-in-Duluth gear in the Lincoln Park Craft District, restaurants and breweries, college sports, and a full calendar of events such as the John Beargrease Dogsled Race, Grandma's Marathon, Bayfront Blues Festival, and Bentleyville, America's largest free walk-through holiday light display. When Bentleyville's 128-foot-tall Christmas tree lights up at Bayfront Park, it helps Duluth earn its "Christmas City of the North" nickname.

Consider this too: More than 130 parks are tucked into the city's steep hills, along its many creeks and rivers and the waterfront. More than 100 miles of trails draw mountain bikers and winter fat-tire bikers as well as hikers—some of whom rigorously tackle the 310-mile Superior Hiking Trail as it stretches to Canada.

Many parks date back to the early part of the 1900s, when the city was still booming with lumber, mining, and shipping—all essential to a quickly growing country. At one point Duluth boasted more millionaires per capita than anywhere else in the United States. Visitors slip into the elegance of that era while riding historic trains, driving by elegant Victorian homes, and touring Glensheen Mansion on the city's east side.

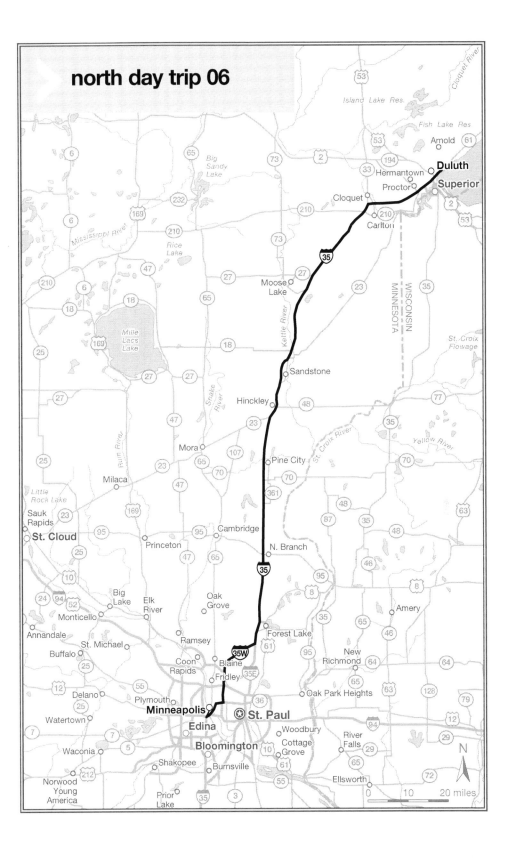

north day trip 06

This chapter roughly groups destinations geographically to make the most of a short visit when you can't find lodging or afford spending the night—or you're craving a new place to explore.

Start any visit with a stop at **Thompson Hill Welcome Center**, 8525 Skyline Pkwy., (218) 723-4938, as you reach the southern outskirts and exit at Boundary Avenue. Grab a fresh visitor's guide to get oriented and pause for a picnic at this scenic spot.

getting there

Follow I-35 north from the Twin Cities for 2 hours and 20 minutes.

skyline parkway

If you start a visit at the Thompson Hill Welcome Center, you're already on the Skyline Parkway Scenic Drive, which stretches 25 miles from Spirit Mountain to Seven Bridges Road. It will continue to climb up the city's steep bluffs until you're traveling high above downtown and Lake Superior. You'll catch the most dramatic views watching the lake glitter and glow as the sun sets and the moon rises.

where to go

Enger Park Golf Course. 1801 W. Skyline Blvd.; (218) 723-3451; golfduluth.com. This 27-hole course in the hills above Duluth takes advantage of the rolling terrain and woods with views of historic Enger Tower. There's also a driving range and short game practice area.

Enger Tower. 1601 Enger Tower Dr.; (218) 730-4300; engertowerduluth.com. This five-story stone tower looming 530 feet above Lake Superior was a gift from Norway in 1939, then rededicated by the king and queen of Norway in 2011. Like Enger Park itself, it's symbolic of Duluth's international ties and rich in history. Stroll through perennial and shade gardens and ring the peace bell in the Japanese tea garden, a gift from sister city Ohara, Japan. Visit in spring to see 4,000 daffodils. Don't miss views from the tower or the ridgeline gazebo and picnic tables.

Lake Superior & Mississippi Railroad. 6930 Fremont St.; (218) 624-7549; duluthrivertrain.com. This volunteer-run narrated excursion train operates twice a day on the weekends mid-June through mid-October. Passengers ride in an open-air safari car or one of two 1912 coaches for a 90-minute to 2-hour trip of 6 miles, much of it along the St. Louis River. Admission: $22, adults; $11, ages 3 and up. Veterans ride free on Sunday.

Lake Superior Zoo. 7210 Fremont St.; (218) 730-4500; lszooduluth.org. Tucked away in West Duluth near Kingsbury Creek, Lake Superior Zoo takes families through indoor and outdoor exhibits with 300 animals such as lions, tigers, brown bears, river otters, kangaroos, and lemurs. The size isn't overwhelming for kids, and they can get up close with animals in the indoor lab. Admission: $18, age 13 and older; $12, children 3–12. Open 10 a.m. to 4 p.m. year-round, with longer summer hours.

Spirit Mountain. 9500 Spirit Mountain Place; (800) 642-6377; spiritmt.com. Summer and fall visitors can enjoy the Timber Twister, a self-controlled alpine coaster, plus a Timber Flyer zip line and nine-hole minigolf course. This variation of a traditional zip line has bench-like seats rather than a harness. It allows a parent and child to ride together. In winter, Spirit Mountain has 22 ski runs, 700-foot vertical drops, 1 super pipe, and the largest terrain park in the Midwest. Families can race down a six-lane tubing park or check out the Lower Spirit Mountain Nordic Center and groomed Nordic ski trails. Spirit Mountain also has disc golfing, scenic chairlift rides, and 73 campsites. Call for details on adventure park and prices, plus seasonal hours.

Superior Hiking Trail. (218) 834-2700; superiorhiking.org. This beloved—and rugged—306-mile trail starts south of Duluth at Jay Cooke State Park and scenically climbs along the city's hilltops and over its creeks and rivers before following Lake Superior's North Shore all the way to the Canadian border. You can find short sections with stellar views from Spirit Mountain and additional trailheads along Skyline Drive.

where to stay

Mountain Villas. 9525 W. Skyline Pkwy.; (866) 688-4552; mtvillas.com. These 14 eight-sided villas sleep up to six with two bedrooms, two baths, a full kitchen, and a living room with a pullout sofa. Right on Spirit Mountain with views of the St. Louis River and Lake Superior, they're especially convenient for skiers and snowboarders, who can get a discount on lift tickets. Open year-round with some pet-friendly units. $$–$$$.

Willard Munger Inn. 7408 Grand Ave.; (218) 624-4814; mungerinn.com. This hotel has long drawn raves for the value of its pine-sided rooms with quilts and amenities such as continental breakfast, free use of bikes and passes to Lake Superior Zoo across the road. The hotel also sits at the foot of Spirit Mountain ski resort, 1 block from the St. Louis River, and right along the Willard Munger Trail. The trail, you may have guessed, was named for the hotel's founder, who passionately supported environmental improvements and projects, including the popular trail between Hinckley and Duluth. Winter guests can hop onto the trail with Nordic skis or nab a winter downhill special. $$.

lincoln park

This neighborhood buzzes with fresh energy as new restaurants and businesses open along Superior Avenue west of downtown Duluth, bordered roughly by Garfield, Piedmont, and 40th Avenues. The city designated it as the Lincoln Park Craft District to recognize its many makers and homegrown businesses, such as Duluth Pack and Frost River, companies that handcraft leather and waxed canvas camping gear and accessories.

where to go

The Back Alley. 2409 W. Superior St.; (218) 464-1786; backalleysurf.com. You can order a hot coffee, learn about the freshwater surf scene, possibly catch some live music, or go big with a new surfboard and the necessary wetsuit to use it on Lake Superior.

Bent Paddle Brewing. 1832 W. Michigan St.; (218) 279-2722; bentpaddlebrewing.com. One of the early businesses to help revive this flagging neighborhood in 2013, this craft brewery has grown into a popular destination, with a green space for live music, yard games, and a heated (if needed) pet-friendly patio. The taproom offers limited brews that you might not find elsewhere, along with nonalcoholic options for families. Their more than two dozen brews, such as cold press black coffee ale, 14 Degree amber ale, Venture Pils, and Wilderness Tuxedo sour ales, are made with water from Lake Superior. It also launched a line of sparkling waters infused with CBD and THC and opened Cann-A-Lounge + Market in 2023 with related CBD products in its original taproom.

Damage Boardshop. 1904 W. Superior St.; (218) 724-4027; damageboardshop.com. Fitting in with the city's get-outdoors focus, this shop blends skateboards, surfboards, and snowboards to take advantage of every season.

Duluth Children's Museum. 2125 W. Superior St.; (218) 733-7543; duluthchildrens museum.org. Curious kids will enjoy getting behind the throttle of a Cirrus airplane to learn about aviation, experimenting with science, making snacks with produce from the museum's greenhouse and gardens, and exploring a St. Louis River estuary wild rice paddy while learning Ojibwe words. Admission: $10, ages 2 and older.

Duluth Folk School. 1917 W. Superior St.; (218) 481-7888; duluthfolkschool.com. Let the handcrafted vibe of this neighborhood inspire you to join classes at this school that started in 2015. Learn to make your own canoe paddle or snowshoes, felt wool, master Swedish or Norwegian folk painting, or make homemade wine. You can also join game nights, community craft nights, and open mic nights or stop in for homemade quiche and locally roasted coffee at the Dovetail Café & Market. Its name comes from the dovetailed cabin within its walls, built from pines from the 2016 blowdown.

Frost River. 1910 W. Superior St.; (218) 727-1472; frostriver.com. This Duluth original grabs attention with its vibrant red storefront and a retail area packed with heritage goods, such as daypacks, shoulder bags, duffel bags, and all manner of outdoor accessories. It's all handcrafted from waxed canvas, leather, and brass hardware in the business's lofted upper story. You can also find clothing and hats, gifts for pets, picnic goods, and cribbage boards.

Two Loons Gallery and Boutique. 2025 W. Superior St.; (218) 481-7727; twoloons.mn. More than 200 local and regional crafters sell at this gallery with stained-glass lamps, jewelry, paintings, clothing, accessories, and home decor with a Great Lakes flair.

where to eat

Clyde Ironworks. 2920 W. Michigan St.; (218) 727-1150; clydeironworks.com.com. Large and spacious, this converted ironworks that once built industrial cranes now stokes up huge wood-fired ovens used for Neapolitan pizzas, stromboli, crusty baguettes that accompany salads, and buns for juicy burgers and sandwiches. Even cheesecakes and apple crisp go into the wood-fired oven. $$.

Duluth Grill. 118 S. 27th Ave. West; (218) 726-1150; duluthgrill.com. This popular break-fast and lunch stop attracts a mix of meat-lovers, vegans, and gluten-free diners who can all feast on meals creatively presented and locally sourced whenever possible—including seasonal produce grown right on the property. Look for fun twists, such as savory pancakes or waffles, bibimbap and Korean flavors, fresh takes on Mexican plates, and desserts such as banana cream pie. $$.

Love Creamery. 1908 W. Superior St.; (218) 576-5639; lovecreamery.com. Look for sea-sonally inspired, creatively crafted small-batch ice cream at this business that started in Lincoln Park and added a shop in Canal Park. They scoop 16 rotating flavors of ice cream (including vegan and gluten-free choices) such as goat cheese with blackberries, mascar-pone with apricot jam, lavender honeycomb, maple bourbon pecan, and malted chocolate with chocolate-covered pretzels. Ice-cream flights, ice cream drenched with espresso, sun-daes, and ice-cream bars and sandwiches are also served. $.

OMC Smokehouse. 1909 W. Superior St.; (218) 606-1611; omcsmokehouse.com. The initials stand for "Oink, Moo, Cluck," a playful nod to the tender pork, beef brisket, and chicken they smoke here. The meats are served deliciously as-is or piled onto loaded macaroni and cheese, layered into tacos, and heaped into burrito bowls. You can also find vegetarian options, plus catfish and gumbo for a little Southern flair to a Northern meal. Sit inside to enjoy the artwork or grab a spot on the patio, where you might find a fire crackling. $-$$.

canal park & downtown

Canal Park, Duluth's hugely popular waterfront district, stretches between downtown and the Aerial Lift Bridge. Its museums, scenery, Lakewalk, restaurants, and boutique shopping can easily fill a day—or several days. The area is easy to navigate by foot, but you can also rent a bike or surrey or even a horse-drawn carriage for an alternative or more romantic way to get around.

Keep an ear out for the blast of boat horns and bells from the bridge, which rises to let charter boats, ships, and gigantic ore tankers that can be up to 1,000 feet pass between Lake Superior and Duluth Harbor. You can't fathom the size of tankers (roughly the length of three football fields) until you're standing in their wake. If your timing's off and ships aren't coming in, head to the S.S. *William A. Irvin* for an in-depth look at one of the Great Lakes' freshwater giants.

getting there

Take I-35 from the Thompson Hill information center into Duluth. Exit at South Lake Avenue to reach Canal Park.

where to go

Bentleyville Tour of Lights. 700 W. Railroad St.; (218) 740-3535; bentleyvilleusa.org. This much-anticipated holiday tradition turns Duluth's Bayfront Park into a Christmas wonderland with more than 5 million lights illuminating a 138-foot Christmas tree and creating large walk-through displays depicting everything from elves to snowmen and dinosaurs to ore boats. Sponsors keep the event free—including cookies, popcorn, cocoa, and marshmallows to roast over the many fires set up to warm cold fingers. Open nightly, Saturday before Thanksgiving to just after Christmas. Parking is $10. Food shelf and new toy donations encouraged.

Great Lakes Aquarium. 353 Harbor Dr.; (218) 740-3474; glaquarium.org. Learn about the fish and wildlife that live in and around the Great Lakes through exhibits and demonstrations, such as divers heading into two-story tanks to swim among sturgeon, salmon, trout, and other freshwater fish. Even more fun: Catch the river otter program when handlers bring them buckets of snow or ice filled with hidden treats such as anchovies and worms. Other live exhibits include seahorses, touch tanks with stingrays, and shorebirds. Get a little wet with a hands-on model of the Great Lakes and the importance of watersheds. Open 10 a.m. to 6 p.m. daily. Admission: $20, adults; $19, seniors; $16, kids 3–17. Parking is $10 per vehicle.

Lake Superior Maritime Visitor Center. 600 Canal Park Dr.; (218) 788-6430; lsmma.com. Learn about Duluth's shipping history and shipwrecks, hear crew members and passengers tell their tales, and take the wheel in a pilothouse facing the lake. Check the front door for listings of ships coming into or leaving the harbor, or go to harborlookout.com. You can get an excellent view from the second-floor windows or out on the pier. Free admission. Open daily in the peak season, then Friday through Sunday when the shipping season stops—usually between December and March when the harbor freezes.

Lake Superior Railroad Museum. 506 W. Michigan St.; (218) 727-8025; lsrm.org. You can still hear a steam engine's whistle and the chug of a train at this attractive 1892 train depot. Explore the Midwest's largest indoor train collection, with vintage steam trains, a model railroad, and re-created turn-of-the-20th-century downtown. You can also catch the North Shore Scenic Railroad here. Museum admission: $14, age 14 and up; $7, ages 3–13.

Lakewalk. (218) 730-4300; duluthmn.gov/parks/. This scenic, almost 8-mile paved path stretches from Bayfront Park and Duluth Entertainment Convention Center to Canal Park, past the Fitger's shopping complex, Leif Erickson Rose Garden, and stretches all the way to Brighton Beach (Kitchi Gammi Park) on the town's eastern edge. Along the way, enjoy the people watching as families skip stones, teens jump off the eerie foundation of an old gravel dock in the harbor, and folks go by on the passenger train.

North Shore Scenic Railroad, 506 W. Michigan St.; (218) 722-1273; duluthtrains.com. Head to the historic Duluth Depot to catch a narrated scenic ride through downtown or along the shore to Two Harbors. The most popular option, the Duluth Zephyr, takes a 75-minute trek through downtown, along the shore, and as far as the Congdon Mansion area. First-class seats include an upstairs viewing area in a sky-view dome car. If you have kids, look for family-focused rides such as weekend pizza trains, fall pumpkin patch trains, or the Christmas City Express, which includes a story time or shuttle to Bentleyville. Daily train excursions run mid-April through late October. Tickets start at $22, adults; $11, children 3–13.

Park Point Beach. At the end of Minnesota Avenue; duluthmn.gov/parks. Cross the aerial lift bridge from Canal Park and follow Minnesota Avenue onto what's considered the world's longest freshwater sandbar. It stretches for 7 miles before reaching Park Point, a favorite hangout with dunes, sandy beaches, picnic grounds, and a play structure shaped like an ore boat. It's also the least-bracing place to take a Lake Superior swim. Water can get up to 72°F. On windy or stormy days, Park Point may attract Great Lakes surfers. Park Point Recreation Area and Trail also draws birders, who look for songbirds and waterfowl resting and refueling during spring and fall migrations.

S.S. *William A. Irvin* tours. 350 Harbor Dr.; (218) 722-7876; decc.org/william-a-irvin/. Someone said "Supersize me" when these mighty ships were built. Stand next to this one and it's tough to fathom that it was retired in 1978 because it was too small at only 610 feet long. It was launched in 1937 to haul materials to Ohio and Indiana steel mills and transport company dignitaries and guests in four luxury cabins. Climb aboard to learn about life on this "Laker" and see the elegant rooms. You also can tour the Lake Superior tug next to the *Irvin*. Open May through October. If you go in October, test your bravery with the Irvin's Haunted Ship—a unique Minnesota scare venue. Tours last 45–60 minutes. $20, adults; $15, children age 11 and older; $10, military and seniors; free for kids under 10.

salties vs. lakers

Duluth welcomes two kinds of ships: "Salties," which travel about 2,340 miles from the Atlantic Ocean via the St. Lawrence Seaway, and "Lakers," which stay on the Great Lakes because they're too big for the seaway. Salties have to be less than 600 feet long, while Lakers are usually 600 to 1,000 feet long—or about three football fields in length.

The William A. Irvin, *a retired Great Lakes flagship of US Steel, boasts a 2,000-horsepower engine and could unload 13.8 tons of ore in less than 3 hours.*

Close to 900 ships arrive and leave the Port of Duluth-Superior each year. They haul coal, iron ore, grain, limestone, cement, salt, wood pulp, and equipment such as gigantic wind turbines that get shipped across the country.

You can track ship schedules at harborlookout.com or with an app such as MarineTraffic.

Vista Fleet Sightseeing & Dining Cruises. 323 Harbor Dr.; (218) 722-6218; vistafleet .com. One of the best ways to enjoy the world's largest freshwater lake is to hop aboard the *Vista Star* or *Vista Queen* public cruises. Ranging from 75 minutes to almost 2 hours, tours include Duluth history, its harbor, shipping, and the ecology of Lake Superior. They are also a chance to go beneath the aerial lift bridge. Special tours include sunset cruises catered by Bellisio's Italian Restaurant, family-focused pizza cruises, and fall color lunch or dinner. Tours run daily May through October, with prices starting at $16.

Wheel Fun Rentals. 365 S. Lake Ave.; (218) 464-7292; wheelfunrentals.com. Among the more distinctive ways to get down the pier, along the Lakewalk, or to the harbor front is pedaling a single or double surrey. You also can rent kids' bikes, mountain bikes, choppers, and deuce coupes. Prices run from $11/hour to $40/hour. Open late May through mid-September.

where to shop

Canal Park and the waterfront are full of shops, galleries, and restaurants. You can easily fill an afternoon browsing the storefronts, but you'll find additional gems tucked into the DeWitt-Seitz Building, a converted warehouse on Canal Park Drive, or Fitger's, a former brewery converted into a historic hotel with shops, restaurants, and a microbrewery. Fitger's (fitgers .com) is walkable from the waterfront (look for the vintage red water tower) or you can park in the ramp next to it. Call shops for hours, which vary by season. More information is available at visitduluth.com/shopping or canalpark.com

Art Dock. 394 S. Lake Ave., Ste. 101; (218) 722-1451; art-dock.com. See the region through the eyes of more than 160 local and regional artists who create pottery, jewelry, paintings, glass, and photographs. You can find everything from batik hangings of blueberries and agate jewelry to stained-glass snowflakes, woodblock prints, and hand-knit items.

Blue Heron Trading Company. 394 S. Lake Ave., Ste. 102; (218) 722-8799; theblue herontradingcompany.com. If watching the Food Network makes you drool, this is your kind of place. It's packed with gourmet ingredients, kitchen tools, a rainbow of pots and pans, playful kitchenware and textiles, and just about anything you need to be a happy host.

Duluth Pack Flagship Store. 365 Canal Park Dr.; (218) 722-3898; duluthpack.com. This shop sells far more than the heirloom canvas bags they've handcrafted for canoe camping since 1882. Look for stylish canvas purses and daypacks, camping supplies, handmade paddles, hats, hammocks, brand-name outerwear and activewear, hiking gear for dogs like pooch packs and collapsible food bowls, and even locally forged tent stakes.

Indigenous First Art & Gifts. 202 W. Second St.; (218) 590-3305; indigenousfirst.org. Find beaded and woven native jewelry and art, paintings, native foods, apparel, and books from 120 contributing artists at this shop dedicated to Lake Superior Anishinaabe (Ojibwe).

Lake Superior Art Glass. 357 Canal Park Dr.; (218) 464-1799; lakesuperiorartglass.com. Take the chill off a cool day watching artisans blow molten glass into new works of art. You can see them swirl colors across clear glass spheres and glasses and join hands-on classes such as making glass pendants or ornaments. The shop sells products by local and national glass artists who may be influenced by the fish, birds, and waves you can see around the Great Lakes.

Siiviis and Sivertson Gallery. 361 Canal Park Dr.; (218) 723-7877; sivertson.com. Expect a joyous flood of color and often humorous touches from more than 60 regional artists such as Liz Sivertson with her dreamy twists on North Shore wildlife, Rick Allen's playful woodcuts, Christian Dalbec's luminous photos of Superior's waves, and jewelry such as Sami bracelets with braided metallic thread on leather. Siiviis and Sivertson Gallery, based in Grand Marais, also specialize in art by Alaskan and Canadian Inuit.

where to eat

Harbor 360. 505 W. Superior St.; (218) 722-8439; harbor360duluth.com. For decades, the top floor of the Radisson Hotel Duluth—Harborview has revolved slowly to offer diners a 360-degree view of the city and its waterfront. This restaurant focuses on fast-casual, affordable food such as a wild rice salad, walleye sandwich, and smash burgers. Open daily breakfast through dinner. $$.

Canal Park Brewing Company. 300 Canal Park Dr.; (218) 464-4790; canalparkbrewery .com. On a balmy, calm day, you can't beat a lakeside seat on Canal Park Brewing's patio.

Combine a flight of award-winning craft beers such as Nut Hatchet brown ale, Hank and Dabs pale ale, Click Drag Kolsch, and Old Avalanche barley wine with fried Ellsworth cheese curds, popcorn-topped beer cheese soup, smoked salmon BLT on cranberry wild rice bread, or a ground chuck patty with white cheddar, beer-glazed onions, and house whiskey sauce. Desserts include a silky Swedish cream topped with lingonberry sauce and berries. $$.

Grandma's Saloon & Grill. 522 Lake Ave. South; (218) 727-4192; grandmasrestaurants .com. Canal Park's best-known restaurant serves classic American fare in a historic building packed with antiques and local memorabilia, from neon signs to a stuffed bear that had the misfortune to crash through a hotel lobby in the 1940s. The restaurant can serve 600 people inside and on the rooftop patio but still may require a wait due its popularity, with a chicken and wild rice salad, beef or wild rice burgers, a triple-decker Monte Cristo, smoked trout on toasted rye, and a walleye shore lunch. The patio overlooks the Lift Bridge and lake. $$.

fun fact: *Grandma's Saloon and Grill may best be known for Grandma's Marathon, which was named for the restaurant when it became a key sponsor in 1977 and began its tradition of a prerace spaghetti feed. The June event with multiple race options has grown to be among the top marathons in the nation, sometimes selling out with 20,000 registered runners coming from all 50 states and from dozens of countries. Few locations can beat the North Shore's scenic lakefront route from south of Two Harbors to the festive finish line in Canal Park. Learn more at grandmasmarathon.com.*

fun fact: *Grandma's Saloon and Grill may best be known for Grandma's Marathon, which was named for the restaurant when it became a key sponsor in 1977 and began its tradition of a prerace spaghetti feed. The June event with multiple race options has grown to be among the top marathons in the nation, sometimes selling out with 20,000 registered runners coming from all 50 states and from dozens of countries. Few locations can beat the North Shore's scenic lakefront route from south of Two Harbors to the festive finish line in Canal Park. Learn more at grandmasmarathon.com.*

Hanabi Japanese Cuisine. 110 N. First Ave. W.; (218) 464-4412; hanabiduluth.com. For a more sophisticated night out, head downtown for close to 80 kinds of sushi, sashimi, and a fusion mix with special rolls. Everything arrives artfully crafted. You also get udon or soba noodles, gyoza, crispy tempura, tuna, red snapper, and other grilled seafood. $$.

Lake Avenue Restaurant and Bar. 394 S. Lake Ave.; (218) 722-2355; lakeaveduluth .com. Locavore chefs at this trendy spot like to surprise diners with unusual and seasonal ingredients. Think lamb meatballs, beet or jackfruit pizza, Szechuan chicken on Japanese milk bread, and colorful seasonal salads. They have some mainstays too, including a brisket sandwich and Lake Avenue burger with house-made pickles. The micro-distillery in back shakes up a creative (and potent) line of cocktails, and you can catch live music on weekends. Open for lunch and dinner daily. $$–$$$.

Little Angie's Cantina and Grill. 11 E. Buchanan St.; (218) 727-6117; littleangies.com. The large patio makes this a popular hangout during balmy days. At night it's downright festive with the playful neon sign and margaritas flowing. If you're eating their Tex-Mex fajitas, burritos, sandwiches, and salads indoors, the collection of Southwestern and vintage cowboy memorabilia gives you plenty to look at. $$.

Northern Waters Smokehaus. 394 S. Lake Ave., Ste. LL1; (218) 724-7307; northern waterssmokehaus.com. For a memorable picnic, order a gourmet sandwich or a selection of salami, bacon, meat sticks, smoked pork, trout, whitefish, salmon, and more—all locally, skillfully smoked for this popular Canal Park destination. Try a Pastrami Mommy with bison meat, smoked whitefish tacos, lox and cream cheese on bagels, or the Hedonist, a liver pâté sandwich with French pickles and all the fixings. Smoked tofu sandwich and vegetarian salads are also available. $$.

Va Bene Caffé. 734 E. Superior St.; (218) 722-1518; vabenecaffe.com. Va Bene taps the area's Italian heritage and claims some of the city's best views of the lake from the solarium. Stroll the Lakewalk from Canal Park to here and you won't feel as guilty indulging in antipasto, Italian sausage soup, rich pastas, and creamy gelatos. $$.

Vikre Distillery. 525 S. Lake Ave., #102; (218) 481-7401; vikredistillery.com. Handcrafted botanical gins infused with the fragrant northern essence of cedar, juniper, or spruce provide the star ingredients at this chic and cozy cocktail room near the base of the aerial lift bridge. Vikre also distills its own aquavit, whiskey, and herbal liqueurs, all of which inspire constantly changing and wildly creative cocktails with seasonal syrups (think blueberry, fig, sage, and chai) plus juice and fruit purees. Vikre taps Northern Waters Smokehaus for local charcuterie, crostini, and snacks. $$.

where to stay

Canal Park Lodge. 250 Canal Park Dr.; (218) 279-6000; canalparklodge.com. The Arts and Crafts design and colorful exterior make this hotel stand out. It includes 116 rooms on three floors, with more than 50 of them facing the lake. There's a pool area that's popular with families, plus complimentary appetizers in the evening and hot breakfast in the morning. $$.

Fitger's Inn. 600 E. Superior St.; (218) 722-8826; fitgers.com. Historic rooms built in the brewery's former bottling department have Lake Superior views and connect to Canal Park via the Lakewalk. Rooms feature the greens, blues, reds, and gold tones of the late 1920s, along with some arched windows, exposed rock walls, and high ceilings. $$.

The Inn on Lake Superior. 350 Canal Park Dr.; (218) 726-1111; theinnonlakesuperior .com. If you smell a campfire and roasting marshmallows along the Lakewalk, it's probably families in front of this 175-room inn. They have nightly story time, campfires, and an indoor pool, plus a heated pool on the roof. Many of the luxury rooms and suites feature lake-view balconies, and all include morning breakfast. Some rooms are pet friendly. $$–$$$.

Pier B Resort Hotel. 800 W. Railroad St.; (218) 481-8888; pierbresort.com. One of the city's newest hotels opened in 2017 near Bayfront Park with views of the harbor as ships come and go. You can also dine at its Silos Restaurant to catch the view. $$$.

Solglimt Bed & Breakfast. 828 S. Lake Ave.; (877) 727-0596; solglimt.com. With gorgeous lake views and a sandy Park Point beach out the back door, this B&B lives up to its name. It translates to "sun on the water." The home also stands out with its modern expansion, artsy rooms, environmental efforts, sprawling gardens, and beautifully presented meals. The three-course breakfasts are served on the patio or in the guest dining room facing Lake Superior. $$–$$$.

South Pier Inn on the Canal. 701 S. Lake Ave.; (218) 786-9007; southpierinn.com. If you love watching ships come in, South Pier's rooms facing the harbor boast the best views, with ships gliding by within 100 feet of the windows. It's also an ideal location for watching the world's largest aerial lift bridge go up and down. Breakfast included. $$.

east duluth, mn

Glensheen Mansion. 3300 London Rd.; (218) 726-8910; glensheen.org. Consider the stats on one of the Minnesota's poshest and storied mansions: 39 rooms, 15 bedrooms, 15 fireplaces, 10 bathrooms, and 1 double murder. That last part gets swept under the carpet with freshly imagined events and tours offering new ways to explore this lakeshore treasure built between 1905 and 1908 with intricate woodwork, stained glass, a solarium that's an Arts and Crafts masterpiece, elegant gardens, marble fountain, stables, and more. Look for whiskey and history talks, craft sessions, flashlight or candlelight tours, self-guided tours, holiday decorations, treasure hunts, and free concerts on the pier Wednesdays in July and August, which attendees listen to from shore or paddle in from the lake. Admission $8 for youth 6 to 17 and $20 for adults for a self-guided tour of the 12-acre estate. Admission varies by tour.

Hawk Ridge Bird Observatory. E. Skyline Pkwy. and 52nd Ave. East; (218) 428-6209; hawkridge.org. Enthusiastic birders from across the country and beyond line up to watch close to 100,000 hawks migrate through each fall. Migrating birds save energy by riding

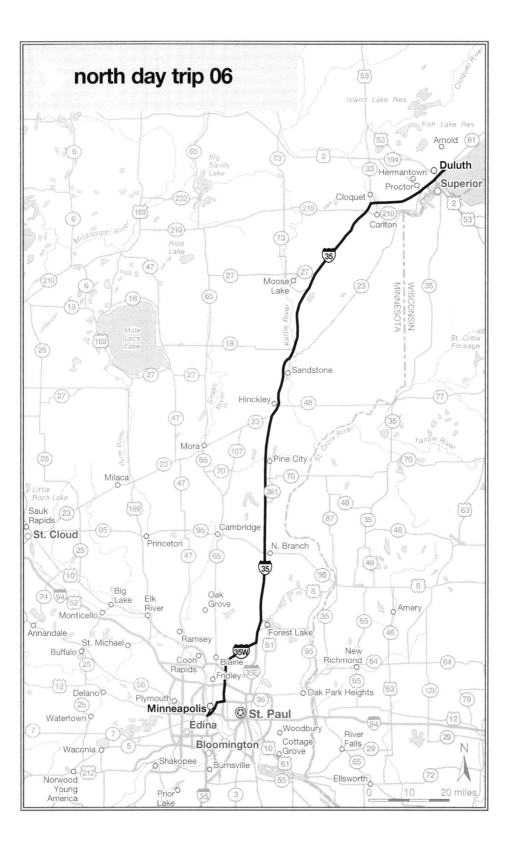

north day trip 06

the warm thermals that rise from Lake Superior's shore to high above the ridge. Most pass through between September 10 and 25, but naturalists with spotting scopes and field guides are usually on hand from September 1 through late October. There are also 4 miles of hiking trails threading Hawk Ridge's 365 acres.

where to eat

At Sara's Table Chester Creek Café. 1902 E. 8th St.; (218) 724-6811; astccc.net. This college-comfy restaurant filled with shelves of books draws appreciative diners, starting with breakfasts such as cranberry wild rice French toast and hippie farm breakfast. Vegetarian and global flavors influence lunch and dinner choices such as whitefish with harissa aioli and slaw on ciabatta, Thai tofu curry, buttermilk chicken and fresh greens salad, Peruvian steak and potato stir-fry, and a nightly hot dish special—a nod to Minnesota, moms, and church basements. $$.

Tavern on the Hill. 1102 Woodland Ave.; (218) 724-0010; tavernduluth.com. This modern restaurant with a charming patio near the University of Minnesota—Duluth campus serves an eclectic and creative menu that includes soft pretzel sticks with beer cheese for dipping, fried avocado street tacos, Italian cioppino, ahi tuna burger, burrata insalata pizza, plus plenty of vegetarian, vegan, and gluten-free choices. $$–$$$.

where to stay

Edgewater Hotel & Waterpark. 2400 London Rd.; (218) 728-3601; duluthwaterpark .com. This hotel with more than 200 rooms and suites draws a family crowd for its 30,000-square-foot Polynesian-themed water park and complimentary minigolf, but you don't need kids to appreciate the lake-view rooms, balconies, heated outdoor pool, and availability of bikes. $$.

northeast

day trip 01

northeast

>>>

ice age geology & scandinavians:
taylors falls, mn; st. croix falls, wi;
scandia, mn; lindstrom, mn

Combine the St. Croix River—considered one of the best canoeing rivers in the nation—with the awe factor of a 200-foot-high ice age gorge (known as the Dalles) and you have a spectacular attraction for outdoor lovers. Whether you're hiking alongside gravel-rock-scoured potholes or gazing at funky rock formations from the water, it's easy to see why this stretch along the Minnesota and Wisconsin borders has been drawing tourists for more than a century.

It's also understandable why citizens rallied to save its beauty when extensive mining and logging were taking a toll on the land and river. The result was the nation's first interstate state park, in 1900. It straddles almost 1,700 acres on both sides of the St. Croix River near the towns of Taylors Falls, Minnesota, and St. Croix Falls, Wisconsin. About 200 miles of the St. Croix and Namekagon Rivers (which connect) are preserved federally as a National Scenic Riverway, which helps keep them pristine and undeveloped. From Interstate State Park paddlers can choose how much of the Lower St. Croix River they want to explore—from easy 2-hour floats to half a day or more, with additional landings and state parks downriver.

Adventurers wanting more action can try cliff jumping and rock climbing, while anyone preferring laid-back touring can take narrated boat tours to admire the Dalles of the St. Croix. History runs deep in this area, beginning with the Dakota and Ojibwe peoples and French fur traders to New Englanders who arrived in the early 1800s seeking to make their fortunes in lumber and natural resources. During one effort to float logs down the St. Croix to sawmills, the logs jammed and backed up for 7 miles, making news around the world. By the later

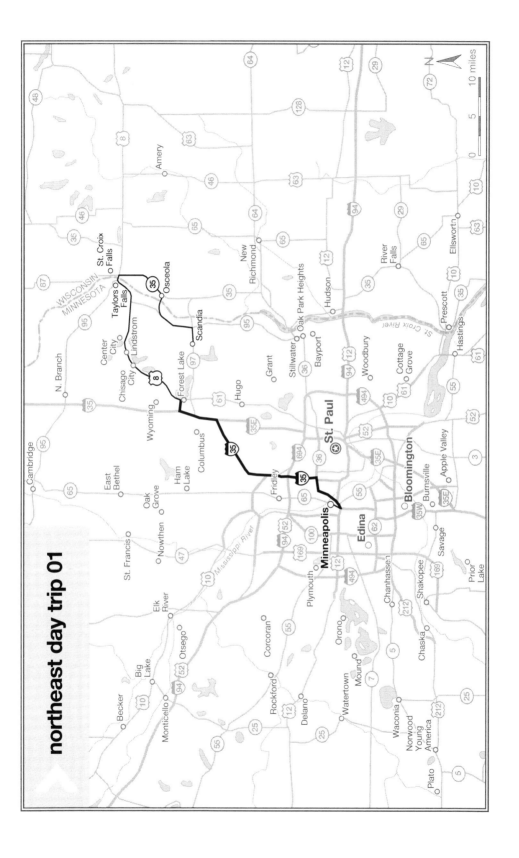

northeast day trip 01

1800s, immigrants from Sweden, Denmark, Norway, and Germany arrived to make a new home in Minnesota.

These days, the area is popular for vineyards, which take advantage of the hilly terrain that's favorable to cold-hardy grape varieties. You could spend a day or more just sampling wine and savoring local cheese and charcuterie plates, with pauses to admire the Franconia Sculpture Park or the work of local artists. A trip to Taylors Falls and St. Croix Falls can wind south to Osceola, Scandia, and William O'Brien State Park and loop back to Lindstrom on the Chisago Lakes in about 40 miles.

Learn more about the area at thestcroixvalley.com and chisagolakes.org.

taylors falls, mn

This getaway wins raves for its outdoor recreation and geology that shows ancient floods of basalt, potholes scoured into rocks, and rippling eskers. Boat rides, paddling tours, and rock climbing make summer a popular time to visit, but autumn may be the most popular. Explosions of red, gold, green, and orange carpet the valley, reflect in the river, and shimmer across the many lakes. Be prepared for weekend crowds as like-minded travelers converge for the seasonal spectacle. Winter visitors can enjoy the town's quiet season, while spring visitors can watch for woodland flowers such as trout lilies and the first hints of green in the valley's canopy of trees.

getting there

From Minneapolis or St. Paul, follow I-35 north to US 8 near Forest Lake. Follow US 8 East to Taylors Falls. It's about 50 miles, or 1 hour, to get there.

where to go

Folsom House. 272 W. Government St.; (651) 465-3125; mnhs.org. History buffs can tour this former lumber baron's mansion in the Angel Hill district above Taylors Falls. Most of the neighborhood's well-to-do homes reflect the community's New England heritage with Greek Revival facades. You can see the family's 1848 rosewood piano, their china set gracing the walnut dining room table, Mr. Folsom's office and book collection, an upstairs nursery stocked with toys and a potty chair, and bedrooms with vintage razors, eyeglasses, a wedding dress, and a Civil War uniform. Admission: $6, adults; $5, seniors and college students; $4, children 5–17. Open daily late May through early October.

Franconia Sculpture Park. 29836 St. Croix Trail, Franconia; (651) 257-6668; franconia .org. You can spot this fanciful attraction 3 miles before reaching Taylors Falls. Outdoors and always changing, this free 50-acre sculpture park with more than 85 pieces ranks among the best and most imaginative places to introduce kids to art. You can see local and international artists creating works in progress from April through December, catch a guided tour May through October, and stay for concerts on Saturdays throughout the summer. The park is open year-round (look for snowshoe events in winter) and includes rotating art shows in the Mardag Gallery at Franconia Commons, open weekends in the offseason; daily mid-April through mid-November.

Interstate State Park—Minnesota. 307 Milltown Road; (651) 539-4500; dnr.state.mn.us. As eastbound US 8 nears the St. Croix, watch for the seasonal visitor center and parking lot for hiking, rock climbing, and catching one of the tour boats down below. Hike the Glacial Pothole Trail to see a unique geologic area. Melting glaciers and gravel that swirled through whirlpools carved out perfectly smooth kettles (or potholes) with names such as Lily Pond, The Squeeze, and the Bottomless Pit, which is deeper than 60 feet. The park includes 37 semi-modern campsites, 22 with electricity. The park spans 298 acres on the Minnesota side, with another 1,330 acres on the Wisconsin side of the river. (see the Osceola section for more details). $7 daily park sticker is required.

Pleasant Valley Orchard. 17325 Pleasant Valley Rd., Shafer; (651) 257-9159; pleasant valleyorchard.com. This seasonal farm 9 miles southwest of Taylors Falls opens for U-pick strawberries in June and again in September and October for U-pick apples, hayrides, apple pastries, pumpkins, and holiday gifts.

Taylors Falls Canoe and Kayak Rental. Interstate State Park—Minnesota; (651) 465-1080; taylorsfallscanoeandkayakrental.com. There are several places to rent canoes and kayaks in the area, but this one has been around since 1910. Paddlers can get onto the water for 2 to 3 hours, finishing at Osceola Landing 7 miles downstream, or spend half a day paddling 17 miles to William O'Brien State Park. Shuttle pickup times vary.

Taylors Falls Scenic Boat Tours. 220 South St. (ticket stand is at the intersection of US 8 and MN 95); (651) 465-6315; taylorsfallsboat.com. Paddlewheel boat tours have taken visitors through the Dalles of the St. Croix River for more than 100 years. Guests can settle into the enclosed lower level or grab a seat on the upper deck as guides point out formations such as the Old Man of the Dalles, Lion's Head, or Devil's Chair. Look for daily tours from 45 to 80 minutes, along with sundown, twilight, and history cruises May through mid-October. Tickets start at $15 for kids 3–15; $26 for adults.

Wild Mountain. 37200 Wild Mountain Rd.; (651) 465-6315; wildmountain.com. This ski and snowboard area includes 26 runs, 4 terrain parks, and a tubing run across 100 acres. It's one of the first Midwest resorts to open each winter and one of the last to close. When it does and spring arrives, visitors can ride go-karts, zoom down an alpine slide, or cool off with Avalanche Alley Water Slides and Wild Adventure Island Waterpark.

Wild Mountain Winery and Pizza. 16906 Wild Mountain Road; (651) 583-2161; wild mountainwinery.com. With its 15-acre location at one of the highest spots in Chisago County, this spot offers some of the best views for sipping local wines and slushies and noshing on pizzas or crackers and locally made Eichten's cheeses. The winery welcomes dogs, hosts live music on Saturdays, and has the Wild Vines Campground for tent camping.

where to eat

The Drive In. 572 Bench St.; (651) 465-7831; taylorsfallsdrivein.com. Look for the giant mug of root beer above this wonderfully nostalgic and tasty summer drive-in where you'll still see carhops taking orders. It's been a landmark for more than 50 years. Get one of the juicy hand-pattied burgers, thick-cut onion rings, and a frosty mug of homemade root beer or a float. The business also includes Adventure Falls Mini Golf. $.

Juneberry Cafe. 360 Bench St.; (651) 240-0105; juneberrycafe.com. You can linger at this seasonal eatery with a steamy espresso, Sebastian's ice cream (handcrafted in Minneapolis), grilled breakfast burrito, salads, and hot-pressed sandwiches such as bacon, cheddar, and fig. They also keep a case of grab-and-go sandwiches for those eager to hit the trails or paddle the river. $.

Tangled Up in Blue Restaurant. 425 Bench St.; (651) 465-1000; tangledupinbluerestaurant .net. Named for a Bob Dylan song, this small blue-hued restaurant earns raves for its seasonal, beautifully presented dinners. Menus may include crab-stuffed salmon or grilled shrimp with cauliflower puree, a spicy-sweet filet mignon, and flaming bananas Foster served over ice cream. High-season reservations recommended. $$$.

st. croix falls, wi

The beauty of the St. Croix River Valley extends across the river from Taylors Falls to St. Croix Falls on the Wisconsin side. Osceola is about 9 miles south of St. Croix Falls.

where to go

Chateau St. Croix Winery. 1998 WI 87; (715) 483-2556; chateaustcroix.com. With stone lions out front and an impressive chateau, this winery takes its inspiration from Europe with a variety of white, rosé, red, and dessert wines made from cold-hardy grapes on their 55-acre grounds. Stop by the deli for flatbreads, paninis, charcuterie platters, and more to savor while sipping wine on-site. The winery also hosts events throughout the year, including a jazz festival, grape stomp, Oktoberfest, holiday weekends with mulled wine and vendors, and a New Year's masquerade party.

Dancing Dragonfly Winery. 2013 120th Ave.; (715) 483-9463; dancingdragonflywinery. com. This winery offers tours, tastings, and wine by the glass, along with handcrafted pizzas, pretzels, paninis, baguettes, and desserts to complement their wines made with Midwest and coastal grapes. They bottle dozens of wines, such as their award-winning dry red Jeté that blends Sangiovese with cold-hardy grapes and Polka, its dry white wine made from Riesling grapes. They also make a nouveau much like Beaujolais Nouveau in late fall.

Fawn-Doe-Rosa Wildlife Educational Park. 2131 US 8; (715) 483-3772; fawndoerosa .com. This family-run attraction opened in 1963 and has given generations a chance to cuddle baby bunnies and interact with farm animals, get close to tame deer, take a pony ride, and learn about regional wildlife from lynxes to foxes. Open seasonally. Admission: $9.50 and up.

Ice Age National Scenic Trail. nps.gov/iatr. Anyone interested in sampling the scenery of Wisconsin's national scenic trail can start at its western terminus in Interstate State Park. Skilled hikers with mammoth ambitions can follow the trail almost 1,200 miles to its eastern terminus in Door County's Potawatomi State Park.

Interstate State Park—Wisconsin. 1275 WI 35; (715) 483-3747; dnr.wisconsin.gov. Wisconsin's oldest state park (established in 1900) sprawls for 1,400 acres along the river. It includes 85 campsites ($12–$20/night) and encompasses Lake O' the Dalles with a swimming beach. Hikers can follow Pothole, Summit Rock and River Bluff Trails with views of the Dalles and its rock formation named "Old Man," or continue onto the Ice Age National Scenic Trail. The Ice Age Interpretive Center offers exhibits and a film about the area's geologic formation. Daily park fee: $8–$11.

Miracle at Big Rock. 1674 WI 87; bigrockcreekwi.com. With a dazzling display of holiday lights on this historic farmstead, visitors can choose a walk-through or drive-through experience to enjoy the displays. There also are sleigh rides, sledding, activities from making s'mores to watching fireworks, and a heated area for indoor vendors, craft cocktails, and activities such as cookie decorating and visits with Santa. Open daily from Black Friday through New Year's Day.

Riverwood Canoe Rental. 254 S. Cascade St.; Osceola; (715) 222-2288; riverwood canoe.com. Rent a solo or tandem kayak and canoes from this place for 7-mile trips between Interstate State Park and Osceola.

St. Croix ArtBarn. 1040 Oak Ridge Dr., Osceola; (715) 294-2787; thestcroixartbarn.org. Formally named the St. Croix Center for the Arts and best known as the ArtBarn, this 110-year-old dairy barn 8 miles south of St. Croix Falls houses a 150-seat theater for plays, musicals, and concert, along with ongoing art exhibits. You also can take classes during the warm season.

St. Croix National Riverway Visitor Center, 401 N. Hamilton St.; (715) 483-2274; nps .gov/sacn. This seasonal visitor center offers a 19-minute film on the St. Croix River, along with nature exhibits, Junior Ranger booklets, and information on where to paddle, camp, hike, or picnic within this 230-mile-long stretch of national park land following the St. Croix and Namekagon rivers.

Trollhaugen Outdoor Recreation Area. 2232 100th Ave., Dresser; (651) 433-5141; trollhaugen.com. This longtime Midwest ski destination with 24 trails, 3 terrain parks, and 10 lanes of tubing takes advantage of the hilly winter landscape. They've been expanding with new trails, more lighting, and new chairlifts. In summer the hills become Trollhaugen's Adventure Park with a six–zip line course that zooms across 3,000 feet of trees up to 50 feet above the ground. An aerial challenge course looks like the elevated paths of a *Star Wars* Ewok village, with multiple courses and levels of difficulty.

where to eat

Dalles House Restaurant and Lounge. 720 St. Vincent St.; (715) 483-3246; dalleshouse. com. Enjoy beef tournedos and shrimp, duck in orange sauce, Friday fish fry, and seafood pasta, with live music Saturday nights. Sandwiches include a Croix burger with bacon, cheddar, coleslaw, and barbecue sauce or a Wisconsin burger topped with cheese curds. Anyone taking the Dam burger challenge—eating a full pound of ground chuck and fries—can earn a T-shirt with bragging rights. $$–$$$.

where to stay

St. Croix Valley Inn. 305 River St., Osceola; (715) 494-1677; stcroixvalleyinn.com. The seven spacious suites come with fireplaces, exposed stone walls, and hydromassage tubs. Breakfasts are delivered to rooms, allowing guests to dine in their bathrobes or on patios overlooking the valley and the river. $$–$$$.

scandia, mn

Along with nearby Lindstrom, Scandia is known for the Nordic heritage of its early settlers.

getting there

From St. Croix Falls, follow WI 35 to Osceola. Cross the St. Croix River to Minnesota and head south on MN 95 less than 9 miles to Scandia.

where to go

Gammelgården Museum. 20880 Olinda Trail; (651) 433-5053; gammelgardenofscandia .org. This "Old Small Farm" open-air museum showcases authentic buildings and a church built by Minnesota's first Swedish immigrants. Look for special events during the year, such as Midsommer Dag (Midsummer Day). Open Friday to Sunday from May 1 to mid-October. Valkommen Hus and Butik (welcome house and gift shop) with Scandinavian books, products, and handcrafted items is open Wednesday to Sunday from May 1 to December 23.

Rustic Roots Winery. 20168 St. Croix Trail North; (651) 433-3311; rusticroots.wine. In addition to a variety of red, white, and rosé wines made with cold-hardy grapes grown on 20 acres, Rustic Roots makes its own hard cider and serves local beers on their three patios. Guests can also bring a blanket and spread out in the estate-style vineyard.

William O'Brien State Park. 16821 O Brien Trail North, Marine On St. Croix; (651) 539-4980; dnr.state.mn.us. Along the St. Croix River and 4 miles from Scandia, this state park encompasses 1,653 acres that draw paddling enthusiasts, hikers, and Nordic skiers for 12 miles of river and savanna trails and families for swimming in Lake Alice, fishing from the pier, and camping between the lake and river. The park includes 114 campsites in two campgrounds, 3 year-round camper cabins, plus 1 seasonal cabin for rent. Visitors can rent canoes, kayaks, and paddleboards and borrow volleyballs, bocce balls, birding kits, and more. $7 for a day pass.

lindstrom, mn

With a historic water tower that looks like a Swedish coffeepot, "America's Little Sweden" proudly preserves its heritage and its role in Swedish literature. Novelist Vilhelm Moberg visited Lindstrom in 1948 and wrote *The Emigrants* about early homesteaders Karl Oskar and Kristina Nilsson, drawing fans from around the world to this tiny town. You'll also find colorful renditions of quilt blocks throughout the community and along the Swedish Barn Quilt Trail on US 8 between Chisago City and Taylors Falls. For additional information on places to go, check out cityoflindstrom.us/visitor-information-tourism.

where to go

Glädje. 13025 Lake Blvd.; (651) 257-1821; gladjegallery.com. This longtime gallery (formerly Gustaf's Up North Gallery) promotes regional artists, including painters inspired by the local landscape, Scandinavian folk artists, potters, jewelers, and handcrafted furniture makers.

Lindstrom Historical Walking Tour. cityoflindstrom.us. Stop by the Chisago Lakes Chamber Building next to the veterans' memorial to pick up a map for a self-guided walking tour. It covers the town's Swedish ties, along with historic buildings and homes.

Swedish Gift Store. 12734 Lake Blvd.; (651) 317-8976; swedishgiftstore.com. Browse hundreds of products that show Swedish heritage—from imported candy, Nordic sweaters, and linens to Sami bracelets, Dala horses, flags, T-shirts, and trolls.

Winehaven Winery and Vineyard. 9757 292nd St., Chisago City; (651) 257-1017; winehaven.com. The founders of this winery 3.4 miles west of Lindstrom started in beekeeping before expanding to wine. That background, plus the area's Scandinavian heritage, led to their Stinger Honeywine (also known as mead), which became an international hit. They make blush, red, white, and fruit wines.

where to eat

Gustaf's on Main Eatery. 13045 Lake Blvd.; (651) 263-0737; gustafseatery.com. Inside this historic building's brick facade and white spindled verandas, you'll find a homey place to grab breakfast, lunch, or snacks, with ice-cream cones, fresh-baked scones, savory egg dishes, a plate of Swedish pancakes, sandwiches, and salads. $–$$

Lindström Bakery. 12830 Lake Blvd.; (651) 257-1374; lindstroem.edan.io. This favorite stop with famed Swedish doughnuts also has classic doughnuts and cookies, cinnamon toast, apple crispies, gingerbread cookies, seasonal rosettes, and more. $.

Northern Lake Tavern and Grill. 10470 South Ave., Chisago Lakes; thenorthernlake tavern.com. With wood paneling, window views of the lakes, and a deck for outdoor dining, this place just west of Lindstrom gets people in the weekend mood—especially for Twin Cities folks headed to northern Wisconsin cabins. Look for pastrami barbecue sandwiches, supersized fried cod fillets, flatbread pizzas, wraps, and burgers. $$.

Panola Valley Gardens Tea. 26026 Olinda Trail; (651) 257-6072; panolavalleygardens .com. This picturesque wedding venue also offers public luncheons and afternoon teas by reservation and themed by what's in bloom throughout the summer. $$$.

day trip 02

northeast

the birkie, fat-tire races & giant fish
hayward, wi; cable, wi

Flanked by the Upper St. Croix–Namekagon River corridor to the west and Chequa-megon-Nicolet National Forest to the east, the Hayward–Cable Lakes area attracts adventurers in search of something big: a trophy fish, a memorable mountain bike trek, a scenic St. Croix paddle, an epic cross-country ski race, or serious relaxation. Together with Cable (17 miles to the east), the Hayward Lakes area offers close to 130 resorts, about 40 restaurants, and countless ways to get your heart pumping among woods, rivers, and lakes.

Forest trails draw Olympic-level athletes and have made the area famous. Consider this: Despite its small-town population of about 1,500, Cable welcomes 20,000 spectators who show up to cheer on 11,000 cross-country skiers in the legendary Birkebeiner Ski Race—the largest in North America. Cable also has hosted International Paralympic competitions.

In the warm season, trails through 850,000 acres of national forest draw mountain bikers who come for fun or training for the September Chequamegon Mountain Bike Festival, which treks through 40 miles of trails and has ranked among the top races in the country for more than four decades.

Altogether, you'll find more than 94 miles of cross-country ski trails, 1,200 miles of snowmobile trails, 400 miles of mountain bike trails, 150 miles of ATV trails, and 125 miles of hiking and snowshoe trails.

A multimillion-dollar development project is underway on the former Telemark Resort site. Plans for new hotel lodging, villas, and condominiums should significantly add to the area's accommodations and provide a new sports hub.

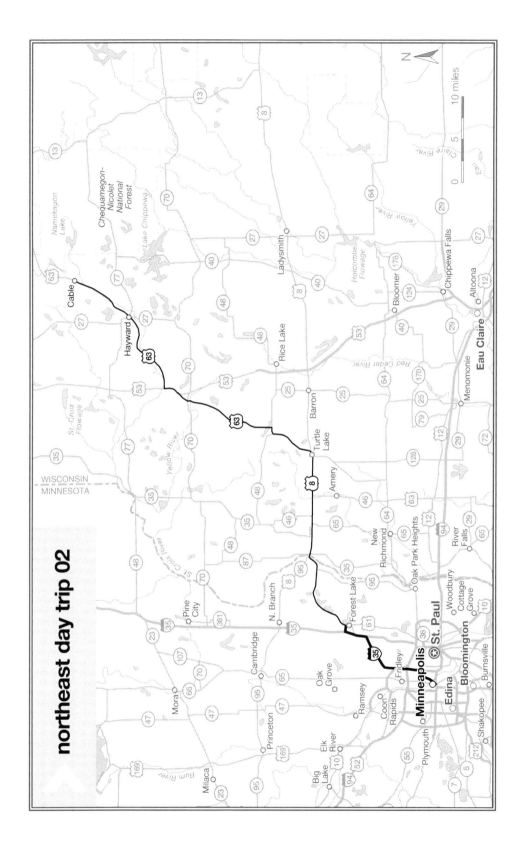

northeast day trip 02

hayward, wi

Hayward boasts one of the Midwest's most eclectic museum buildings and campiest photo opportunity. So go ahead. Don't be shy. Pose like human fish bait in the mouth of a four-and-a-half-story muskie. This icon of Hayward (pop. 16,200) appropriately houses the National Freshwater Fishing Museum Hall of Fame.

During the summer, listen for the buzz of chain saws and thunk of axes during a lumberjack show, or come for the fiercely competitive International Lumberjack Olympics. Inhale the fresh sawdust and enjoy the action. For detailed information, stop at Hayward Lakes Visitors and Convention Bureau, 15805 US 63; (715) 634-4801; haywardlakes.com.

getting there

Follow I-35 north to the US 8 exit, heading east toward Taylors Falls. Follow US 8 about 47 miles. At Turtle Lake, turn north onto US 63 and continue about 60 miles to Hayward. The 140-mile drive takes about 2.5 hours.

where to go

Big Fish Golf Club. 14122 W. True North Ln.; (715) 934-4770; golfbigfish.com. Course designer Pete Dye sculpted hills and hazards into the forest for this 18-hole golf course that's par 72 with five sets of tee boxes.

Freshwater Fishing Hall of Fame and Museum. 10360 Hall of Fame Dr.; (715) 634-4440; freshwater-fishing.org. Everything you wanted to know about fishing can be found in this shrine to anglers everywhere. Look for 100,000 fishing artifacts from bobbers to boats, 1,000 vintage outboard motors, displays honoring top anglers, and an exact replica of the Rapala family's 1950s workshop in Finland. The museum covers half a city block (about 7 acres) and includes a well-stocked pond for catch-and-release fishing during the summer. Open mid-April through October. Admission: $9, adult; $7, ages 3–17.

Moccasin Bar. 15820 US 63; (715) 634-4211. Pop into this saloon to see the world's largest muskie, at 5 feet long and 67 pounds. This has become an unofficial wildlife museum with quirky displays. Think taxidermy meets *Dogs Playing Poker*. Now picture that cult scene with bear cubs, a white rabbit, and an otter pouring a brew. You'll find stuffed raccoons in a boxing ring, chipmunks having an Oktoberfest moment, and a courtroom with a wolf as the judge, a bobcat as the sheriff, and a badger in trouble for poaching. Open 9 a.m. to bar close.

Namekagon River Visitor Center. W5483 US 63, Trego; (715) 635-8346; nps.gov/sacn. On the way to Hayward at the intersection of US 53 and US 63, this National Park Service site includes a movie, exhibits, hands-on activities, and a diorama that explain the area's history and natural resources, including sturgeon—the fish that gave the Namekagon River, a 95-mile tributary of the St. Croix River, its name.

Scheers Lumberjack Village. 15640 CR B; (715) 634-6923; scheerslumberjackvillage. com. Lumberjacks mastered extreme sports long before reality shows and axe-throwing became trendy. Settle into "The Bowl" (Hayward's 1890s holding area for logs) and watch the entertaining skills of flannel-clad competitors. They roll logs, climb poles, saw wood, and even invite kids to be part of the action. The village also includes the River Deck Restaurant, minigolf, a boutique, and cabin rentals. Shows run late May through early September. Admission: $13, kids 4 to 11; $19, adults.

muskie mania

So why is the muskie (or muskellunge) so sought after by anglers? Chalk it up to the fun and challenge of netting these huge fish that put up a good fight. A record-breaking muskie came in at 5 feet long. They have been known to eat muskrats and even ducks. You'll need all your muscles to reel one in and catch Wisconsin's state fish.

Wilderness Walk Zoo. 9503 N. WI 27; (715) 699-1442; wildernesswalkzoo.com. This family animal park includes a petting zoo; northern Wisconsin wildlife such as bears, foxes, wolves, and porcupines; and exotics, including a Siberian tiger and camel. The Western Town has an area for gold panning and refreshments at Crooked Creek Café. Admission: $12–$17. Open May through fall. Check for updated hours.

where to eat

The Angry Minnow Restaurant & Brewery. 10440 Florida Ave.; (715) 934-3055; angryminnow.com. Kick back with an oatmeal stout, a River Pig pale ale, Minnow Lite, or seasonal peach gose while dining on the brick terrace or inside Hayward's oldest building. For dining, look for seasonal flatbreads, soup and spent-grain pretzels, smoked whitefish tacos, smoked pork with barbecue sauce, and a classic Friday-night fish fry with Great Lakes perch or whitefish. $$.

Tremblay's Sweet Shop. 10569 Main St.; (715) 634-2785; tremblaysweetshop.com. If you have kids or adult chocoholics, get a sweet fix at this Main Street confectionary. They've been making fudge, turtles, truffles, chocolates, and pulled taffy since the early 1960s. $.

West's Hayward Dairy. 15848 W. Second St.; (715) 634-2244; westsdairy.com. It's impossible to resist a small-town dairy that's been serving homemade premium ice cream since the 1920s, with flavors like church basement lemon bar, acai berry ice cream, coconut magic bar, and a chocolate-studded red wine ice cream. You can get sandwiches and coffee here too. Open April through October. $.

watch for elk

Keep an eye out for wildlife, especially east of Hayward and Cable nearing Clam Lake. An elk herd of 25 was reintroduced to the forest in 1995. With the addition of more relocated elk, the herd had grown to more than 355 in 2023. Find out more at clamlakewi.com/elk-info or dnr.wisconsin.gov.

where to stay

Hayward KOA Holiday. 11544 N. US 63; (715) 634-2331; koa.com. This family-oriented campground amps up the fun factor with themed summer weekends that might be a 1980s theme and prom, a Bigfoot fest, and more. Guests can enjoy two playgrounds (one themed like a ship), a jumping pillow, outdoor movies, wagon rides, and a 300-foot waterslide and heated pool. The Red Pine Express Café offers family-focused breakfasts, lunch, and dinners. You can bring your own tent or camper, or you can rent one- to two-room cabins and lodges that sleep six and have kitchenettes and bathrooms. Luxury lodges sleep eight and have larger kitchens. The campground also rents tubes, kayaks, and canoes and offers shuttles for trips along the Namekagon River. $.

McCormick House Inn. 10634 Kansas Ave.; (715) 934-3339; mccormickhouseinn hayward.com. This grand 1887 lumber baron's home offers six luxurious guest rooms and made-to-order breakfasts. Guests can soak in a secluded spa or wander the formal English garden with an impressive reflecting pool. The inn has added a restaurant that's open to the public Wednesday through Saturday. Expect a Southern flair, with items such as she-crab soup, shrimp and grits, crab cakes, and fried green tomatoes. Look online for details on the backyard summer concert series. $$–$$$.

Spider Lake Lodge. 10472 W. Murphy Blvd.; (715) 669-3557; spiderlakelodge.com. Rustic, yet elegant and skillfully decorated and restored, this 1923 log lodge was added to the National Register of Historic Places in 2019. Each of the eight rooms has unique decor and comes with breakfast, served on the huge porch overlooking the lake. Guests may also rent the Adirondack-style Ted's Treehouse Cabin. $$–$$$.

Treeland Resorts on Chippewa Flowage. 9630 Treeland Rd.; (715) 462-3874; tree landresorts.com. This resort on the scenic Chippewa Flowage includes 10 motel suites, 29 one- to five-bedroom cabins, a restaurant and bar, a pool, kayaks and paddleboats, pickleball courts, and sand volleyball. $$$.

cable, wi

Despite its popularity with skinny skiers in the winter and mountain bikers in the summer who come to "Trail Town USA," the hundreds of miles of trails and area lakes make it easy to find solitude and serenity. Listen for loons, watch for eagles, and escape into an outdoor adventure. For advice on trails and visitor information, stop by the Cable Area Chamber of Commerce, 13380 CR M; (715) 798-3833; cable4fun.com.

getting there

From Hayward, follow US 63 east about 17 miles to Cable.

where to go

The Birke Trail. (715) 634-5025; birkie.com. You can access the Birke's more than 60 miles off McNaught Road, where the race traditionally starts in Cable, or at multiple trailheads throughout the trail system. Many areas have warming cabins set up. Check online for maps, current trail conditions, and information on the many ski races throughout the season. You'll find information on Birke races for mountain bikers and runners too. Ski passes at $5–$10/day for anyone age 12 and up help fund trail-grooming costs.

Cable Area Fall Color Tour. Grab a map online or at the visitor center for three different guided routes through the national forest during peak fall color weekends. The community also hosts the Cable Area Fall Fest during the last weekend in September, with a variety of events and entertainment.

Cable Natural History Museum. 13470 CR M; (715) 798-3890; cablemuseum.org. If you want a full appreciation for the area's lakes, forests, and rivers, check out the interactive exhibits here. Kids can roam the Curiosity Center, which includes exploring the forest floor, climbing into its tree canopy, and seeing some of the live raptors, reptiles, and amphibians that make their home in northern Wisconsin. Museum staff can recommend trails for interpreted or scenic hikes, loan visitors birding backpacks and cameras (with a refundable deposit), and rent snowshoes for winter exploring. The museum also features the work of local photographers and artists and sells a variety of nature-related gifts. Open Tuesday through Saturday. Free admission on Tuesday. Admission: $5 for adults; free for those age 18 and younger.

Chequamegon Area Mountain Bike Association. cambatrails.org. Plot your foray into the woods through this organization that creates and maintains 130 miles of singletrack trails, more than 70 miles of groomed winter trails, and more than 200 miles of marked gravel routes in and around the Chequamegon-Nicolet National Forest, Bayfield, and northern Sawyer County Forests. Maps also available at the Hayward Lakes and Cable visitor centers.

where to eat

Brick House Café. 13458 Reynolds St.; (715) 798-5432; thebrickhousecafe.net. This quaint house in downtown Cable serves crème brûlée French toast and espresso barbecue pulled pork (both of which were featured on *Diners, Drive-ins and Dives*), plus breakfast burritos, a monster croissant sandwich with three meats, pastrami wraps, soups, and decadent seven-layer cakes and cookies. $$.

The Rivers Eatery at Ideal Market. 43455 Kavanaugh Rd.; (715) 798-3123; riverstogo .com. This high-ceilinged former potato warehouse now holds the Ideal Market, a small bookstore, and a coffee shop, but the best part is the cafe in the back. They crank out more than a dozen creative wood-fired pizzas like the Eau Claire (cranberry barbecue sauce, chicken, cranberries, and cheese), along with salads and vegetarian choices served with wine and cold beer. Decor includes bikes, ski race bibs, and local artwork. $$.

where to stay

Garmisch USA Resort. 23040 Garmisch Rd.; (715) 794-2204; garmischresort.com. East of Cable, this alpine-influenced lodge perches along the shore of Lake Namakagon. Guests can stay in 9 rooms in the lakeside lodge (some with balconies), 4 guest rooms at the Zugspitze Inn, and 13 cabins ranging from a one-room bungalow to a five-bedroom, 3,600-square-foot Blarney Castle with ivy-covered turrets. You can dine at the resort's Bierstube and dining room, which has an outdoor patio overlooking the lake. The menu includes German meals such as schnitzel (breaded pork tenderloins), smoked pork chops, and a popular Friday-night fish fry. $$.

east

day trip 01

east

>>> **shops, cycling & charm on the st. croix**
stillwater, mn

stillwater, mn

Dubbed the birthplace of Minnesota, Stillwater gracefully rises above the St. Croix River like a grande dame who manages to stay chic. Antique shops, artsy boutiques, and tasty restaurants line its historic Main Street that hugs the river. Victorian bed-and-breakfasts beckon overnighters. Gondolas and paddleboat rides woo newlyweds and romance-seekers.

Its historic charm, scenic bluffs, and proximity to the Twin Cities keep the town of 21,000 residents thriving while regularly making national "Best Of" lists for travelers including the best US small-town food scene (*USA Today*), top 10 prettiest towns in America (*Forbes*), America's best towns for fall colors (*Travel and Leisure*), and more.

Trendy clothing boutiques, home and kitchen shops, galleries, garden stores, and bookshops line Main Street, with more than 40 independent owner-operated stores in the community. You'll find antique armoires, vibrant vintage dresses, local wines and gourmet ingredients, and locally inspired art and attire.

Active travelers, too, find their way here, pedaling to Stillwater from St. Paul on the 18-mile Gateway Trail. Cyclists and runners can admire the view of Stillwater from across the St. Croix River on the Wisconsin side when they follow the 4.7-mile St. Croix River

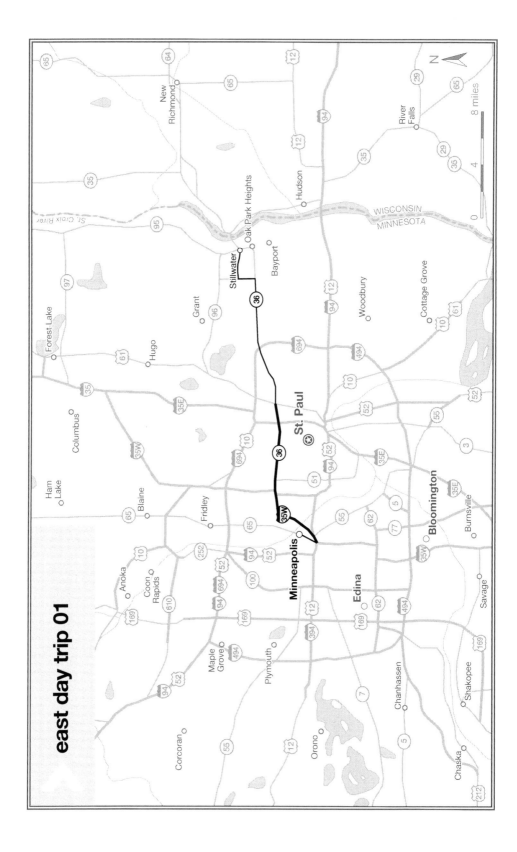

east day trip 01

Crossing Loop Trail. It takes users across the Historic Lift Bridge (reopened after conversion to a pedestrian/bicyclist-only crossing in 2020) into Wisconsin and south before returning to Minnesota via the St. Croix Crossing Bridge (completed in 2017) and looping back to Stillwater.

Stillwater's Chilkoot Hill draws hard-core cyclists, but if steep hills seem daunting, you can rent electric bicycles for leisurely exploring along the 5.9-mile Brown's Creek State Trail or winding through neighborhoods to admire Victorian homes and historic architecture.

Make sure you have time to relax on a rooftop bar or dine on a patio that takes full advantage of the St. Croix riverfront views. With sunset coloring the sky and reflecting off the water, it can be an idyllic date night or evening with friends.

getting there

Follow MN 36 east about 20 miles to Stillwater.

where to go

Aamodt's Apple Farm. 6428 Manning Ave.; (651) 439-3127; aamodtsapplefarm.com. Crowds choose their favorite bags of apples from huge bins in this historic barn. It's loaded with temptations from pies and sugar-coated apple cider doughnuts to pumpkins, gourmet popcorn, and Honeycrisp apple salsa. During the fall peak, you'll find close to a dozen varieties, including Honeygold and Honeycrisp, as well as fresh cider, grilled apple brats, a hay-bale maze, goats to pet, and pedal tractors.

St. Croix Vineyards. 6428 Manning Ave.; (651) 430-3310; scvwines.com. In a rustic barn next door to Aamodt's Apple Farm, this winery founded in 1992 offers tastings, flights of award-winning wines such as Frontenac Gris and Vignoles, and wine by the glass. Among its signature wines are a semisweet red wine that's chilled for warm-weather picnics in the orchard and raspberry infusion, a sweet pairing for chocolate and dessert. Prefer something else? **Thor's Hard Cider** also is on site. Check online for seasonal hours, details on winery tours, and events such as live music, winter snowshoe tours, sauna time, yoga in the vines, and holiday specials.

Stillwater Trolley. 400 Nelson St. East; (651) 430-0352; stillwatertrolley.com. Hop aboard for 45-minute narrated history tours that travel downtown, along the river, and up into the neighborhoods built by lumber barons. Runs daily May through October. Look for additional tours such as the Saturday summer Storytime Trolley for kids in partnership with Valley Bookseller and the Rivertown Terror Tour evenings in October. History tour tickets start at $8 for kids ages 3–16; $14 for adults.

Teddy Bear Park. 207 Nelson St. East; (651) 430-8800; discoverstillwater.com/attractions/teddy-bear-park. This playground 2 blocks uphill from downtown and nestled into the bluff offers a nod to local history with play areas inspired by paddleboats, trains, and the river. Plan a picnic and photo ops by the oversized teddy bear statue that gives this park its name.

Warden's House Museum. 602 N. Main St.; (651) 439-5956; wchsmn.org. Stillwater, home to the state's biggest high-security prison, began with the state's first territorial prison. Visitors can learn more about that early prison and see this 14-room 1853 warden's house Thursday through Sunday. May to October. Admission: $8, adults; $3, children 6–17.

where to shop

The popularity of Stillwater means most shops are open seven days a week and often into the evening hours. Check the Stillwater website for details on themed Ladies Night Out events and full listings of shops, including multiple antiquing destinations.

Darn Knit Anyway. 423 S. Main St., Suite 423b; (651) 342-1386; darnknitanyway.com. Crafters and fiber artists can lose themselves in the array of unique yarns (some locally made), textiles, and wool for felting. You also can find handmade gifts or take a class to learn new skills.

Käthe Wohlfahrt of America, 129 S. Main St.; (651) 275-1236; christmasfromgermany. com. The famed Christmas store from Germany opened its only US location in Stillwater, pulling in shoppers with its glittering ornaments, hand-carved Christmas scenes, music boxes, candleholders, nutcrackers, cuckoo clocks, and souvenirs.

Midtown Antique Mall. 301 S. Main St.; (651) 430-0808; midtownantiques.com. You can easily spend hours in this dizzying three-story collection of antiques that's one of the largest in the state, with more than 80 dealers. Jewelry, music, toys, textiles, kitchenware, and tools fill the lower levels, while the top floor displays antique bookshelves, armoires, tables, and elegant furniture.

Staples Mill Antiques. 410 N. Main St.; (651) 430-1816; facebook.com/staplesmill antiques. Three floors of collectibles and antiques from 30 dealers can be found tucked into this former sawmill.

Stillwater Art Guild Gallery. 402 N. Main St.; (651) 689-0149; artguildgallery.com. This cooperative in the Isaac Staples Sawmill brings together the vibrant work of more than 90 members who are potters, painters, photographers, sculptors, jewelers, glass, and fiber artists.

Stillwater Olive Oil Company. 231 S. Main St.; (651) 472-5789; stillwateroliveoil.com. Sample your way through an array of specialty oils such as black truffle or butternut squash seed oil; extra virgin olive oils infused with basil, mushroom and sage, or bacon; and balsamic vinegars with flavors such as blackberry ginger, fig, and dark chocolate.

find a new way to get around

Ditch your car and find a new way to explore the scenic St. Croix River Valley, whether you're on the river itself or dreamily drifting above it in a hot-air balloon.

Aamodt's Hot Air Balloons. *(651) 351-0101; aamodtsballoons.com. This longtime business departs from Aamodt's Apple Farm and St. Croix Vineyards with small-group flights (up to eight passengers) and private flights to mark special occasions.*

Gondola Romantica. *425 E. Nelson St.; (651) 439-1783; gondolaromantica.com. Gondoliers take couples onto the St. Croix during the day or by the glow of a full moon in authentic imported gondolas that gently rock in the river's current.*

Stillwater River Boats. *525 S. Main St. (651) 430-1234; stillwaterriverboats.com. Brunch, lunch, and dinner cruises let guests dine while enjoying the ever-changing scenery along the St. Croix River. Cruises sail daily.*

where to eat

Dock Café. 425 E. Nelson St.; (651) 430-3770; thedockstillwater.com. This restaurant perched along the St. Croix boasts the best riverside view and patio. The menu offers sandwiches, salads, and entrées such as whiskey-butter salmon, walleye with wild mushroom sauce, and filet mignon with scallops. $$–$$$.

Domacín Restaurant and Wine Bar. 102 S. Second St.; (651) 439-1352; domacin winebar.com. Order a cheese board or elegant appetizer while savoring a pinot noir from the Willamette Valley or a northern Italian vintage from their 25-page wine menu. Entrées may include beef tenderloin with chimichurri and mole butter, duck breast with blackberry-balsamic, and seasonal Mediterranean pastas. Open Tuesday through Saturday. $$$.

Feller. 402 S. Main St. (at Hotel Lora); (651) 571-3501; fellerrestaurant.com. With inspiration from hunting and gathering, the menu blends morning items such as trout Benedict and breakfast pizza with wild boar sausage, appetizers such as pheasant meatballs and foragers crostini, and entrées such as bison ribeye and pecan-crusted walleye. $$–$$$.

Leo's Grill and Malt Shop. 131 S. Main St. South; (651) 351-3943; leosgrill.com. This enduring diner adds a dose of nostalgia to the downtown dining scene and is a good choice for young families, with burgers, homemade skin-on fries, thick malts, and even a walk-up window for cones on a hot summer day. $.

LoLo American Kitchen and Craft Bar. 233 S. Main St.; (651) 342-2461; loloamerican kitchen.com. This original location for LoLo draws diners who linger over trendy seasonal small plates, chef-inspired street food such as pork belly tacos and sticky rice bowls, and craft cocktails. The same restaurant team created Stillwater Proper, a restaurant and bar inside a distillery at 227 S. Main St., and Lolito, which opened in 2023 at 112 N. Main St. with a focus on elevated Mexican cuisine and cocktails. $$

MatchStick Restaurant and Spirits. 232 N. Main St. (at Hotel Crosby); (651) 571-0111; matchstickgrill.com. This farm-to-table restaurant serves small plates such as house-made beet bratwurst, blue crab roll, panzanella, wood-roasted vegetables, braised shellfish, grilled bison, and St. Louis ribs. Desserts include carrot cake bread pudding, cinnamon roll beignets, and an old-fashioned cocktail turned into a bourbon ice cream float. The restaurant stocks hundreds of wines and an extensive selection of spirits, with weekday happy hour specials.

The Tilted Tiki Tropical Bar and Restaurant. 324 S. Main St.; (651) 342-2545; thetilted-tiki.com. For a more tropical mood, this place will deliver a flaming rum-and-juice drink big enough to share or a single-sized beachy drink with a flower and fruit on the top. Graze on ahi tuna bites, Spamwiches, wonton nachos, huli chicken with pineapple barbecue sauce, and vegan tacos. $$.

where to stay

Ann Bean Mansion. 319 W. Pine St.; (651) 430-0355; annbeanmansion.com. This cute Victorian bed-and-breakfast, one of five in Stillwater's historic neighborhoods, features five spacious, comfortable rooms with gas fireplaces, including one room with a trapdoor that leads to the tower with a cozy table for two. $$–$$$.

Hotel Crosby. 232 N. Main St.; (651) 967-7100; hotelcrosby.com. Opened in 2018, this 55-room boutique hotel features a rooftop saltwater hot tub, an on-site spa, a patio and terrace, and MatchStick Restaurant and Spirits. $$$.

Lora Hotel. 402 S. Main St.; (651) 571-3500; lorahotel.com. This 40-room three-story boutique hotel opened in 2018 after extensively renovating the 150-year-old Joseph Wolf Brewery that nestles next to the bluff on the south end of Main Street. Creative design incorporates original stone walls for a blend of old and modern materials. Pets are welcomed with a pet bed and bowls. Guests and the public can grab a hot drink and pastries at Made Coffee, savor happy hour or a nightcap at the Long Goodbye, or have lunch or dinner at Feller. $$$.

The Lowell Inn. 102 N. Second St.; (651) 439-1100; lowellinn.com. Step into the past with 23 rooms furnished in antiques and pastel fabrics, or choose one of the 12 contemporary rooms in the annex of this 1927 hotel built 1 block uphill from downtown. It includes two restaurants, which serve breakfast, lunch, and dinner. Look for afternoon teas served in the George Washington Room and multicourse fondue dinners on weekends in the Matterhorn Dining Room. $$.

Rivertown Inn. 306 W. Olive St.; (651) 430-2955; rivertowninn.com. Built in 1884, this home has been transformed with nine sumptuously decorated rooms, each named for English poets and authors such as Lewis Carroll and Jane Austen. The lavish grand suites in the carriage house—one themed for Agatha Christie's *Murder on the Orient Express*—could pass for a theatrical set. $$$.

Water Street Inn. 101 S. Water St.; (651) 439-6000; waterstreetinn.us. A 2019 expansion added 20 new rooms to this 1890 inn that has the only accommodations along the riverfront. In addition to increasing the number of rooms to 61, a new rooftop restaurant—Papa's—overlooks the St. Croix River Valley. Charlie's Irish Pub, also at the hotel, has a patio overlooking the river and live Irish music Friday and Saturday nights. The Irish theme carries into the new rooms with plaid accents and deep colors on accent walls. Older rooms retain a Victorian look with dark ornate furniture, wallpaper, and curtains. Some rooms have balconies and gas fireplaces. $$–$$$.

day trip 02

east

>>> **red cedar & chippewa river valleys:**
menomonie, wi; chippewa falls, wi; eau
claire, wi

Driving east from the Twin Cities toward Menomonie, I-94 splits in two, swinging around a gorgeous stretch of hardwoods as the road dips into a valley. It's spectacular in the fall, and it's a teaser for the rolling scenery yet to come in west-central Wisconsin.

Bikers and cross-country skiers come for state trails along Menomonie's Red Cedar River and the Chippewa River that runs through Chippewa Falls and Eau Claire. Approximately 16,000 University of Wisconsin students keep the area lively and youthful with campuses in Eau Claire and at Stout in Menomonie. They help fuel fun coffee shops, more than 250 restaurants, and an admirable arts scene that's especially active in Eau Claire, where musician Justin Vernon of Bon Iver has sparked a creative renaissance.

Grab a rural road around these cities—named like alphabet soup with "OO," "E," and "H"—and the pace changes. East of Chippewa Falls in particular, you can catch the *clip-clop* of a Mennonite family's horse and buggy, pass fields polka-dotted with Holstein cows, and taste the cheese that makes Wisconsin America's Dairyland.

menomonie, wi

Only an hour east of the Twin Cities, Menomonie, pop. 16,800 and home to the University of Wisconsin–Stout campus, ranks as a favorite among nature lovers. They bike and hike through shady ravines and across trestle bridges spanning the Red Cedar River and enjoy the scenery of the Red Cedar Valley Trail, Devil's Punchbowl, and Hoffman Hills State

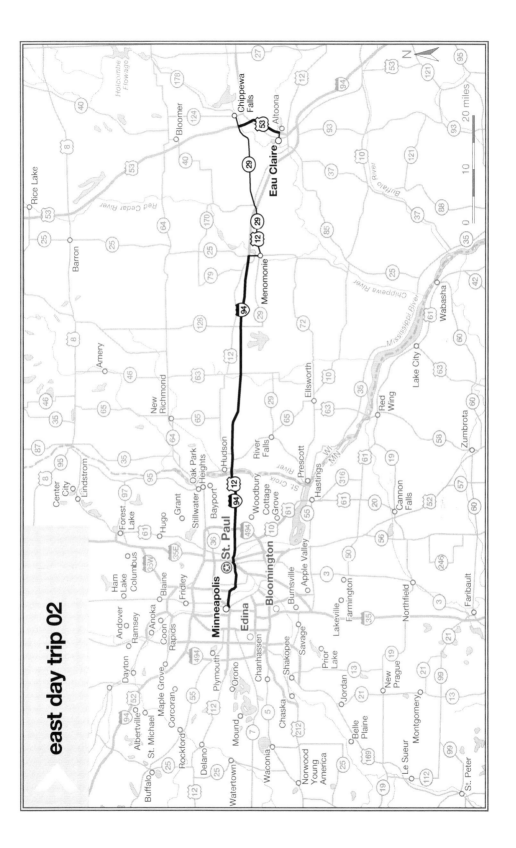

east day trip 02

Recreation Area. Pack a picnic with local meats, cheeses, and brews, or find an outdoor patio with views of Lake Menomin, a reservoir along the river.

More information can be found at the Menomonie Area Chamber of Commerce and Visitor Center, 1125 N. Broadway St.; (715) 235-9087; exploremenomonie.com.

getting there

Take I-94 east about 70 miles to Menomonie.

where to go

Caddie Woodlawn Historical Park and State Wayside. N1250 WI 25 S.; (715) 232-8685; dunnhistory.org. You can see the childhood home of Caroline Woodhouse, the inspiration for the 1935 Newbery Award–winning children's book *Caddie Woodlawn*, 9 miles south of town. Carol Brink wrote the series based on her grandmother's experiences growing up with four siblings in 1860s Wisconsin. Open spring through fall.

Crystal Cave. W965 WI 29, Spring Valley; (715) 778-4414; acoolcave.org. Explore Wisconsin's longest cave with a 1-hour guided walking tour past stalactites, stalagmites, drusy crystals, and rippled flowstone more than seven stories underground and about 20 miles west of Menomonie. Guides cover the history of the cave (discovered more than 70 years ago) and lead guests through rooms such as the Ballroom and Mother Hubbard's Cupboard. Wild caving and custom tours are also offered. Round out a family-oriented day with gem panning, dinosaur-themed minigolf, and browsing one of the Upper Midwest's largest rock shops. Open April to October. Admission starts at $15 for kids ages 3–12; $22 for adults.

Devil's Punchbowl. Southwest of Menomonie on 410th St. (also known as Paradise Valley Road and Rustic Road 89) about 2 miles from the CR P intersection; landmarkwis.org. This geologic "bowl" with a 45-foot waterfall cascading across rims of rock features a mossy, fern-covered microclimate. It was donated to the Landmark Conservancy in 1990, and ongoing improvements have included the addition of stairways and native prairie restoration.

Govin's Farm. N6134 670th St.; (715) 231-2377; govinsfarm.com. This family farm opens its lambing barn for families to visit farm babies late March through early April, pick strawberries beginning mid- to late June, and late September to late October weekends for fall activities, including an 11-acre corn maze and a haunted trail.

Hoffman Hills State Recreation Area. 740th St.; (715) 232-1242; dnr.wisconsin.gov. For some of the best views of fall colors or rolling wooded hills, wetland, and prairie year-round, climb the 60-foot observation tower and hike or ski the trails through this 700-acre site. Free admission, but a state trail pass is required for skiers age 16 or older.

Mabel Tainter Center for the Arts. 205 E. Main St.; (715) 235-0001; mabeltainter.org. This 1889 Victorian theater shows off the grandeur and riches of the city's lumber boom and houses a varying array of arts, from dance performances and concerts to monthly gallery shows and tours. It's also a good place to shop for gifts made by local artists or grab a drink at the Spirit Room Thursday through Saturday during events and before performances.

Russell J. Rassbach Heritage Museum. 1820 John Russell Rd.; (715) 232-8685; dunnhistory.org. Home to Dunn County Historical Society and located in Wakanda Park, this museum's interactive exhibits and photos chronicle the area's history, including early mound-building people, the Victorian era, rise of industry, golden age of American auto design, the Kraft State Bank robbery, Caddie Woodlawn and Dunnville General Store, and Fulton's Workshop encouraging inventions. Open Tuesday to Saturday. Admission $5, kids; $8, adults.

Red Cedar Trail. 912 Brickyard Rd.; (715) 232-1242; dnr.wisconsin.gov. The popular 14.5-mile Red Cedar State Trail lures many to its peaceful riverside route, which you can access at Riverside Park. The highlight? The 846-foot-long railroad bridge spanning the impressive river. The trail joins the Chippewa River State Trail, forming a continuous route of 37 miles between the cities of Menomonie and Eau Claire. In winter, the Chippewa River Trail is used for snowmobiling, while the Red Cedar Trail is groomed for cross-country skiing and snowshoeing. Daily trail passes are required. Bikes can be rented from Simple Sports (400 E. Main St., 715-233-3493).

where to eat

Ellsworth Cooperative Creamery. 3001 CR B; ellsworthcheese.com. The Ellsworth cooperative and cheese factory, which makes cheese curds sold at grocers across the Twin Cities, opened a Menomonie retail shop in 2022 with a huge array of cheeses, meats such as brats and summer sausage, and specialty snacks. You'll also find popular Wisconsin wines and beers from New Glarus Brewery, Wollerscheim, Door Peninsula Winery, and more, plus ice cream, pizza, and sandwiches. $$.

The Raw Deal. 603 S. Broadway St.; (715) 231-3255; rawdeal-wi.com. This casual, artsy coffeehouse serves fair-trade coffee roasted in-house, flavored lemonades, fruit smoothies, and vegan and/or gluten-free foods such as salads, soups, bagel sandwiches, pies, muffins, and bars. $$.

Waterfront Bar and Grill. 512 Crescent St.; (218) 235-6541; thewaterfrontwi.com. You can enjoy views of the lake from the patio here with a plate of fried cheese curds to share, big burgers slathered in sauce, burritos, fried shrimp, pasta specials, and late-night drinks or cold beers. $.

where to stay

Irvington Campground and Rentals. E4176 CR D; (715) 235-2267; menomonie camping.com. These 45 campsites—most with full hookups or water and electric for RVs and campers—sit along the east bank of Red Cedar River about 4 miles from Menomonie's downtown. The campground rents canoes and tubes for river floats and bikes for riding along the Red Cedar Trail, which parallels the west shore. Shuttle service also available. Open May to mid-October. $.

chippewa falls, wi

Chippewa Falls (pop. 14,780) draws visitors with its historic brick Main Street not far from the mighty Chippewa River. Coupled with natural springs, the city has long claimed some of the country's purest water. Much of it goes into making its famous Leinenkugel beer.

A dammed section of the river creates the 6,300-acre Lake Wissota, with Lake Wissota State Park as a popular pine-scented escape. The city also claims a key role in the technology revolution. Cray Computers, builder of the world's first supercomputer, was founded here.

For more information, contact the Chippewa Falls Chamber of Commerce and Visitor Center, 1 N. Bridge St.; (715) 723-0331; gochippewacounty.com.

getting there

From Menomonie, continue on I-94, exiting at WI 29, which leads northeast to Chippewa Falls. The cities are about 30 minutes apart.

where to go

Bridge Street Art & Gifts Cooperative. 304 N. Bridge St.; (715) 226-1921; facebook.com/BridgeStreetCooperative. This art co-op brings together paintings, glass, pottery, accessories, and fiber arts made by area artisans.

Collective Charm. 16 W. Columbia St.; (534) 220-7076; collectivecharmantiques.com. Fans of upcycled goods and one-of-a-kind finds can browse 12,000 square feet of furniture, accessories, and collectibles from more than 65 vendors in the heart of downtown.

Country Fest. 24447 CR S; (715) 289-4401; countryfest.com. With more than 7,000 campsites, 5 stages, and more than 50 bands, this annual three-day celebration—billed as the "nation's largest party in a hayfield"—rocks with some of country music's biggest names, as well as up-and-coming artists. Past performers have included Taylor Swift, Blake Shelton, Miranda Lambert, Keith Urban, and Eric Church.

Irvine Park & Zoo. 125 Bridgewater Ave.; (715) 723-0051; irvineparkzoo.org. Kids love this spacious 318-acre historic public park that's home to tigers, bobcats, cougars, black bears, deer, and bison; a seasonal Red Barn Petting Zoo; and Irvine Park Cave, with a natural spring flowing through it. The park lights up with more than 60,000 lights for its Christmas Village from Thanksgiving to New Year's Day. Open year-round. Free admission, but donations are appreciated.

Jacob Leinenkugel Brewing Company. 124 E. Elm St.; (888) 534-6437; leinie.com. Sign up at the Leinie Lodge for hour-long tours (or a 90-minute behind-the-scenes option) of this popular brewery, from grain storage and mash cookers to the bottling area for everything from its year-round beers to its seasonal brews, such as a grapefruit shandy, Sunset Wheat (with blueberry and citrus flavors), Snowdrift vanilla porter, and Chocolate Dunkel (lager with cocoa nibs). You'll be able to shop for Leinie's and Wisconsin souvenirs at the log welcome center with its massive stone fireplace and comfy leather chairs. Tours start at $15/person and include four 5-ounce samples afterward.

sample wine & spirits

This area may be best known for its beer, but wineries blend local fruits, cold-hardy grapes, and heritage recipes used by early German settlers.

Chippewa River Distillery & Brewster Bros. Brewing. *402 W. River St.; (715) 861-5100; chippewariverdistillery.com. Founded in 2015, this distillery inspires fresh cocktails with a variety of Trumie's vodkas in flavors such as dill, garlic, bacon, jalapeño habanero, apple pie, ginger, black currant, raspberry, and espresso. Other products include Chippewa gin, flavored whiskey, schnapps, craft whiskey, and about a dozen craft beers. Open Wednesday to Sunday.*

Dixon's Autumn Harvest Winery. *19947 CR J; (715) 720-1663; autumnharvest winery.com. Sample fruit and grape wines and gourmet foods, and pick up fresh apples from the orchard, including its signature Champagne apples, a golden variety that's sweet and spicy. Signature wines include Fall Folly with black raspberries, Grandpa's Best elderberry heritage wine, and Blue Heaven, a semisweet red accented with blueberries. You can also kick back with several drinks exclusive to the tasting room, such as Grandpa Mac's Hard Apple Cider, sangrias, and wine slushies. Open May through October.*

O'Neil Creek Winery. *15369 82nd St., Bloomer; (715) 568-2341; oneilcreek winery.com. This winery specializes in fruit wine, dandelion wine, and dessert wine. Open Friday to Sunday, May through December.*

River Bend Winery & Distillery. *10439 33rd Ave.; (715) 720-9463; riverbendwinery .com. Sample award-winning wines made from cold-hardy northern grapes such as Brianna, Frontenac, and Frontenac Gris at this 8-acre vineyard. The family expanded with a distillery in 2016, as well, producing Craftsman bourbon whiskey, gin, and vodka, and a dark smooth Wisconsin whiskey ideal for mixing old-fashioneds, the state cocktail.*

Lake Wissota State Park. 18127 CR O; (715) 382-4574; dnr.wisconsin.gov. Bring your own or rent a boat, canoe, or kayak to get onto the water at this man-made lake created in 1918 by a power-and-light dam. You can camp at 116 sites in the woods (not on the water), swim at the beach, take a hike on 11 miles of trails, or find a scenic picnic spot. Bikers can catch the Old Abe Trail and bike 20 miles to Brunet Island State Park. Park fee starts at $11/ vehicle for out-of-state visitors, $8 for Wisconsinites, and $3 for Wisconsin seniors.

Loopy's Tube & Canoe Rentals. 10691 CR X; (715) 723-5667; 723loop.com. Popular for its summer tiki bar and pizzas, Loopy's also rents canoes, kayaks, and inner tubes and pro-vides a shuttle service up the Chippewa River. The approximately 2.5-hour downriver floats and paddles end at Loopy's Saloon & Grill. Standard tube rates start at $13.

Mason Shoe Outlet Store. 301 N. Bridge St.; (715) 723-4323; masoncompaniesinc.com. Chippewa Falls is home to Mason Shoe's catalog and internet company, giving local shop-pers access to thousands of pairs of shoes through this company that's been around for more than 118 years. The choices are dizzying—and impressive for anyone needing hard-to-find sizes (4–14) and widths (AAAA–EEEE).

Rocque Ridge Guides and Outfitting Service. 30965 WI 27; (715) 517-1100; rocqueridge .com. Stop by this shop for full-service bait and tackle, camping gear and accessories, and to rent pontoons, canoes, kayaks, paddleboards, snowshoes, and ice-fishing equipment.

Spring Street Sports. 12 W. Spring St.; (715) 723-6616; springstreetsports.com. Rent bikes, skis, snowboards, and snowshoes here for exploring area parks.

Yellowstone Cheese. 24105 CR MM, Cadott; (715) 289-3800; yellowstonecheese.com. This dairy makes more than 30 flavors of cheddar, Colby, and Monterey Jack, using vegeta-bles, olives, dill, bacon, and hot peppers for a variety of combinations. Don't miss squeaky-fresh cheese curds or Colby so fresh it's still a little warm. The shop also sells wine, Point root beer, jams and jellies, maple syrup, take-n-bake pizzas, and meats.

where to eat

Olson's Ice Cream. 611 N. Bridge St.; (715) 723-4331; olsonsicecream.com. Good luck choosing a flavor, with 30 daily choices of ice cream and sorbet at this favorite downtown destination. The flavors rotate from 250 recipes the family has developed since the mid-1940s. Look for everything from chocolate monster and caramel cashew to seasonal tira-misu, cotton candy confetti, and black licorice. You can also find close to a dozen gourmet popcorn flavors both here and at its Eau Claire location. Call for seasonal hours. $.

River Jams. 2940 109th St.; (715) 861-3041; river-jams.com. You can sip craft cocktails, catch an open-mic night or live music night and order ahi poke, bruschetta boards, burgers with bacon jam or truffle cream, wings, and Friday fish fries at this restaurant along the Chip-pewa River. $$.

SandBar and Grill. 17643 50th Ave.; (715) 723-1266; lakewissotasandbar.com. This casual eatery with juicy burgers, fried Yellowstone cheese curds, pizza fries, and pizzas offers a perfect waterfront location on summer days and a good place to catch a sunset on Lake Wissota. $$.

Wissota High Shores Supper Club. 17985 CR X; (715) 723-9854; wissotahighshores. com. This sturdy log restaurant has been a destination since 1936 with its spot along the scenic shore of Lake Wissota. You can drive up or boat here and dine on the outdoor patio. It's known for its Friday fish fry, along with steak, pasta, and a salad bar with soup. $$–$$$.

where to stay

The Inn on Lake Wissota. 16649 96th Ave.; (715) 382-4401; innonlakewissota.com. This lakeside B&B takes advantage of Lake Wissota views with a private patio or deck access for some of its five rooms. Multicourse breakfasts are served family-style in the dining room overlooking the lake. $$$.

eau claire, wi

As the hometown to indie rocker Justin Vernon of Bon Iver (who won a Grammy as best new artist in 2012), Eau Claire (pop. 69,450) has seen its popularity rise as its local music and art scene blossomed.

Several large-scale music festivals add to the city's youthful vibe with 9,300 students attending University of Wisconsin–Eau Claire—many of whom choose to stay after earning their degrees. Much of the community's new energy can be found near the confluence of the Chippewa and Eau Claire Rivers, where there's been a significant revival and investment.

You'll find trendy restaurants, taverns, two boutique hotels, the $60-million Pablo Center at the Confluence that opened in 2018, and the Children's Museum, which built a new two-story location that opened in 2023. You can find breakfast and picnic ingredients at the bustling farmers' market along the Chippewa River, stroll or bike through riverfront Phoenix Park, admire views of the Pablo, cross over the Eau Claire River footbridge to spend the day exploring eateries, taverns, galleries, and tattoo shops, or stick to the Chippewa River State Trail for a day of cycling.

Thrillist named Eau Claire of the 16 coolest small cities in the country in 2022, and chances are high you'll want more than a day to thoroughly check it out. To simplify your planning, the Visit Eau Claire staff already has a variety of itineraries for everything from traveling with your dog or kids to a guys' weekend or a cycling adventure. They can also make sure you don't miss concerts at the amphitheater, special events, or watching a game of *kubb*, a Nordic lawn game with a huge following in the area.

You can stop by the Visit Eau Claire office at the Pablo, 128 Graham Ave., or contact them at (715) 831-2345; visiteauclaire.com.

getting there

From Chippewa Falls, take US 53 south about 15 miles to Eau Claire. From St. Paul, Eau Claire is 82 miles east on I-94

where to go

Action City. 5150 Fairview Dr.; (715) 334-8751; metropolisresort.com. This 55,000-square-foot play area that's part of Metropolis Resort blends an outdoor maze, indoor go-karts, minigolf, bowling, a climbing wall, batting cages, arcade, trampoline park, and laser tag. Chaos Water Park also is part of the resort, with slides, lily pads, lazy river, and activity pool. Call for seasonal hours, pricing, and packages bundled with lodging.

Artisan Forge Studios. 1106 Mondovi Rd.; (715) 563-3005; artisanforgestudios.com. Just a few minutes off I-94, you'll see the funky, fun murals on the garage doors of this creative hot spot. More than 30 vendors converge here, offering studio space for artists in all mediums, a guitar factory, music lessons, jewelers, a gallery, and a gift shop. You can order soups, sandwiches, coffee, and gelato from Sweet Driver Chocolates and Café. Their artfully shaped, swirled, and decorated truffles look almost too perfect to eat.

Carson Park. 100 Carson Park Dr.; (715) 839-5039; eauclairewi.gov. If you can go one place in Eau Claire, head to this 134-acre peninsula nestled inside the oxbow Half Moon Lake. It's the hub for attractions such as the Chippewa Valley Museum, Chippewa Valley Railroad, and a sports complex for university and school football games and Northwoods League baseball with the Eau Claire Express.

Children's Museum of Eau Claire. 124 N. Barstow St.; (715) 832-5437; childrens museumec.com. This popular family destination unveiled a new two-story 26,000-square-foot museum in 2023—one that incorporates natural light and trees into its architecture and creates six different galleries for little ones: bitty city, a water play exhibit, toddler forest, fitness and nutrition, outdoor experiences, and body smarts, where kids can crawl through a digestive tract from a mouth to an exit into a toilet. Closed Wednesdays. Admission: $11 for ages 1 and up.

Chippewa River State Trail. dnr.wisconsin.gov. This trail begins at Phoenix Park near the confluence of the Eau Claire River. It crosses a 500-foot-long trestle bridge spanning the Chippewa River and follows it for about 30 miles southeast through river bottoms and prairie, along sandstone bluffs, and through wetlands, connecting with the Red Cedar State Trail in the Dunnville Wildlife Area. A state trail pass is required at $5/day or $25/year to ride a bike, ride horses, or cross-country ski along it.

Chippewa Valley Museum. 1204 E. Half Moon Dr.; (715) 834-7871; cvmuseum.com. This year-round museum makes use of the park's historic buildings to re-create parts of the past: Ojibwe exhibits, a Swedish log home, a one-room schoolhouse, a 21-room doll-house, and a 1950s ice-cream parlor. Open Tuesday to Saturday. You can also check out the nearby multibuilding Wisconsin Logging Museum dedicated to the 1890s timber boom and open daily May through September. Admission: $12, adults; $10, seniors; $5, students ages 5–17.

Chippewa Valley Railroad. 811 Carson Park Dr.; (715) 450-3330; chippewavalleyrailroad .org. Tour Carson Park and see Half Moon Lake while riding in a miniature quarter-size working railroad car powered by steam and gasoline. Open noon to 5 p.m. Memorial Day weekend through Labor Day. Admission: $3, adults; $2, children.

Eau Claire Sculpture Tour. Download maps at visiteauclaire.com/sculpture-tour. More than 70 sculptures from local and international artists can be found through downtown, along with many murals to liven up photo ops. The sculpture tour claims to be one of the largest in the nation. Art ranges from children cast in bronze and imaginative animals to colorful and abstract pieces.

Pablo Center at the Confluence. 128 Graham Ave.; (715) 832-2787; pablocenter.org. This gleaming $60-million arts center opened in 2018 as a collaboration between the community and the university to help drive the creative economy. It brings together a 1,200-seat theater, a 400-seat theater, a dance studio, art galleries, a recording studio, and classrooms for learning. It hosts touring Broadway shows, concerts, open-mic nights, and the Wisconsin Shakespeare Festival, which premiered in 2023.

Revival Records. 128 S. Barstow St.; (715) 514-4202; revivalrecords.com. Right around the corner from the Pablo Center, fans of vinyl can get lost in the vast collection of vintage and new records, along with cassette tapes, CDs, and the audio equipment to play it all.

Riverside Bike & Skate. 937 Water St. St.; (715) 835-0088; riversidebikenskate.com. Rent bicycles (including fat-tire and e-bikes), in-line skates, or ice skates for the Chippewa Valley Trails and next-door Hobbs Municipal Ice Center, or rent a canoe and kayaks for trips on the Eau Claire or Chippewa River.

where to eat

The Brewing Projekt. 1807 N. Oxford Ave.; thebrewingprojekt.com. Edgy with a humorous dose of animated artwork on all their cans, this modern brewery crew makes a Resist series of milkshake IPAs, Smoofee sours loaded with fruits, Puff Tart sour ales, and plenty of pilot beers they test out in the tasting room. If you're not into beer, they make Bomb seltzer in flavors such as piña colada and creamsicle. Watch the schedule for special events such as winter farmers' markets, hands-on art projects, and food trucks. Open daily. $.

Eau Claire Cheese and Deli. 1636 Harding Ave.; (715) 234-2000. Grab picnic fixings, an ice cream, or a mother lode of cheese to take home from this popular stop. $.

The Livery Restaurant and Saloon. 316 Wisconsin St.; (715) 833-7666.; theliveryec.com. With exposed redbrick walls and a cozy outdoor patio, this spot serves pork belly banh mi, a Leinie's beer-battered cod sandwich, and a half-pound burger with bacon onion balsamic jam and Gorgonzola on a brioche bun. If you're craving something fancier, go for salmon with a grain trio, beer-battered chicken with Korean barbecue sauce and soba noodle salad, or a bourbon steak. Socialize in the upstairs game room with pool, darts, and arcade games, or gather around the fire pit on the patio. $$–$$$.

Mona Lisa's. 428 Water St.; (715) 839-8969; monalisaeauclaire.com. Kick back on the patio or inside this exposed brick and contemporary restaurant downtown. The Italian and Mediterranean pastas, salads, thin-crust pizzas, and seafood and steak choices change frequently with seasonal fare. Open for dinner Wednesday to Sunday. $$.

Ramone's Ice Cream Parlor. 503 Galloway St.; (715) 895-8186; ramonesicecream.com. You can find at least 24 Chocolate Shoppe Ice Cream flavors at this dessert parlor, along with malts, pies, and coffee — plus gluten-free, nondairy, and nut-free and sugar-free options. Grab a spot on the patio with a vibrant mural as the backdrop. $.

Ray's Place. 838 Water St.; (715) 832-3991. If you want to settle into a bar that's authentically classic Wisconsin and locally loved, grab a roast beef sandwich with horseradish mustard and a cold beer here. $.

Shift Cyclery and Coffee Bar. 615 Graham Ave.; (715) 514-5060; eaushift.com. Who knew you could have one of the town's best plates of waffles and home-baked goods while you get your bike tuned up at the same time? This combination bike shop and coffee stop helps you and your wheels run more efficiently. You can also rent a bike, e-bikes included, for exploring the city. $,

where to stay

Lismore Hotel. 333 Gibson St.; (715) 318-7399; hilton.com. Named for the Australian town of Lismore, this eight-story hotel underwent a $21 million makeover in 2015. It features a sleek, modern design, offers river views on the upper floors, and sits less than 2 blocks from the Pablo Center at the Confluence. Phoenix Park and the farmers' market are an easy stroll across the Phoenix Park Bridge, a historic trestle bridge illuminated at night. The hotel's gastropub, The Informalist, serves brunch Friday through Sunday and daily dinner with options for vegan and gluten-free needs (theinformalist.com). $$.

The Oxbow. 516 Galloway St.; (715) 839-0601; theoxbowhotel.com. This hip boutique hotel partly owned by Justin Vernon opened in 2016 a few blocks from Phoenix Park. Look for locally written literature and art on the walls and wood tables and doors made from city trees. Guests can borrow complimentary bikes from the hotel, or the public may rent them. You can catch live jazz and music at its restaurant, The Lakely, open for dinner Tuesday through Saturday and seasonally for brunch. It's known for craft cocktails and signature *Koldtbord* (curated "cold table" of appetizers), farm-to-table comfort food, and outdoor patio. $$.

play *kubb*

Forget cornhole. If you want a lawn game to play at a brewery, tavern, music festival, or a park in Eau Claire, grab some of the wooden pieces that compose the Swedish game of kubb (pronounced like "coob" and rhymes with "tube"). Places such as The Lakely and The Complexx at Wagner's Lanes have sets, as do most of the hotels in this city, known as the "Kubb Capital of North America" and home to the US National Kubb Championships in July, drawing up to 125 teams.

Sometimes referred to as "Viking Chess," this popular Swedish game involves throwing wooden sticks at wooden blocks with movements like bowling and horseshoes. Two to 12 people can play a game, and it can be played even in the snow. Area high schools and students, in partnership with the public arts council, built 24 sets for area hotels. If you spend the night, ask to use one.

southeast

day trip 01

southeast

>>> **wisconsin's great river road:**
stockholm, wi; pepin, wi; alma, wi;
fountain city, wi

Colorful small towns dot the Wisconsin side of the Great River Road as it winds its way south of the Twin Cities and around Lake Pepin. Historic villages sit tucked between steep coulees, the Mississippi River, and backwaters strewn with water lilies through which herons stoically stalk their prey.

If you crave a theme, follow the Great River Wine Trail to tasting rooms, each with its own personality. Orchards and vineyards thrive along bluffs and embankments above river valleys, which keep them safe from cold temperatures that creep into lower elevations during spring and fall. Regional vineyards are part of the Upper Mississippi River Valley American Viticulture Area, established in 2009 and embracing varietals of newer cold-hardy grapes.

Even without making any stops (although, trust us, you'll want to), a trip along Wisconsin's Great River Road south to Fountain City provides a perfect laid-back road trip whether you're goofing off with girlfriends or hugging the curves with a motorcycle rumbling beneath you. Keep an eye out for eagles and sailboats as you soak up the scenery along the shore of 21-mile-long Lake Pepin, a widening of the Mississippi where the Chippewa River joins it. You'll cruise through Stockholm and Pepin before driving farther south to Alma and Fountain City.

Don't underestimate these small river towns. They tend to draw seriously gifted artists and visionaries who've used their passions and talents to create picture-perfect pizza farms, unexpected museums (medieval armory, anyone?), and one-of-a-kind attractions such as Fountain City's megalithic Kinstone.

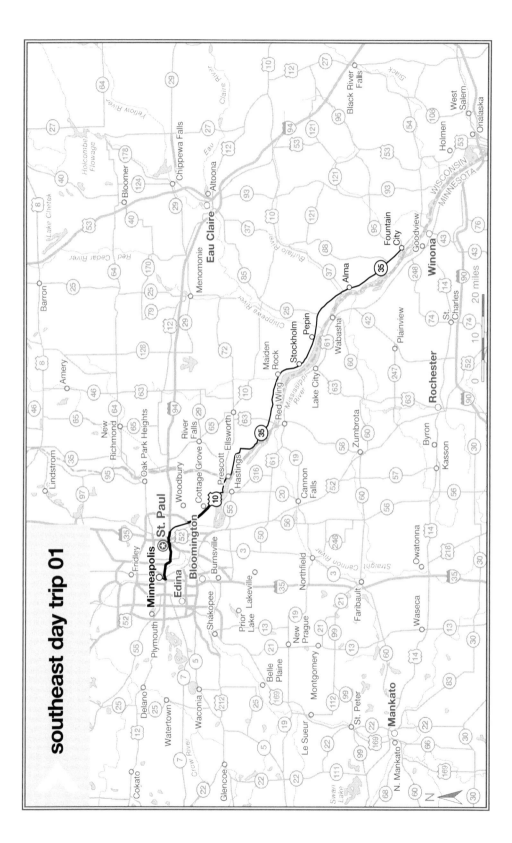

southeast day trip 01

travelers' tip

As you head east from the Twin Cities on US 10 and cross the confluence of the Mississippi and St. Croix Rivers between Hastings, Minnesota, to Prescott, Wisconsin, head to the Great River Road Visitor and Learning Center. On the southern edge of Prescott, this center offers restrooms, travel brochures, and several exhibits on area geology and wildlife, along with viewing scopes and sweeping river valley views from the patio. 200 Monroe St.; (715) 262-0104; freedomparkwis.org. Online, you can find more information on Wisconsin's Great River Road National Scenic Byway at wigrr. com. For more on the Great River Wine Trail, go to greatriverroadwinetrail.org.

stockholm, wi

The population hovers near 75 residents, but this tiny village pulls in a steady flow of visitors. Chalk it up to the colorful charm of a historic river town (founded in 1854) matched with a handful of artsy shops, galleries, cafes, and unique places to rent. They roll out a gracious welcome, with blue bikes for visitors to borrow and blue water bowls for canine guests. Some sites in this section are in nearby Maiden Rock (pop. 114), 8 miles upriver from Stockholm. Look for annual events, such as an art fair in July, at stockholmwisconsin.com.

getting there

Follow US 10 southeast out of the Twin Cities, crossing into Wisconsin at Prescott. Continue southeast on WI 35 (Great River Road) to Stockholm. It's about 60 miles (70 minutes) from downtown St. Paul.

where to go

Indigo Swan Jewelry and Fine Art. N2051 Spring St.; (651) 231-2266; indigoswangallery .com. Enjoy browsing artsy jewelry made by owner Ann Mooney, handbags, original artwork, puzzles, pottery, stained-glass creations, and more. Open seasonally.

Maiden Rock Bluff State Natural Area. dnr.wi.gov. You'll need to head inland and up into the bluffs on CR J from Stockholm, go northwest on CR E, then west on Long Lane to reach the parking area. About 1 mile long and 400 feet high, this bluff offers great views of the valley, a chance to spot nesting peregrine falcons, bald and golden eagles, and migrating birds, along with common and rare prairie wildflowers.

Maiden Rock Winery and Cidery. W12266 King Ln.; (715) 448-3502; facebook.com/WineryCidery. This winery makes apple wines and artisanal hard ciders such as Honeycrisp Hard, Scrumpy, and Bitter Love. In the fall, you get the best deal: hard ciders and wines, plus fresh apples from the Maiden Rock Orchard and stunning colors along the bluffs.

The Palate. W12102 WI 35; (715) 442-6400; thepalate.net. This gourmet kitchen store features a little of everything enthusiastic hosts love: stylish aprons and linens, great glassware, colorful kitchen pots and pans, gourmet foods, and inspiration for seasonal gatherings. You also can order a fine wine and cheeses to savor in the shop or look for cooking classes and events to join.

Rush River Produce. W4098 200th Ave.; (715) 594-3648; rushriverproduce.com. If you visit in summer, have a cooler handy for the produce of this farm about 6 miles north of Stockholm and 3 miles inland from the river. Look for asparagus in May; red, white, and black currants and gooseberries from July through early August; plus fall raspberries and autumn apples. The biggest attraction: 9 acres with 14 varieties of U-pick blueberries, including some that grow on vines. Call before visiting to check what's ripe and available.

Stockholm Gardens. W12014 WI 35; (715) 442-3200; stockholmgardens.com. Enjoy browsing for organically grown perennials, herbs, annuals, peonies, heirloom vegetables, and shrubs at this historic barn and greenhouse. Open April to October.

where to eat

Little Larke Bakery. N2055 Spring St.; (715) 615-0210; facebook.com/littlelarkebakery. Stop in for sweet temptations such as frosted turtle doughnuts, apple cheesecake kolaches, and mini carrot cakes, or go for savory with focaccia and artisanal breads. Outdoor seating available. Call for seasonal hours. $$.

Stockholm Pie and General Store. N2030 Spring St.; (715) 442-5505; stockholmpie.com. As you can guess, this cafe with sandwiches on homemade bread and quiches has built its reputation on pie. Look for chicken or beef pies for lunch, or skip to dessert with lingonberry lemon, caramel apple crunch, and pumpkin pecan. Gluten-free options available. $$.

Vino in the Valley. W3826 450th Ave., Maiden Rock; (715) 639-6677; vinointhevalley.com. Soak in the scenery of the Rush River Valley and ambience of this charming vineyard on Thursday, Friday, and Saturday nights with pizzas, pastas, salads, meats, and cheeses plus Sunday buffets. Sip Wisconsin beers or wines made by Cannon Valley Winery. It's also open for a Sunday buffet. May through September. $$.

where to stay

Journey Inn. W3671 200th Ave., Maiden Rock; (715) 448-2424; journeyinn.net. This eco-retreat tucked into a coulee north of Stockholm features four rooms named for the elements and a one-bedroom cottage. Amenities include organic fabrics, green practices, balconies or patio, and a seasonal organic breakfast with fair-trade coffee and tea. $$$.

Maiden Rock Inn. N531 CR S, Maiden Rock; (715) 448-2608; maidenrockinn.com. This 16,000-square-foot sturdy stone school has found a new purpose in its second century with a conversion to an inn with four colorful guest rooms and an event center. $$.

pepin, wi

Pepin (pop. 730) is known worldwide thanks to the popularity of Laura Ingalls Wilder, who wrote about her early years here in *Little House in the Big Woods*. You can sit back and ponder those simpler times while eating a sophisticated meal, sipping a local wine, gazing across the marina, or getting onto the lake.

getting there

Continue south on WI 35, driving 6.5 miles south of Stockholm, to reach Pepin.

where to go

Laura Ingalls Wilder Museum. 306 Third St.; (715) 513-6383; lauraingallspepin.com. This small but endearing museum shares artifacts from the pioneer days and stories about the famous author, who was born by Lake Pepin. If you want to see a replica of her cabin, drive 7 miles through farmland to the Little House Wayside on CR CC. Pepin also marks the beginning of the Laura Ingalls Wilder Historic Highway, which links the places where she lived, including sites in Minnesota and South Dakota. Open May 1 through October 30.

Villa Bellezza Winery. 1420 Third St., Pepin; (715) 442-2424; villabellezza.com. Enjoy a taste of Italy with this winery and vineyard that aims for an old-world atmosphere with not only its wines but also its food, whether served at its onsite restaurant, Il Forno Ristorante, or outdoors on the Piazza Bellezza. The staff makes ample use of its brick oven for pizzas baked twice and golden-brown cheesy pastas and paninis. You can sign up for small hands-on cooking classes to learn how to make pasta or pizzas from scratch and cooking with herbs from their gardens. At the end of the year, they host a lively Christmas market with art, crafts, and tasty goods to eat and drink.

where to eat

Harborview Café. 314 First St.; (715) 442-3893; harborviewpepin.com. Consider this restaurant the granddaddy of the Great River Road culinary scene. Its seasonal opening in March sparks road trips for foodies across the Twin Cities. They come for locally sourced lamb, pork, and artfully plated seasonal vegetables with soups, salads, and artisanal breads. Don't miss dessert either, with temptations like chocolate buttercream pie. Check their

Facebook page for updates on the menu. Seating is first come, first served. Open March through late November. $$$.

Nelson Cheese Factory. S237 SR 35, Nelson; (715) 673-4725; nelsoncheese.com. A cheese shop and dairy since the mid-1800s, this shop 8 miles southeast of Pepin has evolved into a sophisticated place with gourmet and imported foods, a restaurant, a cheese store, and an ice-cream stop. Grab a savory soup, sandwich, or pizza for indoors or out on the patio. Or pull together your own picnic basket with a wide selection of wine, meats, cheese, and crackers for a favorite spot along the river. If you go on a nice weekend, be prepared to wait. $.

where to stay

Harbor Hill Inn. 310 Second St.; (715) 600-2466; harborhillinn.net. Pick one of three rooms in this 1870 Victorian home with a tower, or rent the guest room for a kitchen and space for two couples or a family. An English breakfast is served in the morning. $$.

alma, wi

Like Stockholm, this river town may be little (pop. 713), but it offers big surprises, like its Castlerock Museum and Rieck's Landing, a top spot to see swans and waterfowl that stop here during migration. You'll find a handful of sweet boutiques and shops, such as Alma General Store, with the work of local artists in the colorful Main Street buildings, many built in the mid-1800s. Self-guided walking tours highlight the best of Alma's 200 buildings on the National Register of Historic Places. The town was settled by families emigrating from Switzerland and celebrates those cultural roots with Swiss Heritage Days each July. Find more information through the Alma Area Chamber of Commerce at almawisconsin.org.

getting there

Continue on WI 35 22 miles to Alma.

where to go

Buena Vista Park. Buena Vista Road; almawisconsin.com. Enjoy one of the best views in the area with this overlook 540 feet above the Mississippi. You'll be able to see islands, sandbars, and barges heading through Lock and Dam No. 4. You can drive here along CR E or hike up from a trailhead at Second Street and Elm by the Wings Over Alma Nature & Art Center.

Castlerock Museum. 402 S. Second St.; (608) 685-4231; castlerockmuseum.com. Fans of *Game of Thrones*, Vikings history series, *Forged in Fire*, and more will appreciate the mind-boggling array of historic arms and armor at this museum that opened in 2010. Collections span from Ancient Greece and Dark Ages warriors to Vikings, Normans, the Crusades, Feudal Age knights in chain mail, and armored cavalry of the 1700s. Check for details on special events, such as Fire in the Shire, an event with demonstrations and reenactors, or Castlerock in the Park. Usually open Friday and Saturday afternoons, as well as Sundays during the summer. Admission: $6, adults; $4, students age 5 and up.

Danzinger Vineyards & Winery. S2015 Grapeview Ln.; (608) 685-6000; danzingervineyard.com. Among their many award winners are Waumandee White, a semidry wine made with LaCrescent grapes, and Mississippi Mist, White Volvet, Golden Sunrise, and Late Harvest, all semisweet or sweet white wines. You can find close to a dozen red wines from dry to sweet at the tasting room, as well. Check for seasonal hours.

Great Alma Fishing Float. 204 S. Main St.; (507) 398-7073; almafishingfloat.com. There's a small dock across the tracks by the foot of Pine Street where you can lift a signboard and signal you want a shuttle ride to the Great Alma Fishing Float. Most visitors opt to fish all day and can use either a Minnesota or Wisconsin fishing license. Pizza and snacks can be purchased, as well as fish-cleaning services and bait and tackle. Advice is free. $23/adult to fish all day; $10 to visit.

Rieck's Lake Park & Observation Deck. WI 35; (608) 685-3330. About 3 miles north of Alma, this is the best place to see waterfowl such as widgeons, pintails, mallards, wood ducks, and thousands of tundra swans as they eat and rest while migrating between mid-October through freeze-up. You can get swan watch updates by calling the above number. The park also has a dozen first-come, first-served campsites.

Wings Over Alma Nature and Art Center. 110 N. Main St.; (608) 685-3303; wingsoveralma.org. This nonprofit center offers a great overview of the community with historic photos, local art, and exhibits on the area's wildlife—including what's migrating through. There's a 50-foot viewing platform with binoculars and a spotting scope to look for eagles and other birds.

quick tip: take earplugs

If you're staying the night along either side of the Mississippi River and consider yourself a light sleeper, take earplugs to muffle the sound of train whistles. There can be about 30 trains a day passing through the area. If you stand on a walking bridge over the tracks by Lock and Dam No. 4, you can watch trains pass below you.

pizza farms

Owners of three working farms stoke fires in brick ovens during the warm season. The savory aroma of bubbling cheese, crisp crust, spicy meats, basil, and roasted tomatoes wafts across fresh-cut fields and a happy lineup of customers who find their way into the coulees, up in the bluffs, and down gravel roads.

The experience is about more than eating: it's about paying homage to the local harvest, saying hello to the livestock, listening to music (either planned or spontaneous), and celebrating the countryside and camaraderie. Most of all, it's a chance to let passionate farmers and bakers work their magic.

AtoZ Bakery—The Pizza Farm. N2956 Anker Ln., Stockholm; (715) 448-4802; atozproduceandbakery.com. Decorative lights and pots of herbs add to the atmosphere here, where everything comes from their farm, including the sausage, bacon and pepperoni, grains, and a rainbow of heirloom vegetables from eggplants to exotic peppers. Bring your own blanket or table and chairs, utensils and napkins, and drinks. All garbage (including the pizza box) must go with when you leave. Open second and fourth Tuesday of each month May to September, but reservations required.

The Stone Barn. S685 CR KK, Nelson; (715) 673-4478; thenelsonstonebarn .com. A few miles south of Pepin, this vintage stone barn welcomes customers with creative pizzas such as Alaskan (smoked salmon, capers, and dill) and Modena (marinated chicken, feta cheese, mushrooms, and snap peas). Open Friday evenings and for lunch and dinner Saturday and Sunday, early May through October, with seating inside the well-lit, airy barn hung with artwork.

Suncrest Gardens. S2257 Yaeger Valley Rd., Cochrane; (608) 626-2122; suncrestgardensfarm.com. Take the kids to this family-friendly farm with a playground and room to roam 10 miles from Alma. Bring your own picnic blanket and chairs and leave time to say hello to the chickens, llamas, and other livestock while you wait for pizzas vibrant with vegetables and heirloom tomatoes. Open Friday and Saturday evenings from the first weekend in May through the end of September. Live music scheduled Memorial Day through Labor Day.

where to stay

The Blue Door Inn. 331 S. Main St.; (608) 685-4067; bluedooralma.com. This 1850s building was renovated to blend modern touches with the historic character, such as exposed stone and brick walls and a side porch with a river view. Guests can rent the full inn or one of four suites and a one-bedroom apartment in downtown Alma. Blue Door Properties rents additional rooms and lodging along Alma's Main Street at Inn at Big River Theater, 12 Mile Bluff Inn, and Cottage at The Blue Door Inn. $$.

Burlington Hotel & Bar. 809 N. Main St.; (608) 685-3636; theburlingtonhotelalma.com. This 1891 hotel built for railroad employees and passengers includes five guest rooms and a shared kitchenette. The bar opens on Friday and Saturday evenings. $.

fountain city, wi

As with the Castlerock Museum in Alma, one person's passion can become an astonishing attraction. Just outside Fountain City (pop. 790), visitors can enjoy Kinstone, a megalithic rock garden inspired by ancient stone circles and places such as Stonehenge, or can enjoy the folk art of Prairie Moon.

getting there

Follow WI 35 about 17 miles south from Alma to Fountain City.

where to go

Kinstone. S3439 Cole Bluff Ln.; (608) 687-3332; kinstonecircle.com. Created to both rejuvenate 30 acres of her family's former farmland and to create a sacred sanctuary for visitors, owner Kristine Beck began installing what's considered the largest modern or privately owned stone circle in 2011. Each installation has its own story and strikes a different chord, from stones that thrust upward from a wetland with cattails to a dry-stacked-rock sculpture, *The Three Witnesses*, which frames the vernal and autumnal equinox with circular windows. The property erupts into waves of colors as native plants bloom, and paths lead to a labyrinth, megalithic stone sculptures, and the Chapel of Creation, made with cordwood construction and colored glass bottles. Open daily May 1 to October 31. $10 per person age 8 and older; $5 for children 3–7.

Prairie Moon Museum & Sculpture Garden. S2921 CR G; (608) 685-6290; kohler foundation.org. What started out as a hobby for retired farmer Herman Rusche in 1952 became a full-blown folk-art experience about 8 miles north of Fountain City. Rusche created close to 40 concrete sculptures such as dinosaurs, a woodsman fighting a bear, a rocket, a huge arched border, and a two-story turret. They're embellished with paint, seashells, broken glass, mirrors, and pottery shards. The site, now managed by the Kohler Foundation, includes a museum with Fred Schlosstein's rock art modeled after local buildings. He also put trolls in the hillsides to scare hikers. The garden is open during daylight hours; the museum is open Sunday afternoons May through October. Free admission.

Seven Hawks Vineyards. 17 North St., Fountain City; (608) 687-9463; sevenhawksvine yards.com. With 17,000 northern hybrid grape vines, this is considered one of the larger vineyards in the Midwest. They produce about a dozen wines, all featuring eight northern grape varietals. Their signature blends of northern white grapes (Smiling Moon) and reds (Hunter's Blend) have both won awards. Look for special reserves, too, along with port-style red and white dessert wines. Make it a longer outing on a warm day by ordering one of their handcrafted 12-inch pizzas or sharing a charcuterie board and wine flights. Open daily in the summer. Closed Monday and Tuesday in the offseason.

where to stay

Hawk's View Lodges & Cottages. 320 Hill St.; (866) 293-0803; hawksview.net. If you want someplace a little roomy and luxurious, Hawk's View offerings include five two-story, one-bedroom cottages tucked into the wooded bluffs, two hillside lodges (four-bedroom Blackhawk and two-bedroom Osprey), and two one-bedroom studio suites above the Seven Hawks Vineyards tasting room in downtown Fountain City. $$–$$$.

Merrick State Park. S2965 WI 35; (608) 687-4936; dnr.state.wi.us. Camp at one of 65 sites in this 322-acre state park that encompasses Mississippi backwaters about 2 miles north of Fountain City. Join the anglers or look for herons, egrets, muskrat, and even otters. The park rents canoes for scenic paddles, or you can hike and snowshoe along 2 miles of trails. Daily pass: $8–$11.

day trip 02

southeast

>>> **boots, pottery & riverboats:**
red wing, mn

red wing, mn

You can feel Red Wing's pride in its history, craftsmanship, and products among the exhibits at the Red Wing Boot Museum or posing next to a size 638½ boot downtown. You can feel it in the heft of sturdy Red Wing pottery that draws a few thousand collectors for an annual convention, and you can taste it in the Sturdiwheat pancake mixes that keep the town's agricultural roots served up on breakfast plates.

Even without those products and the shopping they often inspire, Red Wing offers a unique getaway with its historic downtown—one of the oldest in the state—and its scenic location along the Mississippi where islands and bluffs beautifully converge. To truly appreciate the landscape, drive to the top of Sorin's Bluff, where Memorial Park has several sweet overlooks across the river and valley. Plan a picnic, take a hike, play a round of disc golf, or check out one of the mountain bike loops. Interpretive panels offer history lessons too.

You may catch sight of Minnesota's last passenger train—Amtrak's *Empire Builder*—as it stops at Red Wing's depot or see a steamboat or cruise ship docking downtown. Visit Red Wing keeps a calendar of when cruise ships are in port, including the Viking River Cruise that launched in 2022 and American Cruise Lines' *American Splendor* or *American Melody*. For more details, contact Visit Red Wing, 120 Broad St.; (651) 385-5934; redwing.org.

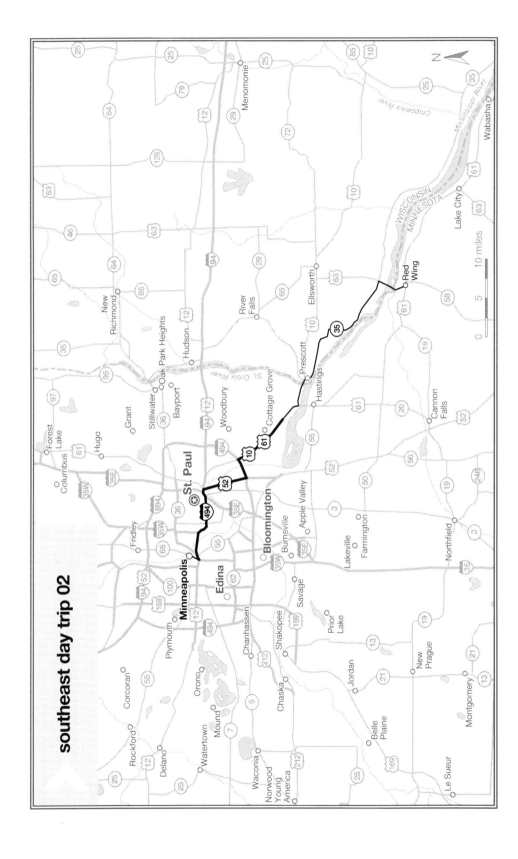

southeast day trip 02

getting there

From I-94 east of downtown St. Paul, take US 61 south (also labeled as the Great River Road) and follow it about 45 miles to Red Wing.

where to go

Cannon Valley Trail. (507) 263-0508; cannonvalleytrail.com. You can access this popular trail for biking and cross-country skiing near the riverfront. It stretches 19.7 miles east to Cannon Falls along the former Chicago Great Western Railroad line. You can rent an e-bike from Rolling River Bike Rental (rollingriverbikerental.com) and have an easy cruise from Welch to Red Wing. You can add miles by connecting with the Mill Towns State Trail to the west and the Goodhue Pioneer State Trail as it heads south to Hay Creek and connects to trails through the Richard Dorer Memorial Hardwoods State Forest. $7 trail pass required to bike the CVT or use the groomed cross-country trails in winter.

Colvill Park. 515 Nymphara Ln.; (651) 385-3674; red-wing.org. Besides being a lovely park along the Mississippi, this is a local hot spot for eagle watching in March, when there may be 100 eagles roosting in the trees or along the bluffs. It's a favorite destination for children in the summer, with a playground and the Red Wing Water Park with large slides, diving board, interactive play area, and zero-depth entry. $2 to $7/person.

Falconer Vineyards. 3572 Old Tyler Rd.; (651) 388-8849; falconervineyards.com. During peak season, the vineyard opens its bistro with wood-fired pizzas, including their signature Grapes of Wrath (zesty sausage, red grapes, green pepper), loaded potato, or Thai chicken pizza. Tastings are $8 for up to five wines, including its award-winning Frontenac rosé; Prairie Star, a Chardonnay-style with oak-barrel aging; and a rich port. The vineyard also makes Lumberjack hard ciders. Check for seasonal hours.

He Mni Can (Barn Bluff). red-wing.org. Long before European settlers reached the area, this 340-foot-high riverside landmark (pronounced Heh-Meh-NEE-Cha) helped guide native travelers along the Mississippi and is considered a sacred place to the Mdewakanton Dakota people of the Prairie Island Indian Community. Hikers can park along East Fifth Street and ascend the bluff at the Kiwanis stairs and find more trails at the top for viewing a former quarry or the bluff-top prairie.

Hobgoblin Music and Stoney End Harps. 920 MN 19; (651-388-8400); stoneyend.com. This quaint barn in rural Red Wing houses a music store featuring a variety of Stoney End harps from lap to floor-sized, mountain dulcimers, banjos, and bodhrans (Irish drums) that are handcrafted here by a handful of experts. You can also find penny whistles, Bouzouki and Octave mandola, mandolins, and concertinas. Watch for folk concerts in the Music Loft or outdoors with a scenic view of bluffs during balmy weather.

Pottery Museum of Red Wing. 240 Harrison St.; (651) 327-2220; potterymuseumred wing.org. In the 1860s, a German immigrant harvested the local clay for durable stoneware with salt glazes. He fashioned bowls, crocks, and jugs for the state's pioneers. With mechanization in the early 1900s, the company became one of the biggest pottery manufacturers in the world. With photos, more than 6,000 vintage pieces, and 13,000 square feet to display them, the museum shows the company's evolution from utilitarian kraut crocks and liquor jugs to elegant dinnerware in the company's mid-century heyday. Serious fans gather for the Red Wing Collectors Society Annual Convention in July. Free admission. Open Tuesday to Sunday.

Red Wing Shoe Store & Museum. 315 Main St.; (651) 388-6233. Head past the two-story boot (size 638½) and upstairs to this museum with an intriguing look at the evolution and importance of the all-American work boot. For more than 100 years the company has built boots tailored to each trade. They have helped build skyscrapers, drill for oil, clear forests, run farms, and hunt for food. The company also made the country's first ski boots. A high point: World War II, when Red Wing provided boots in 200 sizes for America's soldiers. Kids can try on costumes for several trades and pretend to walk on a skyscraper. The building's main floor shows off Red Wing's fashionable lifestyle shoes that are sold globally, sporty hiking boots and shoes, and hardworking boots with optional steel toes, Kevlar, or antistatic soles for various trades. Open daily.

Sheldon Theatre. 443 W. Third St.; (651) 388-8700; sheldontheatre.org. Restored and updated in 2018, this theater shines with turn-of-the-20th-century elegance such as French tiled mosaic floors, Italian marble columns, and Austrian crystal chandeliers. It hosts local and traveling shows and concerts to its stage year-round, but visitors can also take a self-guided tour to appreciate this 1904 gem.

Welch Village Ski and Snowboard Area. 26685 CR 7, Welch; (651) 258-4567; welch village.com. With 360 feet of elevation here, you'll find 60 ski runs, 9 chairlifts, and 140 acres of skiable terrain, along with terrain parks about 20 minutes west of downtown Red Wing. Rental equipment and lessons are available. Lift tickets must be purchased online. They start at $60 for all day and drop to $38 for after 6 p.m.

where to shop

Pottery Place. 2000 Old West Main St.; (651) 388-1161; potteryplaceredwing.com. This 1877 redbrick building comprises several stores beneath its roof and is among several destinations for shoppers along Old West Main Street, which is now called the West End District. You can find several shops on Main Street in the heart of downtown as well.

Pottery Place Antiques. 2000 Old West Main St.; (651) 388-7765; potteryplaceantiques .com. With about 50 dealers, this sprawling collection of Red Wing collectible pieces and aisles dense with floral juice glasses, Watts ware, rare bottles, vintage hats and aprons, rare toys, beer glasses, old books, and colorful quilts can be nirvana for antiques lovers.

Red Wing Arts. 418 Levee St.; (651) 388-7569; redwingarts.org. Check out the work of local and regional artists at the Depot Gallery and Shop or at the **Clay and Creative Center,** 1920 Old W. Main St., which houses a gallery, teaches workshops, and seeks to keep the community's heritage for working with clay a part of the present as well as the past.

Uff-Da Shop. 202 Bush St.; (651) 388-8436; uffdashoponline.com. Browse a lovely assortment of Scandinavian imports such as silver jewelry and charms, Finnish linens and glassware, cookware, and holiday ornaments such as woven straw stars and colorful gnomes.

where to eat

Hanisch Bakery and Coffee Shop. 410 W. Third St.; (651) 388-1589; hanischbakery.com. Whether you're a bakery afficionado or among the fans of this shop's playful TikTok videos, there's much to love among the sweetly crafted doughnuts, flaky pastries, colorful cakes, and homemade breads. You can also enjoy a sit-down breakfast or lunch with quiche, French toast, sandwiches, salads, and soups. Open Tuesday to Saturday. $.

Harbor Restaurant, Bar & Marina. N673 825th St., Hager City; (715) 792-2417; harbor bar.net. Right across the river channel from Red Wing, this casual eatery rocks with summer music festivals, authentic Jamaican jerk seasonings, and great Mississippi views. Get a swamp burger with Cajun seasonings, or try red snapper, tiger shrimp, and chicken with jerk seasoning and a side of Jamaican rice and beans with a kick of coconut. Live music starts every weekend from late May to late September with rock, reggae, blues, and country festivals in the mix. $$.

Red Wing Brewery. 1411 Old West Main St.; (651) 327-2200; redwingbrewing.com. As the first brewery to open in Red Wing in 60 years, this local craft brewer opened in 2011 to a thirsty audience that has grown as they expanded to about a dozen beers, including Work Boot Red and Cokins Bavarian Style, plus some heritage recipes that inspired Red Wing Premium and Remmler's Royal Brew. They also make Good Old Zimmie's Root Beer and bake pizzas that hit all the favorite toppings and beyond with offerings like potluck-inspired pickle roll-up and Tater Tots hot dish pizzas. $$.

Scarlet Kitchen and Bar. 406 Main St.; (800) 252-1875; st-james-hotel.com. This popular restaurant at the St. James Hotel claims a stellar location with its outdoor rooftop patio on sunny summer days and indoor seating near windows with river views. Start the day with seasonally changing meals such as orange cranberry Sturdiwheat pancakes with apple cider caramel sauce, wild rice soup, Mediterranean bowl, pulled pork tostadas, Swedish meatballs, and a trio of homemade desserts. $$.

The Smokin' Oak Rotisserie and Grill. 4243 US 61; (651) 388-9866; thesmokinoak.com. Enjoy the scent of wood-fired rotisserie foods at this log-and-stone-clad restaurant. Look for saucy ribs, chicken, tenderloin roasts, and hand-cut steaks. If you can't decide, go big with the sharable rotisserie sample platter. $$

Stoneware Cafe. Historic Pottery Place, 2000 Old West Main St.; (651) 376-8993; stoneware-cafe.com. Dig into the comfort of a crock of chili, slow-roasted beef or Korean barbecue sandwiches, cranberry chicken salad wrap, or skip to desserts, including Stockholm Pie's fruit and cream pies. $.

where to stay

Moondance Inn. 1105 W. Fourth St.; (651) 212-6305; moondanceinn.com. This stone 1875 home with purple trim offers five spacious rooms and a guesthouse next door for groups. Guests can enjoy weeknight happy hour with wine and hors d'oeuvres or weekend desserts, plus breakfasts such as stuffed omelets, Dutch oven pancakes, fruits, and pastries. Gathering places range from a formal dining room with Tiffany chandeliers and rich woodwork to a cozy area on the third floor with a round window. Downtown and the river are a few blocks away. $$.

Pratt-Taber Inn. 706 W. Fourth St.; (651) 388-7392; pratttaber.com. Elegant porches invite guests to kick back and relax at this restored 1876 brick home with white trim and historic decor in its four seasonally inspired rooms that include fireplaces. $$.

Round Barn Farm B&B. 28650 Wildwood Ln.; (651) 360-1535; roundbarnfarm.com. This property has always drawn attention with its distinctive round barn south of Red Wing, which has become a popular wedding venue. When it isn't booked, you can enjoy a getaway in one of its five rooms, including the spacious Willow Suite with a twig swing facing the fireplace and an alcove bed positioned to catch moonlight. $$$.

St. James Hotel. 406 Main St.; (651) 388-2846; st-james-hotel.com. This four-story 1875 Italianate hotel retains the elegance of an earlier century with spacious accommodations, Amish quilts, rooms named for riverboats, and hallways built wide enough to allow ladies in hoop skirts to pass each other. Each room is different, and you can request a river view. Don't miss the cozy library and organ pipes in the original lobby. Look for holiday decor and special events such as wine tastings, Mardi Gras dinners, eagle-watching, or other seasonal packages. $$.

Treasure Island Resort and Casino. 5734 Sturgeon Lake Rd., Welch; (800) 222-7077; ticasino.com. About 11 miles upriver from Red Wing, this 788-room Caribbean-themed hotel owned by the Prairie Island Band of Ojibwe ranks among the largest hotels in the state. The casino includes more than 2,200 slot machines, 44 table games, a 6-table poker room, and a 550-seat high-stakes bingo hall. The resort includes The Lagoon water park and wave spa, a 2,800-seat event and convention center that draws national tours and entertainment, an amphitheater for outdoor music festivals, a 137-slip marina, a 95-site RV park, a bowling alley, and a 125-passenger yacht for guests yearning to get onto the Mississippi River. $$.

day trip 03

southeast

eagles, toys & lake pepin:
lake city, mn; wabasha, mn

Downriver from Red Wing, the Great River Road makes its way along steep embankments, below scenic bluffs, and through towns full of treasures. You'll find everything from the largest marina on the Upper Mississippi River at Lake City to a national eagle museum with world-class birding to a hand-carved carousel near Wabasha.

Lake Pepin, a 21-mile-long widening of the Mississippi River that doesn't completely freeze during winter, ranks as one of the best places to see eagles, especially in March when trees haven't leafed out and famished eagles are migrating north to join those who never left the state. They rest along the Mississippi, feasting on fish and small game and roosting along bluffs and in wooded lowlands.

It isn't hard to spot their white heads as the birds perch on bare branches. But if you do have difficulty, you can rely on the experts. Five resident eagles at Wabasha's National Eagle Center drop their calm, watchful demeanor and alert visitors when wild eagles come into view far across the river and make it abundantly clear how the term "eagle eye" came to be.

lake city, mn

This town was the birthplace of waterskiing and still hums with the happy energy of people heading out for a day on the water. You can camp along Lake Pepin, stroll its 2.5-mile

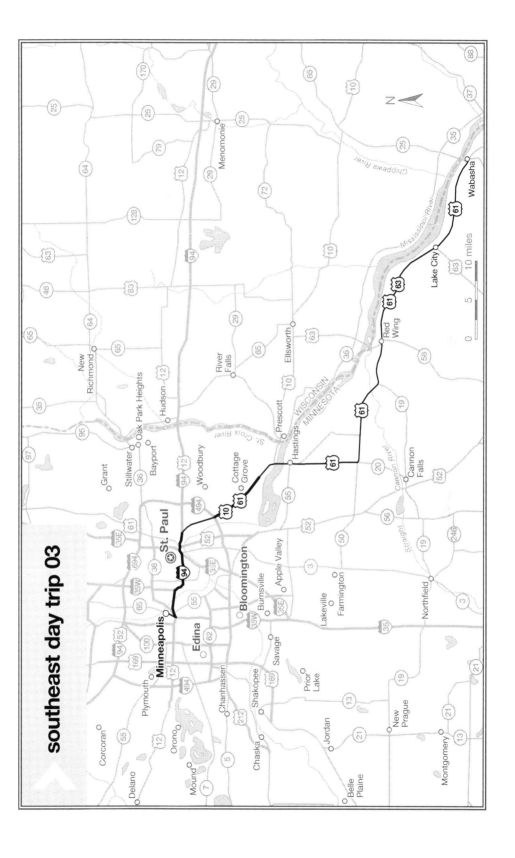

southeast day trip 03

walkway, count the sailboats and barges, and catch a beautiful sunset along the water-front marina.

getting there

Follow US 61 southeast out of the Twin Cities. It's about 70 miles from downtown Minneapolis to Lake City.

where to go

Frontenac State Park. 29223 County 28 Blvd., Frontenac; (651) 299-3000; dnr.state.mn .us. More than a dozen miles of hiking trails thread along the bluffs leading to the Mississippi. Be warned: If you hike down the bluff, it's a steep hike back up. The reward? Immersing yourself into Mississippi bottomlands and finding surprises such as yellow lady's slippers in bloom and more than 260 species of birds that live nearby or visit during migration. In winter, close to 9 miles are groomed for skiing. The campground includes 58 sites, plus 6 rustic walk-in and 2 backpack sites. If sites are full, ask about four inland campgrounds at Richard J. Dorer Memorial Hardwood Forest. Entrance fee: $7.

Hok-Si-La Municipal Park. 2500 N. US 61; (651) 345-3855; hoksilapark.org. This 252-acre city park sprawls along Lake Pepin, offering visitors a riverside beach, picnic areas, and 38 campsites. Open April through October.

Lake Pepin Pearl Button Company. 226 S. Washington St.; (651) 345-2100. This shop was named for the long-ago business that carved buttons from locally collected Mississippi River clams in this historic brick building. You can see one of the drilled clams and browse through a mix of antiques, replicas, and home decor.

Lakeside Antiques. 106 E. Center St.; (651) 345-4800. Around the corner from the Lake Pepin Pearl Button Company, this place sells an assortment of vintage crocks and house wares, toys, fishing gear and watches, with surprises such as a tree trunk carved with "Wizard of Oz" characters.

Pepin Heights. 1755 S. US 61; (651) 345-2305; pepinheights.com. One of the state's most recognized orchards opens seasonally in Lake City to sell its line of fresh ciders and blended juices, sparkling apple juice, doughnuts, caramel apples, pastries, and snappy fresh apples such as Honeycrisp and the much-desired SweeTango, a University of Minnesota hybrid of Honeycrisp and Zestar.

where to eat

Chickadee Cottage Café. 317 N. Lakeshore Dr.; (651) 345-5155; chickadeecottagecafe .com. It's easy to feel at home in this early-1900s lodging surrounded by gardens. They serve breakfast and lunch, with choices such as wild rice porridge, meat loaf muffin, turkey asparagus melt on cranberry–wild rice bread, and a daily shrimp dish. Open Tuesday to Sunday, April through October. $$.

where to stay

John Hall's Alaskan Lodge. 1127 N. Lakeshore Dr.; (651) 345-1212; sleepalaska.com. This log lodge–style hotel offers lake-view suites with a cabin feel. All have a microwave and minifridge or a full kitchen, and the resort is pet friendly. $$.

Willows on the River. 100 Central Point Rd.; (651) 345-9900; willowsontheriver.com. Each of these modern condo units offers sweeping river views with floor-to-ceiling corner windows and a fireplace, plus full kitchens and balconies, plus an indoor pool and fitness center. $$–$$$.

wabasha, mn

Wabasha (pop. 2,500) provides a playful family getaway with hands-on exhibits at the National Eagle Center and LARK Toys, which is like Santa's workshop and a free antique toy museum rolled together in the nearby town of Kellogg (pop. 425). LARK's whimsical hand-carved carousel alone is worth a stop.

Wabasha is also known as the setting for the *Grumpy Old Men* movies with Jack Lemmon and Walter Matthau. While the movie wasn't actually filmed here, you can dine at Slippery's (as mentioned in the film) or time a visit with their annual Grumpy Old Men Festival in late February for an ice-fishing contest and hot-dish luncheon. You can join the Riverboat Days celebration the last weekend in July or Kellogg's Watermelon Festival the weekend after Labor Day.

You can download maps online for walking tours of Wabasha's downtown, with 50 buildings on the National Register of Historic Places. Go to the Wabasha-Kellogg Area Chamber of Commerce; 137 Main St.; (800) 565-4158; wabashamn.org.

getting there

It's about 14 miles from Lake City to Wabasha, following US 61 (Great River Scenic Byway).

where to go

Broken Paddle Guiding. 213 Main St. West; (651) 955-5222; brokenpaddleguiding.com. Whether you're a beginner or an experienced paddler, this guide company provides equipment and expertise to get you onto the Mississippi to see eagles and into serene floodplain forests where trees arch overhead and herons perch on the branches. There's also a sunset tour paired with the Read's Landing brewpub. They also can arrange paddleboarding and fat-tire bike or road bike tours that maximize the driftless scenery. Look for the Broken Pedal 50, a September gravel-road race.

Coffee Mill Golf. 180 Coffee Mill Dr.; (651) 565-4332; coffeemillgolf.com. The course's 18 holes are built along the bluffs with views of the river valley. Rates begin at $10 for anyone age 12 and under for 9 of the 18 holes. Driving range available.

Coffee Mill Ski Area. 99 Coulee Way; (651) 565-2777; cmskiarea.com. Less crowded than Twin Cities ski hills and more affordable than most, these 11 runs and a terrain park feature 425 feet of vertical drop. Open Wednesday through Sunday. Lift tickets start at $35, child; $45, adult.

LARK Toys. 63604 170th Ave., Kellogg; (507) 767-3387; larktoys.com. You can get happily lost for hours in America's largest independent toy shop 6 miles south of Wabasha. The extensive (and free!) toy exhibits coax the kid out of every generation with Howdy Doody dolls, metal robots and Erector sets, Barbies, and pedal cars. In the various shops, you'll find magic tricks and gags, wind-up toys, musical instruments, tea sets, wooden pull toys, fuzzy puppets, and puzzles galore. Lark makes its own line of classic wooden toys. The complex includes a snack cafe, a bookstore, and even outdoor minigolf, but the biggest "Wow!" goes to the hand-carved carousel made from Minnesota basswood. Among the 19 creatures that whirl around every half hour, you'll see an otter, a flamingo, a cat with a fish, a hairy troll, a wizard riding a dragon, and a reindeer. Carousel: $3/ride. Open daily spring through fall; Friday to Sunday in January and February.

National Eagle Center. 50 Pembroke Ave. South; (651) 565-4989; nationaleaglecenter. org. The National Eagle Center, which began a $27 million renovation and expansion in spring 2022, includes two floors of exhibits and artwork that explain the lives of eagles, their habitat, and their cultural significance, especially to Native Americans. One exhibit is dedicated to Old Abe, an eagle that followed soldiers into 37 Civil War battles, and the expansion makes room for the 25,000-piece collection from Preston Cook. Each weekend in March the center offers Soar with the Eagles special events that include speakers and demonstrations, along with family activities. Year-round daily programs give visitors an up-close look at the rescued and rehabilitated resident eagles. There's even a chance to pose nose-to-beak for photos. Leave time to stroll the riverfront near the museum with a fountain and sculpture of Chief Wapasha. Open daily. Admission: $12, adults; $10, ages 4–16.

eagles make a comeback

With a stern look, keen eyesight, majestic flying, and fierce, fish-shredding legs, the bald eagle has long been America's national symbol of strength. They're also one of the country's best comeback stories.

Consider this: In 1953 there were 1,000 eagle pairs in the lower 48 states. A decade later, they were down to 450 pairs after the chemical DDT thinned their egg-shells, causing eaglets to be crushed to death when their parents sat on the eggs. Between 1968 and 1972 there was a single nesting pair left along a 260-mile stretch of the river. The chemical was banned, and eagles slowly made their comeback.

Lake Pepin has been a key area for the eagles' comeback, with its often-open winter water making fishing possible year-round. Minnesota's population was up to 2,300 nesting pairs of eagles in 2007, when they were removed from the Endan-gered Species list. By 2017 the Minnesota Department of Natural Resources esti-mated there were nearly 10,000 nesting pairs in the state.

where to eat

Chocolate Escape. 152 W. Main St.; (651) 565-0035; thechocolateescape.com. If you truly need an extra nudge to duck into this chocolate shop with chocolate-covered bacon, handmade turtles, truffles, ice cream, and more, tell yourself it's educational. A 70-foot-long mural shows the history of chocolate and how it's made. $

Reads Landing Brewing Company. 70555 202nd Ave.; Reads Landing; (651) 560-4777; rlbrewingco.com. The winning combination of craft beers and chef favorites, such as shrimp and creamy grits, cioppino, Philly cheesesteak flatbread, risotto, and ribeye, would make this a popular destination without any extras, but the patio and river views make it a must-stop. You might be able to watch dredgers excavating sand pushed into the Mississippi from the Chippewa River on the opposite shore. $$.

Slippery's Bar & Restaurant. 10 Church Ave.; (651) 565-4748; slipperys.com. Being part of the *Grumpy Old Men* mystique makes this a busy tourist stop for burgers and Ameri-can fare, but it also has an idyllic location, with decks right on the river and docks for diners arriving by boat. Open seasonally. $$.

where to stay

AmericInn Wabasha. 150 Commerce St.; (651) 565-5366; americinn.com/hotels/mn/wabasha. Don't let the chain ownership of this hotel throw you off. This is no ordinary

AmericInn thanks to the efforts of local businesses and artists, who designed 14 themed suites that represent Wabasha. The Carousel, inspired by LARK Toys, includes a hand-carved headboard with an otter, and the Fisherman's Suite includes decor from the Loon Lake Decoy Company. Some of the hotel's 64 rooms have kitchenettes, and all include a hot breakfast and use of the heated pool and sauna. $$.

Historic Anderson Hotel House. 333 Main St. West; (651) 565-2500; theandersonhouse hotel.com. Minnesota's oldest hotel opened in 1856 for guests traveling up the Mississippi and was once known for letting guests choose a resident cat to share their room. It closed in 2009 for a few years and has new owners. Guests can dine on Dutch pancakes, French toast, and omelets at the restaurant, play Ping-Pong and air hockey in the game room, or grab a drink and pizza at the Speakeasy, which opens on Friday and Saturday evenings. $$.

Turning Waters Bed, Breakfast, and Brewery. 136 Bridge Ave.; (651) 564-1568; turning watersbandb.com. This colorful 1902 home with a wraparound porch has five rooms only a block from the Mississippi, which is handy for guests eager to hit bike trails or paddle the river and backwaters. It's even better for beer lovers who can sample their brews in the converted garage and outdoor space that's home to Hoppy Girl Brewing and rotating taps from regional craft brewers. Guest can enjoy five-course farm-to-table breakfasts, welcome drinks, and ice cream. $$$.

day trip 04

southeast

>>> **the island city below the bluffs:**
winona, mn

winona, mn

Winona, a college town sandwiched on an island between the Mississippi River and Winona Lake, can claim first-class arts and culture with its Minnesota Marine Art Museum and summer theater and music festivals that draws artists from across the country. It also features intricate stained glass and architecture throughout the state's biggest Victorian commercial district, but there's a hip, youthful spirit, too, with its college-student population and the viral tongue-in-cheek *Miami of Minnesota* videos.

To truly appreciate the city's unique landscape and location, head up the 530-foot-high Garvin Heights bluff for sweeping views of the river as barges or riverboats glide by. You'll be able to spot the Winona State University (WSU) campus, which, combined with St. Mary's University, has about 12,000 enrolled students. WSU hosts the annual Great River Shakespeare Festival and the Beethoven Festival, popular summer traditions that stretch over several weeks.

You also can see downtown and the spires of churches. Like Duluth on Lake Superior, Winona's prosperity exploded in the late 1800s thanks to its Great River location that allowed it to get lumber and materials to a booming nation. Millionaires showed their wealth by building Victorian homes and businesses.

Modern residents and visitors alike paddle the Mississippi's serene backwaters, cycle paved and gravel trails, hike its bluffs to enjoy birding and fall colors, and climb rocks in

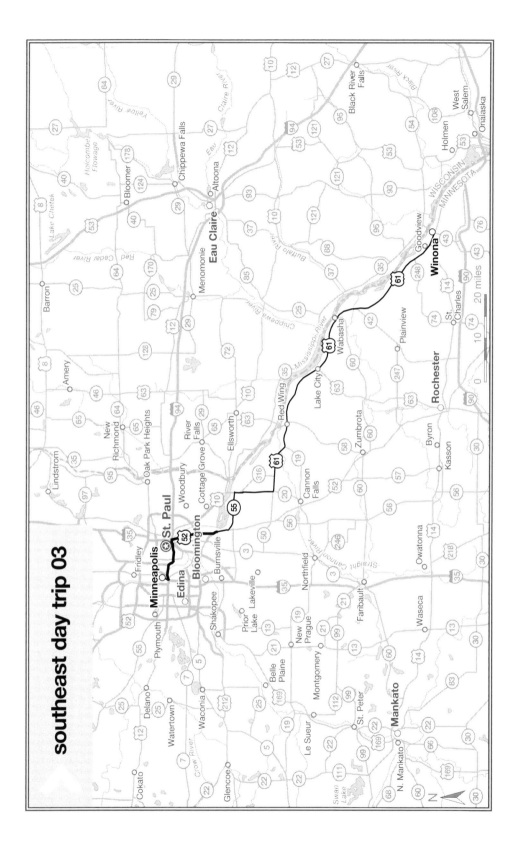

southeast day trip 03

both summer and winter when the ice park opens. The community playfully dubbed itself "the Miami of Minnesota" for being in the southeast corner of the state and consistently having warmer temperatures. You could argue that it has some sweet sandy islands and sunsets too.

winona's stained-glass legacy

Winona is known as Minnesota's stained-glass capital. Part of that is due to its many Victorian buildings, but the city also became a hub for producing stained glass. Here are a few of the dozens of places to enjoy this artwork.

Merchant's Bank. *102 E. Third St.; (507) 457-1100; merchantsbank.com/ locations/winona-downtown. Inside one of Minnesota's prettiest banks—a nod to the talent of Louis Sullivan and Prairie School influences—you'll find a mural of the river valley and Sugar Loaf bluff on one wall and a glowing, colorful display of art glass on the other.*

St. Stanislaus Catholic Church. *625 E. Fourth St.; (507) 452-5430; ssk-sjn .weconnect.com. This white-domed cathedral visible from the bluffs was built in 1895 by the local Polish community with stained-glass windows depicting lives of Eastern European saints.*

Watkins Administration Building. *150 Liberty St.; (507) 457-3300; watkins1868 .com. The company's George Maher–designed administration building cost more than a million dollars in 1913. It features a beautiful dome, art glass windows depicting Winona's Sugar Loaf bluff, plus Italian marble, mahogany, and mosaic accents and trim.*

Winona County History Center. *160 Johnson St.; (507) 454-2723; winonahistory.org. The stained-glass windows in this converted 1915 armory tell the stories of Winona's past, as do the many exhibits, a replicated Main Street, and hands-on exhibits for kids, who can crawl into a cave, a tipi, and a riverboat pilothouse.*

WNB Financial. *204 Main St.; (507) 454-8800; wnbfinancial.com. George Maher of Chicago also designed this 1874 Egyptian Revival bank featuring ornate metalwork, white marble staircases, green marble accents, and ornate art glass windows from the Tiffany Studio in New York. There's also a safari museum with taxidermy trophies.*

For "Miami of Minnesota" and other local souvenirs, stop at the **Winona Visitor Center,** 924 Huff St.; (507) 452-2278; visitwinona.com. You can get a photo op along Lake Winona with Sugar Loaf in the background and the giant "Winona" sign in the foreground. The staff will orient you with information, including walking maps for Winona's historic downtown. Open daily.

getting there

Take US 61 southeast out of the Twin Cities. Winona is about 40 minutes south of Wabasha. You also can take Amtrak's *Empire Builder* train from the Twin Cities or Red Wing.

where to go

Garvin Heights Vineyards. 2255 Garvin Heights Rd.; (507) 474-9463; ghvwine.com. This scenic winery in the Upper Mississippi River Valley Viticultural Area sells a variety of wines made from northern varietals, such as Minnesota's Frontenac or Sabrevois red from southern Quebec. Look for St. Urho and Bluff Country blends, rosé and blush wines, dry blends, and more. Open Thursday through Monday, May to October; Friday and Saturday in April, November, and December.

Great River Bluff State Park. 43605 Kipp Dr.; (507) 643-6849; dnr.state.mn.us. Enjoy the scenic overlooks along the wooded bluffs that rise 500 feet from the Mississippi River Valley 12 miles south of Winona. To get one of the 31 campsites at this 3,067-acre park, you'll have to reserve early for peak fall weekends, when maple-basswood and oak forests are ablaze. Have binoculars handy for hikes overlooking one of the country's busiest flyways during spring and fall migration. Winter visitors can use the sliding hill or cross-country ski trails, while spring and summer visitors can look for wildflowers, watch for migrating birds, and learn about the goat prairie habitat on steep bluffs. Daily fee: $7.

Great River Shakespeare Festival. 163 E. Second St.; (507) 474-7900; grsf.org. This professional theater festival runs about six weeks from late June to early August, using Winona State University's 435-seat DuFresne Performing Arts Center for favorite dramas and comedies from William Shakespeare. It celebrated its 20th season in 2023.

Kashubian Cultural Institute and Polish Museum. 102 Liberty St.; (507) 454-3431; polishmuseumwinona.org. This museum celebrates Winona's Polish roots, which started 150 years ago with a flood of immigrants who came from the northern region known as Kashubia for the booming lumber work in the 1870s. They could earn $1 a day ($1.25 if they could sharpen a saw). Exhibits include a variety of books, photos, Polish-language newspapers, Kashubian folk costumes and embroidery, the art of paper cutting, and a Polish Solidarity banner signed by nine Cold War–era world leaders, including US President George H. W. Bush. Check for seasonal hours.

Minnesota Marine Art Museum. 800 Riverview Dr.; (507) 474-6626; mmam.org. This impressive riverfront museum devotes itself to paintings, photography, and sculptures that reflect life on the water, from historic and impressionist paintings of ships, naval battles, and oceans to indigenous, contemporary, and multisensory art inspired by the Mississippi, Great Lakes, and smaller bodies of water. Leave time to stroll the waterfront and gardens with the museum's scenic setting. Open Tuesday to Sunday. Admission: $10, adults; $8, seniors; $5, children ages 5 and up.

paddlers' paradise

The name "Wenonah" graces the sides of canoes that have been manufactured in Winona for more than five decades. Family-owned Wenonah Canoe has 40 designs, including high-performance canoes and kayaks that are paddled around the world.

Sanborn Canoe Company, maker of handcrafted wood paddles, and Merrimack Canoe Company, custom canoe builders using wood and composites, also operate and manufacture their own designs in Winona.

You can stop by **Winona Outdoor Collaborative,** *4110 W. Fifth St.; winonaout doorcollaborative.com, a collaboration with Sanborn and Merrimack to help people get onto the river and area lakes. The collaborative offers expert guides, equipment to rent, and all you need to get onto local waters or plan a trip to the Boundary Waters. You can also rent camping bundles, backpacking gear, rock-climbing equipment, and cycling essentials. They offer snowshoeing in winter and share tips for cold-weather camping.*

For a casual paddle on Lake Winona, you also can stop at **Lake Lodge Recreation Center,** *113 Lake Park Dr.; (507) 453-1955, cityofwinona.com. The city's recreation department offers seasonal kayak, canoe, and SUP rentals. You can also rent bikes, a hammock, disc golf discs, a longboard, or skates for the winter ice.*

Sugar Loaf. You can drive to the Garvin Heights overlook, but to see the view from the local icon of Sugar Loaf, a little farther south on US 61, you'll need to hike up the bluff. It's worth it. Park along Lake Boulevard (essentially a frontage road near Edina Realty) and look for the path behind it. It takes 20 to 30 minutes to follow switchback trails to the top, where the view stretches for miles into driftless country and down the river valley.

Watkins Heritage Museum. 150 Liberty St.; (507) 457-6095; watkins1868.com. At the turn of the 20th century, this company with its line of spices, extracts, health tonics, and cosmetics was bigger than Procter & Gamble is today. It started in 1868 as the country's first direct-selling company and became its oldest more than 140 years later. Open Monday to Saturday. It's free, but you'll likely want a tin of cinnamon, a bottle of vanilla, minty lip balm, or liniment for aching muscles.

where to eat

Acoustic Café. 77 Lafayette St.; (507) 453-0394; acousticcafewinona.com. This affordable cafe serves soups and sandwiches on home-baked breads and authentic pitas, plus coffee roasted on-site. Bands play live music on the weekends. $.

Bloedow Bakery. 451 E. Broadway; (507) 452-3682. The line might snake out the door at this cherished 1924 corner bakery. It's tough to resist that sugary, yeasty aroma and the cases packed with doughnuts, rolls, maple long johns, and every variation of Bismarck. You can get breads and cookies too. Open Tuesday through Saturday. $.

Blue Heron Coffeehouse. 162 W. Second St.; (507) 452-7020; blueheroncoffeehouse .com. Creative, local ingredients make this cafe a favorite breakfast and lunch spot. Look for quiche or frittata with homemade sausage; moist, sweetly glazed cardamom scones and other baked goods; chai oatmeal; egg salad and other sandwiches on home-baked breads; and seasonal salads. Vegetarians and vegans will find several lunch options, including soups. You can relax on the outdoor patio or stroll to the Mississippi riverfront 2 blocks away. Open Wednesday through Sunday. $$.

Heirloom Seasonal Bistro. 155 E. Third St.; (507) 615-0124; facebook.com/Heirloom SeasonalBistro. Consult the chalkboard not only for the evening menu but also for which local farms provided the meat and produce that inspired it. You can find a mix of casual eats, such as smash sliders with bacon marmalade on Bloedow Bakery buns, *elote* fries with crema and cotija cheese, or something that pairs with a nice wine, such as mussels in vodka and tomato broth, gnocchi, or bucatini carbonara. $$.

Lakeview Drive Inn. 610 E. Sarnia St.; (507) 454-3723; lakeviewdriveinn.com. Take a trip into the past at this nostalgic drive-in that's served made-to-order burgers (look for a Sugarloaf Mountain burger), elk burgers, pork sandwiches, brats, and more since 1938. You can still drink their homemade root beer served in a frosted glass mug when dining on-site. Look for classic cars on Wednesday nights mid-June through mid-September. $.

Nosh. 102 Walnut St.; (507) 474-7040; noshrestaurant.com. This beloved Lake City destination for foodies moved in 2019 to Winona, where it buzzes with happy diners. The menu here changes as chefs present in-season produce (from fiddlehead ferns and rhubarb to sweet corn and tomatoes) for dishes often served with a Western Mediterranean influence, including their popular paella and fresh seafood. They have a small plate menu, too, to go with creative cocktails enjoyed indoors or outside. Open 4 to 9 p.m. Tuesday through Saturday. $$–$$$.

Sapori di Sicilia. 211 Main St.; (507) 474-6155; cafesaporidisicilia.com. If watching food and travel shows stirs your appetite, enjoy a taste of Italy with this Sicilian bakery cafe, led by a chef who learned how to make the breads, cannoli, tiramisu, rich soups, and from-scratch seasonal pastas while in Sicily. You'll find pastries, biscotti, coffee, and gelato too. $$.

where to stay

Alexander Mansion B&B. 274 E. Broadway; (507) 474-4224; alexandermansionbb.com. Lush and opulent, this Victorian mansion boasts incredible woodwork and a sprawling porch that's perfect for balmy days. There are five guest rooms with historic decor and the local Watkins body care products. The D.C. Alexander Suite also has an antique fireplace, original soaking tub, a window seat overlooking the gardens, and a private sunroom. A multicourse formal breakfast in the dining room includes pastries, fresh fruit, a savory egg frittata or quiche, and a sweet dessert, sometimes featuring vintage favorites from Watkins cookbooks. $$.

Carriage House B&B. 420 Main St.; (507) 452-8256; chbb.com. This B&B opened in 1986, creating four guest rooms in the multistory carriage house of an 1870 Victorian home. Artisan breakfasts may include crème brûlée French toast, crepes, or potato eggs Florentine. $$.

Express Suites Riverport Inn. 900 Bruski Dr.; (507) 452-0606; riverportinn.com. While this inn features mostly typical hotel rooms and a pool, it stands out for its 1957 and 1959 Chevy Suites. The two classic cars were turned into beds for these one-of-a-kind 1950s-themed suites. $–$$.

Prairie Island Campground. 1120 Prairie Island Rd.; (507) 452-4501; prairieislandcamp ground.com. Whether you're trying out one of the two tiny houses here (Warbler and Pot-luck) or bringing your own RV, camper, or tent, the views of the river and bluffs on the shore make this a peaceful getaway. Look for weekly concerts that are open to the public, natural-ist activities for kids, and chances to paddle the calm backwater areas of the Mississippi. $$.

day trip 05

southeast

>>> **caves, trails & root river floats:**
lanesboro, mn; preston, mn; houston, mn

You can feel yourself relax as you trade urban traffic for the gently winding Bluff Country Scenic Byway along MN 16 through the Root River Valley. This Driftless area of the state, which escaped the flattening power of ancient glaciers, retains its hilly hardwood forests; 300-foot dolomite bluffs; spring-fed streams for fly-fishing, river paddles, or floats; and Minnesota's coolest caves. You can explore the area's historic small towns by vehicle or along the popular Root River Trail to discover everything from a thriving theater company and the International Owl Center to a pioneer town and tours of Amish farms.

lanesboro, mn

No matter what the season, it's breathtaking to follow a bluff and then dip into the valley to the town of Lanesboro, the area's artsy hub for travelers.

In winter, snowflakes swirl over the historic brick downtown and the many elegant, colorful Victorian homes that have made this the Bed and Breakfast Capital of Minnesota. By spring there's a haze of bright-green buds and the rush of the Root River as it parallels the main street and curves around the bend. By summer, bicyclists whir along trails and paddlers float by on the Root River, while Amish buggies *clip-clop* to the bountiful farmers' market with produce and home-baked treats. By fall, brilliant colors sweep through the bluffs and into the surrounding Richard Dorer State Forest.

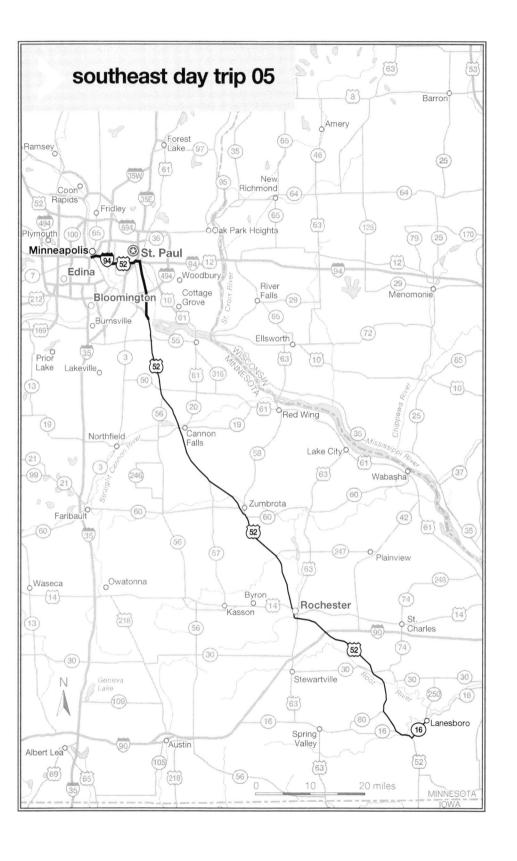

southeast day trip 05

The scenery helps infuse Lanesboro (pop. 720) with creative residents who run gracious B&Bs, contribute to galleries, and support the thriving local theater scene. Most of all, there's a tangible neighborly feeling of a small-town community that encourages you to downshift and unplug from the distractions of work and city life.

For more information, stop by the Lanesboro Area Chamber of Commerce, which is alongside the Root River State Trail at 100 Milwaukee Rd.; (507) 467-2696; lanesboro.com. Most businesses stay open daily through the summer, but restaurants often cut back to Thursday through Sunday in the winter.

getting there

Follow US 52 from the southeast Twin Cities toward Rochester. It's about 130 miles to Lanesboro. Exit at MN 16 East and continue about 6 miles to downtown.

where to go

Amish Backroads Tour. (507) 459-6999; amishbackroadstour.com. Download or rent a USB flash drive or CD from Amish Experience (105 Parkway Ave. North) or Stone Mill Hotel (100 Beacon St. East) for a narrated audio tour of rural Amish shops between Lanesboro and Harmony. Drive time is about 90 minutes, plus time to stop and meet the Amish families who make handcrafted furniture, baskets, quilts, rugs, soaps, jams, pies, and more. Amish shops are generally open Monday through Saturday and accept cash or checks. Audio tour: $29.

Bluffscape Amish Tours. 102 E. Beacon St.; (507) 467-3070; bluffscape.com. These 3-hour narrated tours by 14-passenger minibus include five to six stops with the chance to buy quilts, baskets, furniture, leather goods, and baked goods from Minnesota's largest Amish community, plus the chance to see the 1856 Lenora Stone Church. Tours, offered spring through fall, depart from the Feed Mill in downtown Lanesboro. Rates: $30, adults; $20, teens; $10, kids ages 6–12.

Commonweal Theatre Company. 208 N. Parkway Ave.; (800) 657-7025; common wealtheatre.org. This professional company has entertained audiences with family-friendly comedies and musicals since 1989. Even if you don't have time for a show, pop inside to admire how they've transformed a former cheese factory into a 192-seat thrust stage with funky lobby art. Be sure to look up at the upside-down chairs hanging from the ceiling and decorated thematically. Interior wood- and stonework was salvaged from barns, with dioramas tucked into the walls. Even the restrooms are fun, with farm-tool handles on the stalls.

Lanesboro Art Gallery. 103 Parkway Ave. North; (507) 467-2446; lanesboroarts.org. Browse through a classy collection of work by close to 90 artists who create everything from wearable art and turned wood bowls to paintings inspired by the Bluff Country scenery. Open Tuesday through Sunday in the offseason, with expanded summer hours.

Lanesboro Farmers' Market. Sylvan Park, 202 Parkway Ave. South; (507) 467-2358. Look for grass-fed beef and pork, rhubarb soap, perennials, fresh produce, pies, jams, jellies, lefse, and Amish cashew crunch made with butter, sugar, and cashews. Great time to visit: the Rhubarb Festival in early June. Open 9 a.m. to noon May through October.

underground wonderlands

Southeast Minnesota's Bluff County boasts some of the state's best scenery, but there's another side to it. To fully appreciate the area's geology, head underground.

Filmore County has about 400 known cave systems. It's part of what's called karst topography. The glaciers missed this area, and it's filled with sinkholes, natural springs, and streams that dip underground and disappear.

You can see some of this landscape at Forestville/Mystery Cave State Park. One-hour seasonal tours give visitors a sample of the glossy flowstone and sta-lactites found throughout its 13 miles and finds such as a prehistoric squid fossil. You can gaze into dark shallow "aquariums" along a rock shelf and admire an oth-erworldly underground pool. The cave closes in the offseason when thousands of bats winter here.

If you head about 16 miles south of Lanesboro, you can take 1-hour tours into Niagara Cave, a trendy and quirky place to get married in the late 1930s and 1940s. There were more than 400 weddings at its underground chapel.

Modern visitors head down 275 steps past a 60-foot waterfall and onto a tour that includes stalactites, undulating rock draperies, 450-million-year-old fossils, delicate soda straws hanging from the ceiling, and an intriguing echo chamber. A highlight includes walking through the mazelike limestone canyon with walls as high as 100 feet.

Mystery Cave. 21071 CR 118, Preston; (507) 352-5111 (park office) or (866) 857-2757 (tour reservations); dnr.state.mn.us. Open May through October, with daily tours Memorial Day through Labor Day. There are several options for seeing the cave: 1-hour accessible scenic tour ($10–$15/person), a more rugged 1-hour lantern tour ($10–$15/person), and a rigorous 4-hour wild caving tour ($55/person).

Niagara Cave. 29842 CR 30, Harmony; (507) 886-6606; niagaracave.com. Open March through October. Call for seasonal tour times. Tickets: $20, ages 13 and up; $12, ages 3–12. Additional aboveground activities include gemstone panning, minigolf, a picnic shelter, and a playground.

Little River General Store. 105 Coffee St.; (507) 467-2943; lrgeneralstore.com. Conveniently located along the Root River Valley Trail, this shop offers an array of bikes from tandems and recumbents to electric-assist bikes. They have a shuttle service if you don't want to backtrack and tubes if you'd rather float than pedal along the river.

Root River Outfitters. 101 S. Parkway Ave.; (507) 467-3400; rootriveroutfitters.net. You can tube down the Root River or try your hand at paddling kayaks or canoes. The river is generally gentle and undeveloped, flowing through the Richard J. Dorer Memorial Hardwood Forest.

Root River State Trail. Trailhead in downtown Lanesboro; rootrivertrail.org. The 42-mile trail runs parallel to the river, connecting small towns such as Whalan, Peterson, and Rushford. It's a gentle route. You can bring your bike, rent one, or check Bike Share availability. If you crave a better workout with hills, connect to the 12-mile Harmony-Preston Trail.

where to eat

Aroma Pie Shoppe. 618 Main St., Whalan; (507) 467-2623; facebook.com/aromapie shoppe. This is the best incentive for a 4.7-mile bike ride from Lanesboro to Whalan. Get in line at this seasonal homey cafe that goes through 50 to 100 cream and fruit pies a day. It also offers sandwiches, wild rice brats, wraps, and soups, but pie's the real allure. Try the rhubarb custard. $.

High Court Pub. 109 N. Parkway Ave.; (507) 467–2782; highcourtpub.com. Cool off from a bike ride and recharge with a craft beer, wine, or loaded bloody Mary and wings or flatbreads, such as chicken bacon ranch or Krab Rangoon. This pub also offers a shady, relaxed place to gather on the riverside patio for games of cornhole or *hammerschlag*. The pub was named for the building's third floor, which was once the area's courtroom and is now a refurbished loft with a kitchen for guests to rent. $$.

Juniper's Restaurant, 109 Parkway Ave. South; (507) 467-4040; junipersrestaurantmn .com. While it's casual, with counter service, expect elegantly plated homemade ravioli, pork Bolognese, smash-style burgers, veggie bowls, and small plates at this dinner-only restaurant with balconies and outdoor seating overlooking the Root River and the historic state trail bridge. $$

Lanesboro Pastry Shoppe. 202 Parkway Ave. North; (507) 467-2867. Locals heartily recommend this as a favorite breakfast spot. Tell them what you want, and they'll whip it up. Lunch specials could be roast beef with morel mushrooms or tomato pesto soups, quiche, or a plate of biscuits and gravy. They always have a salad too, with shrimp or salmon, plus monster-size cookies and sticky buns, but don't dawdle. They close by 1:30 p.m. most days. $$.

Pedal Pushers Café. 121 Parkway Ave. North; (507) 467-1050; pedalpusherscafe.com. This family-friendly cafe serves a tasty, eclectic menu mixing comfort foods such as burgers and chicken potpie with Korean pork or mango shrimp bowls, vegan falafel, local brews, and classic milkshakes. $$.

Sylvan Brewing. 100 Beacon St. West; (507) 467-4677; sylvanbeer.com. Lanesboro's first brewery in more than 100 years poured its first beers in 2020 in a former granary. Look for choices such as Lanesbrew American lager, Bucksnort nut brown ale, Brook Stout, and amaretto sour Weisse. $.

where to stay

Berwood Hill Inn. 22139 Hickory Rd.; (612) 867-3614; berwood.com. With a 200-acre hilltop location and whimsical gardens, this 1870 farmhouse makes it easy to stay put and relax or plan a special occasion. There are four guest rooms, including a spacious owl-themed suite in the attic. The rustic Garden Cottage offers another option for warm-weather overnights. With so many objects creatively tucked into the gardens—cherubs, a giant rooster, statues, farm equipment, and frogs—it's become its own attraction, with nonguests able to book a tour. Look for breakfasts such as yogurt topped with fruit and granola, crème brûlée French toast, a potato–green-pepper hash with Canadian bacon, a Brie quiche with hollandaise sauce, and rhubarb crunch for dessert. $$–$$$.

Cedar Valley Resort. 905 Bench St., Whalan; (507) 467-9000; cedarvalleyresort.com. Nestled into the valley along the Root River in nearby Whalan, this resort ranks as a favorite spot for social gatherings, with plenty of room and amenities: bike trail, yard games, disc golf course, ski trails, ice rink, sleigh rides, and canoe, tube, and kayak rentals that are also available to nonguests. Eleven modern log-sided cabins range from three to eight bedrooms. The largest can accommodate up 38 guests. $$.

Historic Scanlan House B&B Inn. 708 Parkway Ave. S.; (507) 467-2158; scanlanhouse .com. Having welcomed guests for more than three decades, this 1889 Queen Anne Victorian built by Lanesboro's founder ranks as one of Minnesota's most venerable B&Bs. Vintage furnishings, stained glass, elaborate woodwork, and alcoves add character to its seven guest rooms, three of them suites and two located in the grand turret. $$.

Root River Inn & Suites. 106 Parkway Ave. S.; (507) 467-2999; rootriverinn.com. Built into the hillside, this downtown hotel stands out with its wraparound balcony, five standard rooms, and four suites named for towns along the Root River State Trail, which is right out the front door. $$.

Stone Mill Hotel & Suites. 100 Beacon St. E.; (507) 467-8663; stonemillsuites.com. Located right downtown, this former mill retains some of its rustic charm with stone walls and wood beams. The 13 rooms and suites feature a local theme and include an expanded continental breakfast. $$.

keep going

Whether you pedal your way east or drive the Bluff Country Scenic Byway, take the winding 30-mile journey to Houston, home of the International Owl Center, 126 E. Cedar St.; (507) 896-6957; internationalowlcenter.org. As the only bird center in the country devoted to owls, it hosts an annual International Festival of Owls every March and is in the process of planning a major expansion. Visitors can browse exhibits and meet their eight ambassador owls (rescues or raised in captivity) or attend activities such as an owl prowl to seek the birds in the wild and learn their calls. $9, adults; $6, 4–17 years old.

preston, mn

At the junction of MN 52 and MN 16, Preston (pop. 1,316) ranks as the biggest town on the Root River State Trail and is known as "Minnesota's Trout Capital." The state trail rolls by its historic train depot and boxcars and a preserved chimney that provides a home for the state's largest population of chimney swifts. They're considered one of the world's fastest creatures and help keep mosquito populations down. More details can be found at the Preston Chamber of Commerce, (507) 765-2153; prestonmnchamber.com.

what to do

Driftless Fly Fishing Company. 208 St. Paul St. SW; (507) 327-4276; minnesotaflyfishing. com. Whether you're new to the sport or seasoned, these local guides help visitors find and fish the best local streams and rivers famed for trout. The business also offers classes, rents kayaks and gear, and has a suite above the shop available to rent.

Harmony-Preston Valley State Trail. This 18-mile multiple-use trail built on a former railroad track connects Harmony and Preston, rolling through forests and farm fields and across streams and rivers. It connects to the Root River State Trail for an additional 42 miles. The trail is groomed for skiing in winter. During warm months, check at City Hall for available Bike Share bikes, which can be used free of charge.

Historic Forestville. 21899 CR 118, Preston; (507) 765-2785; mnhs.org/forestville. A drive 3 miles south of MN 16 and across a bridge will plunge you *Brigadoon*-style into

1899. Historic Forestville, a town that died out when the railroad bypassed it, comes to life each summer with costumed interpreters. Start at the visitor center and follow self-guided tours to visit barns; browse the tonics, tools, union suits, and boots that were left behind at the Meighen store; and learn about the wheat boom and crash that contributed to the town's demise. Open Thursday through Sunday Memorial Day weekend through Labor Day. Rates: $10, adults; $8, seniors and children age 5 and older.

where to stay

Forestville/Mystery Cave State Park. 21071 CR 118; (507) 352-5111; dnr.state.mn.us. With both the cave and historic site to explore, plus hiking and horse trails, this state park can fill up its 73 seasonal campsites, 55-site horse camp, and 5 year-round camper cabins that sleep five to six people. $.

Old Barn Resort. 24461 Heron Rd.; (507) 467-2512; barnresort.com. Once a farm, this property now holds 276 campsites, 4 rentable rooms in the historic barn (including a room with 16 bunk beds), an 18-hole golf course, a restaurant and bar, a three-season swimming pool, a spot along the Root River State Trail, easy access to trout fishing, and games such as sand volleyball and basketball. Both guests and the public can rent tubes for floats down the river. $.

where to eat

Four Daughters Vineyard and Winery. 78757 MN 16, Spring Valley; (507) 346-7300; fourdaughtersvineyard.com. About 20 miles west of Preston, you can kick back at this attractive vineyard that serves brick-oven pizzas with fresh buffalo milk mozzarella paired with toppings such as pepperoni and house-smoked corn on the cob or Italian sausage with pistachios and rosemary. Or order an artfully presented cheese and charcuterie board while sampling flights of Four Daughters wines (which have been served at the SXSW film festival and Sundance Film Festival) or its Loon Juice hard ciders. Follow it with their pinot noir dark chocolate cake layered with caramel gelato. If that's not enough temptation, the Traditionalist Distillery and Lounge serves triple-meat ragu over polenta, bourbon-fed local beef, and an array of bourbon drinks and cocktails. $$.

south

day trip 01

south

>>> **legacy of health & hospitality**
rochester, mn

rochester, mn

Rochester, Minnesota's third-largest city, long ago mastered medical tourism on a global scale. The benefit for travelers who aren't in need of its world-famous health care is that much of the community ranks as experts in hospitality, well-accustomed to helping visitors find their way around, welcoming them with a wide variety of cuisine, a blend of artsy and sophisticated shopping, running and bike trails for healthy excursions, and close to 6,000 rooms for those who want to spend the night.

The Mayo Clinic, founded in 1889 with 27 beds, has grown into a sprawling medical campus that draws more than 1.3 million people from across the United States and 137 countries. Visitors keep the downtown lively with its belowground shops and tunnels connecting medical buildings and hotels and aboveground skyways. Thursdays Downtown, an event that runs from 11 a.m. to 8:30 p.m. brings together a blend of art, food vendors, and live music in the summer. Other events include Roller Disco (with installation of an outdoor rink) and Dogs Downtown in October, and Social-ICE with live music, ice bars, and frozen works of art in February.

Look for event and visitor information at Experience Rochester, located in Mayo Civic Center, Ste. 200, 30 Civic Center Dr. SE; (507) 288-4331; experiencerochestermn.com.

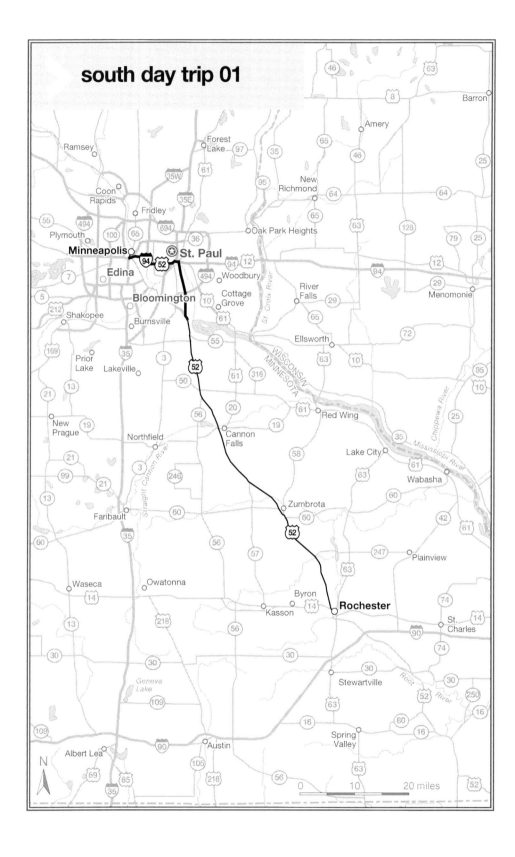

south day trip 01

getting there

From I-94 on the southeast side of the Twin Cities, exit at US 52. Follow it about 90 minutes to Rochester.

where to go

Mayowood Mansion. 3720 Mayowood Rd. SW; (507) 282-9447; olmstedhistory.com. The best time to see Dr. Charlie Mayo's 38-room country home is during the summer, when extensive gardens bloom, or during the holidays, when lavish Christmas decorations and lights make it twinkle. The regular spring through fall tours cover highlights of Dr. Charlie's career and famous houseguests, and showcase the property itself overlooking the Zumbro River Valley. There are extensive limestone terraces and walls, ponds, a long pergola, and a teahouse, and once there were such innovations as a hydroelectric dam and man-made lake on what used to be a 3,300-acre estate. Open April through October. Admission: $20, adults; $10, children 3 to 12. Check for current hours and tour days.

Quarry Hill Nature Center. 701 Silver Creek Rd.; (507) 328-3950; qhnc.org. This is one of the top family attractions, with its free nature center that's home to snakes, frogs, turtles, a resident saw-whet owl, a honeybee hive, and a 1,700-gallon aquarium with fish. Look for naturalist programs, and search for ancient sea fossils, find sandstone caves, or hike, bike, or rent snowshoes or skis to explore this 320-acre park. Free admission.

Rochester Art Center. 30 Civic Center Dr. SE; (507) 722-2552; rochesterartcenter.org. This modern museum has a gorgeous riverside location and fun museum shop an easy walk from downtown. Exhibits change monthly. Don't miss artist Po Shu Wang's 30-foot-long and 15-foot-high sculpture outside the Civic Center. Open Wednesday through Sunday. Admission: $8, adults 21 and older. Free to Olmsted County visitors, military personnel and anyone under 21.

Rochester Trolley & Tour Company. 972 14th Ave. SW; (507) 421-0573; rochestermn tours.com. This company is best known for 2-hour city tours in their five classic trolleys, but seasonal tours also include the Wine Trail, Haunted Rochester, Holiday Lights, Old Order Amish Country, and Scenic Mississippi River Valley.

Silver Lake Park. 840 Seventh St. NE; (507) 328-2525; rochestermn.gov. This widening of the Zumbro River ranks among the prettiest places in the city, with the added attraction of paddleboats, canoes, bikes, and bicycle strollers to use on the 1.8-mile loop around the lake. The open water in winter has drawn more than 35,000 giant Canada geese and helped nurture the species' comeback from near extinction in the 1960s. In summer you can also take a dip in the outdoor pool, try fishing for bluegills or crappies, or take the kids to the accessible playground.

Whitewater State Park, 19041 MN 74, Altura; (507) 312-2300; dnr.state.mn.us. About 25 miles east of Rochester, this state park known for its spring wildflowers and lack of mosquitoes also boasts peaceful hikes along the Middle Branch of the Whitewater River or a more strenuous trek up Chimney Rock Trail for sweeping views of the valley, a beach and swimming hole along the river, and rock formations along the bluff. $7 fee.

a closer look: the mayo clinic

Mayo Clinic's daily weekday clinic and art tours are open to patients and their families, but you can easily pop into its gorgeous, modern Gonda Building (200 First St. SW) to admire a huge Chihuly sculpture and other renowned artworks, not to mention the building's interior design. You might even catch an impromptu concert if someone steps up to the baby grand piano in the atrium. Ask at the info desk for self-guided brochures of its impressive art collection.

Permanent history displays also tell tales of Mayo's beginnings, which were sparked by a devastating 1883 tornado that left the Franciscan sisters scrambling to care for the injured. They asked Dr. William Mayo to lead what became the cutting-edge St. Mary's Hospital in 1889. Their efforts expanded to a world-class medical system with top surgery techniques, research to support new medicines, and a unique philosophy of team care.

You can find historical displays in these locations:

- *Mayo Clinic Heritage Hall. Mathews Grand Lobby of the Mayo Building.*

- *Mayo Historical Suite and preserved offices of Drs. William J. and Charles H. Mayo in the Plummer Building. You can't miss this ornate 1928 building that rises above downtown with gargoyles and a 56-bell carillon. The office suite includes the Mayo brothers' degrees, honors, and photos of presidents and dignitaries, as well as examples of how crude early surgical instruments were.*

- *Main lobby, St. Mary's Hospital, 1216 Second St. SW. The lobby gleams with green marble that surrounds a central courtyard with gardens. The hospital includes a beautiful cathedral.*

where to shop

Counterpoint II and Counterpoint Home. 111 S. Broadway; (507) 280-6419; counterpointhome.com. Browse two stories of classy, colorful, and just plain fun home furnishings, kitchenware and gadgets, clothing, kids' stuff, purses, funky shoes, and Marimekko designs.

James Krom Natural Images Art Museum Gallery. 101 First Ave. SW (subway level), Ste. 42; (507) 272-2415. The glow of art glass sculptures, life-sized wood carvings, and elegant paintings of pastoral landscapes pull visitors into this gallery with work from more than 100 Upper Midwest and national artists.

The Nordic Shop. 111 S. Broadway; (507) 285-9143; thenordicshop.net. A downtown staple for more than 40 years, this shop offers a nod to Minnesota's Scandinavian heritage with warm Norwegian sweaters, Helly Hansen sport clothing, Royal Copenhagen dinnerware, and Kosta Boda crystal.

SEMVA Art Gallery. 20 Second Ave. SW; (507) 281-4920; semva.com. Southeastern Minnesota Visual Artists sell the best of their work here, including paintings, photography, metalwork and jewelry, blown glass, sculpture, and fiber arts from vivid hand-dyed scarves to boiled wool hats. The area's hardwood forest and Nordic folk roots also assure plenty of handcrafted pieces that make the most of swirling wood grains and luminous colors for vases, decorative bowls, rosemaled plates, and ornaments. Open Tuesday through Saturday.

where to eat

Bleu Duck Kitchen. 14 Fourth St. SW; (507) 258-4663; bleuduckkitchen.com. You can enjoy a delicious date night with a contemporary vibe and a touch of whimsy, such as a rendition of the *Girl with a Pearl Earring* painting that pictures a blue duck hanging on their brick walls. Seasonal meals may be tender lamb with pasta, duck with butternut squash, or steelhead trout with risotto and a Thai coconut curry seafood stew. $$$.

The Canadian Honker. 1203 Second St. SW; (507) 282-6572; canadianhonker.com. This is a home-cooked, comfort food kind of place, run by two generations since 1984. Think eggs Benedict, sweet rolls, prime rib melt, 4-hour slow-cooked ribs, or hot beef sandwich. There's outdoor seating and live music on the weekends, and sweet excuses to linger with their most beloved dessert—Bunnie's coconut cake—plus a decadent peanut butter pie with an Oreo cookie crust and chocolate raspberry cake. $$.

Chester's Kitchen and Bar. 111 S. Broadway, Ste. 108; (507) 424-1211; chesterskb .com. Hip and stylish, this Galleria at University Square restaurant deservedly draws steady diners with a wood-fired oven, creative twists on traditional meals, and outdoor seating on the Peace Plaza. Menu favorites include crispy, beer-battered walleye on ciabatta bread, wood-fired rotisserie chicken, grilled barbecue salmon, and a salad with pulled chicken, sweet corn, bacon, and apples. Try the banana cream pie on a walnut-almond crust or the dessert flight. Brunch includes endless mimosas, prime rib hash, lobster bisque, and healthy veggie bowls. Open Monday through Saturday for lunch and dinner, Sunday for brunch. $$–$$$.

Chocolaterie Stam. 111 S. Broadway, Ste. 208; (507) 536-2722; stamchocolate.com. These exquisitely crafted Dutch chocolates come in an array of shapes such as seashells, acorns, and even tiny ears of sweet corn that may remind you of Rochester's iconic Ear of Corn Water Tower. Take your favorite chocolates to go and grab a dish of gelato or sorbetto, freshly made in flavors such as strawberry, forest berry, pistachio, and crème brûlée. $$.

Forager Brewery. 1005 Sixth St. NW; (507) 258-7490; foragerbrewery.com. You won't want to rush a beer or a meal here, with its indoor decor using artistically salvaged (or foraged) materials and handcrafted tables plus an outdoor patio perfect for a balmy evening. The Scratch Kitchen uses produce from local farms for salad and noodle bowls, burgers and vegan sandwiches, and creative wood-fired pizzas inspired by Reuben sandwiches, eggs Benedict, and more. Brews range from a wild ale and a pumped-up Belgian quadruple to the Coastal Sunshine series of sour fruited ales and Humble Bumble hard seltzers. $$

Mango Thai. 318 S. Broadway; (507) 288-2360; facebook.com/mangothai.rochester. Expect colorful and beautifully plated meals such as salads with shrimp or grilled tuna with mango and strawberry, Korean beef with kimchi, basil- or ginger-roasted duck, red curry sea bass or green curry walleye. Coconut custard with sweet sticky rice and green tea ice cream offer a sweet finish. $$–$$$.

Pasquale's Neighborhood Pizzeria. 130 Fifth St. SW; (507) 424-7800; pnpizza.com. With shelves of imported pasta and olive oil and the heady aroma of fresh-baked pizza in the air, this place offers a taste of Italy and New York City–style pizza. Diners can grab a patio spot or a table indoors before ordering pizzas, calzones, stromboli, soups, antipasti plates, and more. Big family? They make a 30-inch Brontosaurus. $$.

Twigs Tavern and Grille. 401 Sixth St. SW (at Centerstone Plaza Hotel); (507) 288-0206; twigstavernandgrille.com. Gluten-free diners can eat here with confidence, knowing their food was prepped in an exclusively gluten-free kitchen. A second kitchen prepares food for customers without gluten issues. Twigs stands out for its vegetarian meals, street tacos and poke bowls, and hot rock grilling that allows diners to cook their own sliced meat and seafood with dozens of sauces and a tabletop rock that heats to 650°F. The patio is popular on warm days. $$.

where to stay

Centerstone Plaza Hotel Soldiers Field. 401 Sixth St. SW; (507) 288-2677; soldiersfield .com. A few minutes from downtown, this 214-room hotel offers courtesy shuttles so you don't have to hassle with parking fees. Stays also include a pool, fitness center, outdoor patio, light breakfast buffet, and pet-friendly and pet-free rooms. $$.

Kahler Grand Hotel. 20 Second Ave. SW; (507) 280-6200; kahler.com. Rochester's grande dame started in 1921, when the Mayo brothers needed a classy hotel to cater to global visitors. It's the place to go for visiting presidents and royalty too, with its exclusive International Hotel within the Kahler. There are more than 660 rooms in the general hotel with a large indoor swimming pool beneath a rooftop dome. Guests also have indoor access to the Grand Shops of Kahler and Marriott Hotels, plus University Square and the Peace Plaza outside the front door. $$.

day trip 02

south

>>> **cannon river, colleges & jesse james:**
northfield, mn

northfield, mn

With two of the nation's top liberal arts colleges (Carleton and St. Olaf), a historic downtown with dozens of restaurants and shops, and enough community chutzpah to chase the Jesse James Gang out of town in 1876, Northfield has always been able to make a big impression while maintaining its small-town feel.

John Wesley North started the community in 1855 after sizing up the Cannon River. He harnessed its hydropower to run a sawmill and gristmill, and that legacy lives on with the Malt-O-Meal Company wafting the aroma of wheat cereal across the outskirts.

A decade after its founding, Northfield welcomed its first college. Today, Carleton College and St. Olaf draw close to 5,000 students who keep the town vibrant, youthful, and cultured with plays, concerts, and art shows throughout the year. The beloved St. Olaf Christmas Festival, one of the oldest musical celebrations of Christmas in the country, is broadcast nationally and beyond.

You'll also find a weekend-long international Vintage Band Festival in late July, followed by the chance to hear the thunder of hooves and blast of guns as folks reenact the historic bank raid the weekend after Labor Day for the Defeat of Jesse James Days. The multiday festival brings together crafts, food, a rodeo, a car show, and bike tours that highlight the area's rolling scenery.

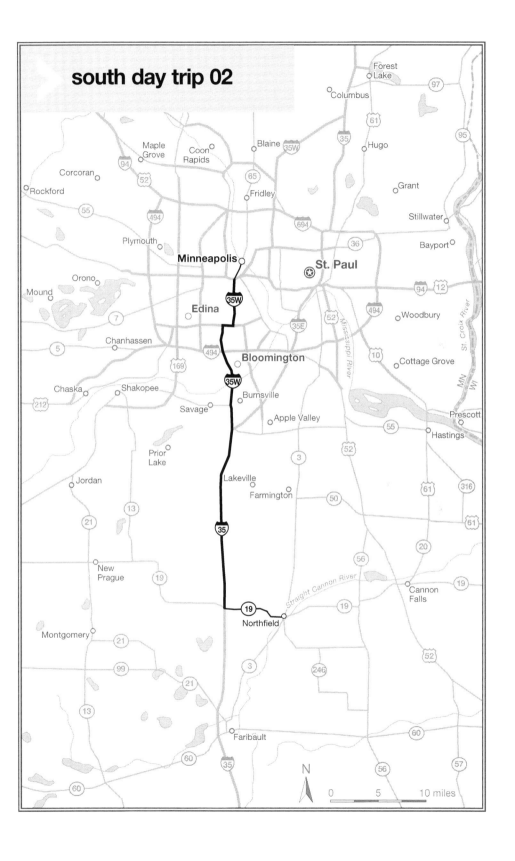

south day trip 02

getting there

Follow I-35 about 30 miles south of the Twin Cities. Exit at MN 19.

where to go

Carleton College. 1 College St.; (507) 222-4000; go.carleton.edu. Enjoy the picturesque campus by strolling the Garden of Quiet Listening with its Japanese design and the 880-acre Cowling Arboretum with views of the Cannon River. The arboretum ranks among the top places in the state to go for a run. Another draw at this top-10 liberal arts college is the Perlman Teaching Museum (at 320 Third St. in the Weitz Center for Creativity), which is open daily and exhibits art from around the world intended to spark conversation.

Nerstrand Big Wood State Park. 9700 170th St. East, Nerstrand; (507) 333-4840; dnr .state.mn.us. This nearly 3,000-acre remnant of original Big Woods forest sits about 7 miles from Northfield on the way to Faribault and offers one the state's best places to see spring wildflowers (and the state's endangered dwarf trout lily), enjoy the Prairie Creek waterfall, and camp at one of 51 modern campsites or 4 primitive walk-in tent sites. Trails offer 13 miles of hiking, 8 miles of paths for cross-country skiing, and 5 miles for snowmobiling. $7 daily fee.

Northfield Arts Guild. 304 Division St. S.; (507) 645-8877; northfieldartsguild.org. When you're in a town with two nationally known liberal arts colleges, you know that even the off-campus art scene will be solid. With a hub in the heart of downtown, the Northfield Arts Guild showcases work by more than 100 regional artists in its gift shop, offers a lively lineup of exhibits, teaches hands-on art classes, and has presented theater productions (at 411 Third St. West) for more than six decades.

Northfield Historical Society Museum and Historic Bank Site. 408 Division St. S.; (507) 645-9268; northfieldhistory.org. Get the details on why the Jesse James Gang came all the way from Missouri and why this robbery was considered by some to be the last battle of the Civil War. The outlaws were apparently after bank funds belonging to two despised carpetbaggers. It's also a good place to catch a video showing the annual reenactment and to grab maps and brochures for historic buildings downtown, the home of Norwegian-born author O. E. Rølvaag, and other James Gang sites on the Outlaw Trail as it heads through Minnesota.

Riverwalk Market Fair. On Bridge Square between Division and Fourth Street along the Cannon River; riverwalkmarketfair.org. This favorite weekly hangout blends a little of every-thing: live entertainers; locally crafted pottery, jewelry, and other art; local farmers selling everything from self-harvested homespun yarns to gourmet cheeses and soaps; gourmet breads, jams, pastries, and coffee; and fresh produce, eggs, and flowers 9 a.m. to 1 p.m. Saturdays from late May through mid-October. Look for winter markets, as well, between Thanksgiving and Christmas.

St. Olaf College. 1520 St. Olaf Dr.; (507) 786-3556; wp.stolaf.edu. Like at Carleton College, you can find ongoing public art performances from orchestral to dance, along with sporting events, on this historic campus. Check out free exhibits at Flaten Art Museum on the main floor of the Center for Art and Dance.

Willingers Golf Club. 6900 Canby Trail; (952) 652-2500; willingersgc.com. This 6,809-yard course was built along a 40-acre forest and among 60 acres of open water and wetlands, achieving Audubon Cooperative Sanctuary status. It's been recognized as one of Minnesota's top courses in *Golf Digest* and is easy to reach at 1.5 miles from I-35.

where to shop

You'll find plenty of quirky, hip, and also thrifty shops concentrated along and near Northfield's Division Street. Most are open seven days a week, but call ahead for details on hours.

Makeshift Accessories Gallery & Studio. 418 Division St. South; (612) 353-8862; makeshiftaccessories.com. Find handcrafted rings, cuff bracelets, money clips, and more cleverly fashioned from upcycled coins, decorative silverware, machinery plates, metal rulers, and more.

MN Soulstice Boutique. 425 Division St. S.; (507) 366-1386;www.mnsoulsticeboutique .com. This shop strikes the right note for anyone who is passionate about buying from companies with a cause. About 80 percent of its inventory, such as hats, scarves, and jewelry, comes from brands dedicated to supporting nonprofit organizations.

Monarch Gift Shop. 405 Division St. S.; (507) 663-7720; monarchgiftshop.com. This well-established shop provides a go-to spot for gifts such as handblown glass spheres, playful and fragrant bath and body products, jewelry, and accessories.

Northfield Yarn. 314 Division St. S.; (507) 645-1330; northfieldyarn.com. Whether you shop by color or texture, this shop fills its shelves with temptations from sturdy wools and soft alpaca to funky buttons for everyone from newbies to experienced knitters looking for heirloom-worthy projects. Look for how-to and special project classes or open-knit nights.

The Rare Pair. 401 Division St. S.; (507) 645-4257; rarepair.com. This corner shop below a redbrick turret in the heart of downtown has been in business more than 40 years, selling comfortable shoes from Birkenstocks to UGGs, along with casual clothes and accessories for men and women.

The Sketchy Artist. 315 Division St. S.; (507) 645-2811; facebook.com/thesketchyartist. With vibrant decor, playful merchandise, and inviting displays, this shop caters to anyone seeking the perfect sketchbook, a groovy new pen, stationery and cards, art supplies, and creative gifts.

Vintage, etc. 411 Division St. S.; (507) 366-4411; facebook.com/vintageetc2016. This is one of several Northfield shops that specialize in vintage or gently used clothing and accessories, as well as antiques to liven up home decor. Thank students on a budget for Northfield's breadth of bargain shopping less than an hour from Minneapolis. Each shop strikes a different vibe with always-a-surprise inventory that shifts as seasons and fresh goods come and go.

where to eat

The Contented Cow. 302B Division St. S.; (507) 663-1351; contentedcow.com. You can order flatbreads, nachos, or pretzels plus shepherd's pie on weekends at this Welsh pub, but it's the atmosphere more than the food that keeps people coming to this 1876 riverside restaurant—especially when balmy days make its patio and deck the place to be. Opened in 1999, it promises "no lame beer" and more than a dozen taps. Another promise: a family-friendly place focused on conversations, live music, and limited TV or sports. Annual events include the MayFly Music and DylanFest in late May, JuneBugMusic Festival, July JazzFest, and New Year's Eve party. $$.

Fielders Choice Tap & Table. 2300 Gleason Ct.; (507) 645-4500; fielderstapandtable .com. You could easily fill up on appetizers, from fried cheese curds and lettuce wraps to street tacos and pretzel bread sticks, and sampling the three dozen (mostly Minnesotan) beers on tap, but leave room for wood-fired pizzas and burgers such as the Strawberry Hill (beef topped with peanut butter, strawberry jam, bacon, and pepper-jack cheese) or Pickle Lucy (beef patty stuffed with cheddar cheese and topped with fried pickles and buttermilk mayonnaise). $$.

George's Vineyards. 1160 S. MN 3; (507) 645-0100; georgesvineyard.com. This casual eatery with an Italian focus serves up meatball grinders, Greek and Caesar salads, and dozens of pizzas. $.

The HideAway Coffeehouse and Wine Bar. 421 Division St. S.; (507) 664-0400; the hideawaynorthfield.com. This longtime coffeeshop makes its drinks with freshly roasted St. Paul–based Truestone coffee beans. You can also get salad and ciabatta sandwiches, soups, and breakfast entrées from burritos to avocado toast on seven-grain bread—also using many locally sourced ingredients. $.

Imminent Brewing. 519 Division St. S.; (507) 646-2327; imminentbrewing.com. Open since 2017 in a renovated former National Guard armory garage, this brewery and taproom offers choices such as its Norstralian sparking ale, Dragon Squirrel Juice IPA, a seasonal brew made with locally grown tart cherries, and a robust porter. It draws beer lovers to socialize indoors or on the dog-friendly patio. Check for updates on live music, visiting chefs, and local food trucks (such as Delicious Pupusas, a thick Salvadorian tortilla), special events (even dog training sessions) and, of course, new brews. $–$$.

Keepsake Cidery. 4609 135th St. East, Dundas; (413) 552-8872; mncider.com. For another twist on local spirits, sample the ciders made from this Cannon River Valley orchard and wild yeasts, yielding flavors from dry and tart to mildly sweet, from sparkling to still. You can also choose from simple tasty fare too, such as cheese and olive plates, toasty sandwiches, soups, and applesauce in season. Look for a wider selection during Friday Night Cookouts. Enjoy live music on Saturday evenings, cidery tours on the first Sunday of the month, and jazz brunch on the third Sunday of the month. Open Friday, Saturday, and Sunday. $–$$.

Loon Liquors. 1325 Armstrong Rd., #165; (507) 581-7527; loonliquors.com. Northfield's craft distillery debuted its first spirits in 2014 and makes award-winning organic whiskey, gin, vodka, and coffee liqueur from local ingredients. Grab a spot indoors or on the patio, or reserve one of its outdoor tents for dozens of creative cocktails from refreshing citrus gin fizz to complex blends with homemade syrups and sodas, bitters, and hints of smoke. Open Thursday, Friday, and Saturday. $$.

Ole Store Restaurant. 1011 St. Olaf Ave.; (507) 786-9400; olestorerestaurant.com. Near St. Olaf, this Nordic-inspired restaurant blends a homey yet upscale feel with its beloved sweet caramel Ole rolls, veggie hash, wild rice porridge, fried walleye, Church Basement Wild Rice Soup, and Swedish meatball dinners. You can enjoy a simplified menu at its outdoor Lena's Lawn area with a picnic beneath the twinkle lights, $$–$$$.

Red Barn Pizza Farm. 10063 110th St. East; (507) 664-0304; redbarnfarmweddingsmn. com. This 10-acre farm offers a winning combination of country charm, live music, farm animals (horses, chickens, outdoor cats), and wood-fired pizza with homegrown ingredients. Open for pizza Wednesday nights and the third Sunday of the month. Open May through mid-October on Wednesday nights and the third Sunday of the month. Cash or check only—and bring your own tables or blankets, utensils, side dishes, beverages, and garbage bags. $$.

Reunion. 501 Division St. South; (507) 366-1337; reunioneatdrinkgather.com. Enjoy a little of everything at this restaurant with craft cocktails, sesame ahi tuna, wood-fired grilled pork chops with bacon jam, wood-fired grilled walleye, and garlic shrimp risotto, followed by desserts such as coffee cheesecake and baked apple tart. $–$$

Tanzenwald Brewing Company. 103 Water St. North; (507) 366-2337; tanzenwald.com. Opened in April 2017, Northfield's first brewery also serves up hearty fare, such as housesmoked pulled pork, mac-and-cheese, and sausages from Kramarczuk's to accompany IPAs, a Belgian golden, *Dunkelweizen*, and ginger and lime hard seltzer. $–$$.

where to stay

Contented Cottage Bed and Breakfast. 5 Walden Place; (507) 301-3787; contented cottage.com. Nestled into a bluff near St. Olaf College, this bed-and-breakfast has three rooms for guests and three-course breakfasts. $$

Fairfield Inn and Suites. 114 Second St. W.; (888) 236-2427; marriott.com/mspnf. With 80 rooms, this is the largest of Northfield's five chain hotels. It overlooks the Cannon River and downtown and allows pets. $$

Lake Byllesby Campground. 7650 Echo Point Road, Cannon Falls; (651) 480-7770; co.dakota.mn.us/parks. In addition to campsites at Nerstrand Big Woods State Park, you can find 35 modern sites and 22 primitive sites at Lake Byllesby Regional Park, about 15 miles northeast of Northfield in Cannon Falls. If you have bikes, you can pedal along the Cannon River into downtown Cannon Falls, where you'll find a winery, an ice-cream and coffee shop, a diner, and more. $.

day trip 03

south

>>> **I-35 river towns:**
faribault, mn; owatonna, mn

If you beeline straight south of the Twin Cities on I-35, you'll reach Faribault only an hour south of Minneapolis and Owatonna in another 20 minutes. Each of these river towns flourished with Minnesota's 1858 statehood and strategic locations on the Cannon and Straight Rivers to power their mills and supply water, followed by railroads and then highways that became essential components of modern industries. Their early success left a legacy of sturdy brick downtowns andgrand Victorian homes, plus a long history of academics thanks to state schools.

Shattuck St. Mary's, an Episcopal boarding school, opened in the first year of Minnesota's statehood. It draws more than 400 students from 37 states and 20 countries to its 250-acre campus. Faribault's Minnesota State Academy for the Deaf opened five years later, in 1863, and is still going strong on its historic 40-acre campus.

Owatonna was home to Minnesota's State School for Dependent and Neglected Children from 1886 to 1945. More than 10,000 children lived on the sprawling redbrick campus with elegantly towered buildings. The Orphanage Museum preserves the poignant tales of children left without families to care for them and left to seek camaraderie and security among other wards of the state. The impressive campus now houses several public and nonprofit community groups, including the Owatonna Arts Center.

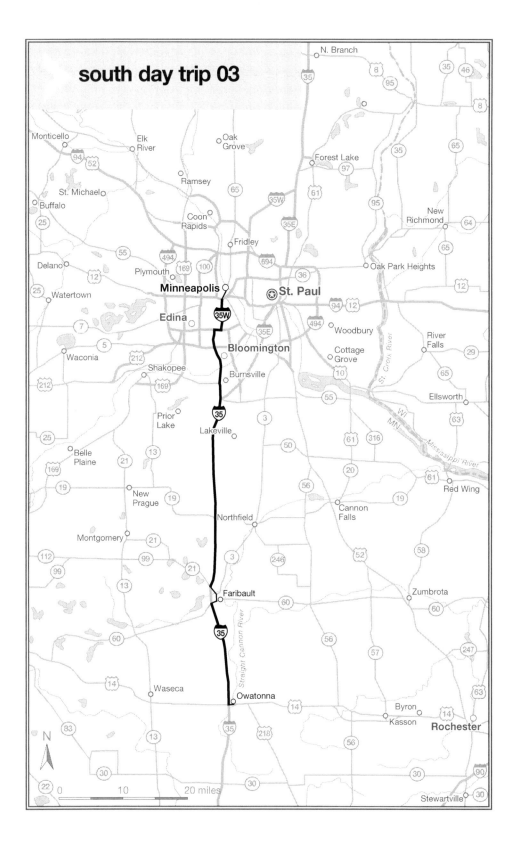

faribault, mn

The name Faribault (aka "Faribo") is known across the country for its woolen blankets. They keep beds toasty in winter, laps warm during fall football games, commemorate events such as the Olympics, and re-create the iconic stripes of fur-trade blankets. Faribault Woolen Mills—the last wool-to-blanket mill in America—briefly closed before a rebirth as one of America's enduring heritage brands.

Visit this town of 24,400 residents in the summer and you may see the distinctive canning trucks hauling fresh peas, green beans, and sweet corn for Faribault Foods, which cans Butter Kernel vegetables, along with many brands of beans, pasta and sauce, and chili and soup, which keep the town's agricultural roots running deep and firmly planted.

You'll also find 10 lakes within 10 miles, Sakatah Singing Hills State Park, and the 39-mile Sakatah Singing Hills State Trail. Don't miss a detour into the historic downtown, which doubled as Wabasha in the movie *Grumpy Old Men.* You'll find murals depicting local history, including the invention of the Tilt-A-Whirl carnival ride, which has made generations joyously dizzy since 1926. Look for the two Tilt-A-Whirl cars that let you take a seat and a selfie.

Grab maps at the Faribault Area Chamber of Commerce & Tourism, 530 Wilson Ave. NW, which is within 0.5 mile of the Sakatah Singing Hills State Trail, (507) 334-4381; visit faribault.com. You can also rent bikes across the street.

getting there

Follow I-35 south to Faribault, about 50 minutes south of the Minneapolis–St. Paul Airport.

where to go

Donahue's Greenhouse. 420 10th St. SW; (507) 334-7156; donahuesclematis.com. Garden lovers shouldn't miss these explosively colorful greenhouses. While they have a variety of plants (especially geraniums and hanging baskets), they're known for more than 130 varieties of clematis vines, which they sell to garden centers across the country. Open for spring sales mid-April to June.

The Faribault Mill. 1500 NW 2nd Ave.; (507) 412-5534; faribaultmill.com. You can stop by the mill store and see photos of the wool-to-blanket process at this historic site that made more than 100,000 blankets during World War II and has operated since 1865. Tours are offered every Friday and Saturday; reservations encouraged. Tours: $10, adults; $5, children.

Paradise Center for the Arts. 321 Central Ave. N.; (507) 332-7372; paradisecenterfor thearts.org. Look for gifts made by regional artists, take a class, or catch a show at this arts hub and historic theater building on the foundation of an 1885 opera house.

River Bend Nature Center. 1000 Rustad Rd.; (507) 332-7151; rbnc.org. This 750-acre blend of woods, prairie, and pond wraps around the surprisingly windy Straight River. It's a favorite place to see the seasons change, with 10 miles of hiking and biking and 5 miles of cross-country skiing. Families can enjoy nature displays in the interpretative center.

Sakatah Singing Hills State Trail. Trailhead at 900 Lyndale Ave. N. dnr.state.mn.us. This 39-mile state trail heads west along Cannon Lake, Sakatah Lake State Park, and small lakeside towns before reaching Mankato. In winter, the trail is groomed for snowmobiling.

caves of faribault

Faribault's sandstone caves were carved out in the 1850s for a brewery until Prohibition shut it down. In the 1930s a cheesemaker used the cool, humid caves to age the first blue cheese produced in America (after years of importing from France). In this century, Caves of Faribault produces internationally award-winning premium blue cheeses, including AmaBlu, AmaGorg, and St. Pete's Select. It can be found at grocers and co-ops across the state.

where to eat

Depot Bar and Grill. 311 Heritage Place; (507) 332-2825; faribaultdepotbarandgrill.com. Named for the former railroad depot that houses it, this dining spot is one of the best places to enjoy a meal with cheeses aged in local caves. Start with deep-fried Reuben bites, Caves of Faribault cheese curds (made across the tracks), or five-onion soup draped in broiled cheese. Try salads made with local blue cheese, gyro flatbread, a burger stuffed with beer cheese and topped with curds, and adult mac-n-cheese with aged gouda. $$.

Redemption Kitchen and Cocktails. 31 Third Ave. NE; (507) 323-8054; get-redemption .com. This converted 1870s downtown warehouse sizzles with the sound of grilled meats and the scent of wood fires and barbecue. Look for meaty eats such as cheesesteak egg rolls, rotisserie chicken, dry-aged porterhouse steak, whiskey-glazed salmon, or homey chicken and dumplings. For drinks, look for cocktails crafted with Minnesota spirits, such as a Blue Ox, Rojo margarita, or apricot gimlet. $$.

where to stay

Historic Hutchinson House. 305 Second St. NW; (507) 323-8107; historichutchhouse .com. The periwinkle blue and pink colors make this turreted 1892 Queen Anne Victorian with three guest suites stand out, as does its ornate wraparound porch and vibrant baskets of flowers. $$.

Sakatah Lake State Park. 50499 Sakatah Lake State Park Rd., Waterville; (507) 698-7851; dnr.mn.state.us. About 17 miles west of Faribault, this park is popular in the spring and fall for 62 drive-in campsites, 5 more remote bike-in sites, 1 camper cabin, and canoeing and fishing on this widening of the Cannon River. It does not have a beach, and algae can bloom in the shallow water during the hottest summer stretches. The Sakatah Singing Hills Trail takes bicyclists to nearby towns such as Waterville and Elysian for more lakes and beaches. It's mostly used by snowmobilers in the winter. $.

owatonna, mn

In addition to Owatonna's orphanage museum, Owatonna (pop. 23,000) offers another gem: the National Farmers' Bank. It's attractive with its brick exterior, terra-cotta green trim, and arched windows, but that's just a hint of the opulence inside. It's considered one of Minnesota's architectural masterpieces.

Owatonna's downtown, which includes 75 buildings in 12 city blocks surrounding Central Park, was recognized as a National Historic District in 2015. You can see images from the town's history with its Gateway Mural at the corner of West Bridge Street and the Muckle Bike Trail.

Central Park hosts a Saturday seasonal farmers' market, along with concerts and holiday lights. Get a historic walking tour guide from the Owatonna Area Chamber of Commerce and Tourism: visitowatonna.org.

getting there

Grab I-35 at Faribault and drive about 16 miles south to Owatonna.

where to go

Cabela's. 3900 Cabela Dr.; (507) 451-4545; cabelas.com. You can argue this is a mega box store, but the 150,000-square-foot showroom in Minnesota's first Cabela's also has about 100 game mounts, an African diorama with an elephant, three aquariums, and outdoor workshops.

Minnesota State Public School for Dependent and Neglected Children (also called the **Orphanage Museum**). 540 W. Hills Circle; (507) 774-7369; orphanagemuseum.com. Once close to 300 acres, this former state orphanage with 16 historic cottages and other buildings is now home to city offices, an art center, and this museum, which touchingly gives a voice to the 10,635 children who lived here between 1886 and 1945. The museum includes pictures, artifacts, and personal stories, and Cottage 11 was restored to look as it did when boys lived here around the 1930s. There are six stations with audio narration on the self-guided tour, including an orphan's memorial and a cemetery. The museum is open daily; Cottage 11 is open afternoons Tuesday to Sunday March through December. $2 donation appreciated.

National Farmers' Bank (now Wells Fargo). 101 N. Cedar Ave.; visitowatonna.org. This bank has been called a jewel box, a symphony of color, and one of the best examples of Prairie School architecture. Louis Sullivan, creator of the skyscraper, designed this bank, which was finished in 1908. Light filters in through huge stained-glass windows, glitters across gold leaf and 2.25-ton cast-iron chandeliers with intricate scrolls and oak leaf designs, and warms the palette of greens, browns, and ambers throughout the building. Visitors can admire the bank from its lobby or walk up to the balcony for a closer look at detailing and a beautiful mural depicting farmers in the field. Open Monday through Friday and Saturday morning. Free admission.

Reptile and Amphibian Discovery (RAD) Zoo. 6750 West Frontage Rd., Medford; (507) 455-1465; theradzoo.com. This collection of all things scaly and amphibian in the Outlet Mall at nearby Medford includes more than 150 snakes, turtles, crocodiles, toads, and frogs. Visitors can see the albino boa constrictor once owned by singer Justin Bieber; "Big Al," the 12-foot-long American alligator; and an Everglades Encounters show with feedings on the weekends. From fall through spring, groups can stay overnight at the zoo for a "Camp with the Crocs." Open daily. Admission: $11.75, adults; $9.75 children 3 to 12 and seniors.

where to eat

Costa's Candies. 112 N. Cedar Ave.; (507) 451-9050; costascandies.com. This downtown landmark has been making handmade caramels, toffees, nut clusters, truffles, and gooey chocolate-covered cream candies for more than a century. Open Monday through Saturday.

Mineral Springs Brewery. 111 N. Walnut Ave.; (507) 413-6281; mineralspringsbrewery.com. Whether you're enjoying a balmy day across from the Straight River or tucked into a wintertime igloo, this brewery pours more than a dozen locally inspired beers, such as Cinder Hill cream ale, Ringmaker Rye (a nod to Jostens, a local company that has made class rings since 1897), and Hope Chocolate Milk Stout (a partnership with nearby Hope Creamery). Food trucks, such as Delicious Pupusas (El Salvadoran stuffed corn tortillas) and Linos Taqueria, offer a variety of food. Open Wednesday to Sunday. $$.

where to stay

River View Campground. 2554 SW 28th St.; (507) 451-8050; riverviewcampground minnesota.com. Not far from the southwestern edge of the city and alongside the Straight River, this place has tent and RV campsites with a minigolf course, heated pool, playground, and other amenities. $.

southwest

day trip 01

southwest

>>> **minnesota river valley orchards & sweets:**
jordan, henderson, st. peter, mn

Southwest of the Twin Cities, US 169 heads into the wide valley of the Minnesota River. It's a favorite destination in September and October, with river bluffs carpeted in fall colors and orchards such as Ferguson's Minnesota Harvest beckoning families with much more than fresh-picked apples.

The biggest magnet? Minnesota's Largest Candy Store, a massive screaming-yellow building south of Jordan. It's like South Dakota's Wall Drug in that there's so much stuffed into this jaw-dropping wonderland that it's hard to explain without experiencing the quirky animatronics, pop-culture icons, murals, and United Nations of candy for yourself. Even if you don't have a sweet tooth, you'll find aisles of hot sauces, pastas, popcorn, gag gifts, more than 200 flavors of novelty sodas, and hundreds of puzzles.

You can also find hikes and scenic roads along the Minnesota River, which ambles and twists through rolling farmland, small towns, wooded floodplains, and shaded ravines. Keep your eyes open for deer and eagles along the water's edge.

jordan, mn

This city of about 8,000 residents on the outer ring of the Twin Cities retains its historic character with brick-and-sandstone buildings and homes tucked into steep hills. Find more information at the Jordan Chamber of Commerce, 315 Broadway St.; (952) 492-2355; jordanchamber.org/about-us.

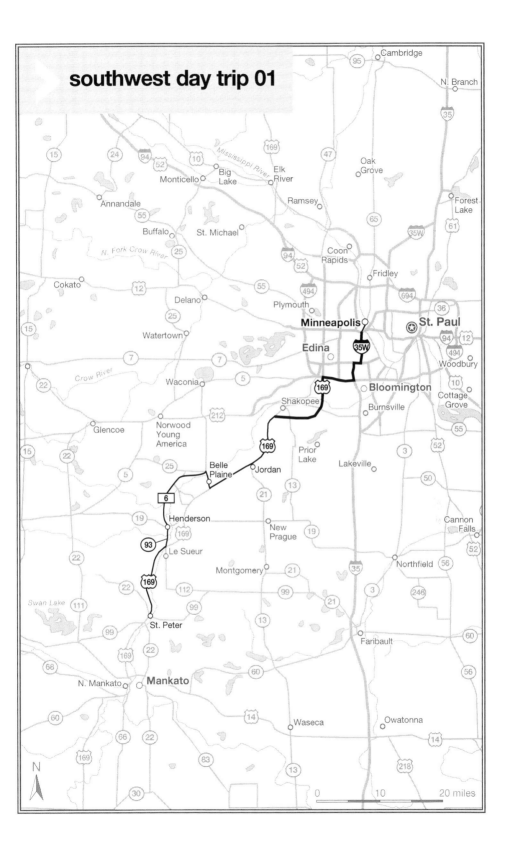

southwest day trip 01

getting there

Follow US 169 south out of the Twin Cities about 35 miles to Jordan.

where to go

Ferguson's Minnesota Harvest. 8251 Old Highway 169 Blvd. at Apple Lover's Ln.; (952) 492-2785; fergusonsorchard.com/twin-cities-home/. This has ranked among Minnesota's most beloved fall destinations for generations, and plans are to significantly expand after being purchased by the Ferguson family, Upper Midwest fall destination specialists, in 2022. Look for a hard cider bar, wagon rides, country store and bakery, U-pick pumpkins and apples, a corn maze, and farm animals on close to 300 acres.

Minnesota's Largest Candy Store. 20430 Johnson Memorial Dr. (US 169); minnesotas largestcandystore.business.site. This screaming yellow roadside attraction was once Jim's Apple Farm, an apple and produce stop, until it decided to supersize—and keep growing. You can still find local produce, such as autumn squash, pumpkins, and bushels of crunchy, sweet apples, along with pies (try the caramel apple), pastries, jams, and jellies. Candy, from nostalgic to imported and obscure, dominates the aisles. Soda pop fans will find funky flavors from across the country, including Minnesota's own Spring Grove sodas and Killebrew root beer. Our advice: Go midweek if you can; take your patience (in case of crowds), cash or check; and enjoy taking photos with all the fun props and displays, including a Dr. Who phone booth and superheroes galore from Groot to Ironman and *Monsters Inc.* characters. Open May through Thanksgiving.

Wagner Apple Farm and Bakery. 18020 Xanadu Ave.; (952) 492-2367. The giant red apple grabs the attention of US 169 road-trippers and lures them in for seasonal local produce including Honeycrisp apples, Haralsons, Cortlands, and outside tables piled high with bright orange pumpkins. Inside you'll find their own honey from nearby hives, apple pies, apple butter, jams and jellies, and gourmet popcorn.

where to eat

Feed Mill Restaurant. 200 Water St.; (952) 492-3646; thefeedmillrestaurant.net. While this century-old former feed mill looks a bit ho-hum on the outside, step inside for lovely views of a wooded Minnesota River tributary from the restaurant's generous windows. It's a peaceful view for enjoying American classics such as hefty morning omelets, hot beefs, and Czech or German soups that tap the area's ethnic heritage. Open Wednesday to Sunday for breakfast and lunch. $.

Suzette's Restaurant. 20251 Johnson Memorial Dr. (MN 169); (952) 492-2422; suzettes restaurantmn.com. Chef Banrith Yong, who escaped from the Khmer Rouge in Cambodia, trained in French cooking in some of the top Swiss restaurants before bringing those skills to his own French restaurant in Jordan in 1998. Savor chicken Wellington, beef tenderloins with French wine sauce, seafood, and crab cake dinners, followed by soufflés and flaky fruit Napoleons. Open for dinner Wednesday to Sunday. $$$.

where to stay

Minnesota River State Recreation Area. 19825 Park Blvd.; (952) 492-6400; dnr.state .mn.us. There are 25 rustic sites at the Quarry Campground (no running water or flush toilets), in the Lawrence unit south of Jordan. A handful of the sites are along the water and make it easy to forget you're anywhere near a metropolitan area. $.

Nicolin Inn B&B. 221 Broadway St. South; (800) 683-3360; nicolinmansion.com. This five-room B&B sits in the heart of downtown with a shady side garden. Rooms all have their own feel, from the rich colors and stately look of the Nicolin Room to the Mertz Room's Art Deco reds, blacks, and zebra stripes. Breakfasts may include Scotch eggs, frittatas, crepes, quiches, and an array of creative scones, such as chocolate ginger. $$$.

henderson, mn

Henderson's downtown—only a few blocks long—ambles from bottomlands uphill into the wooded bluffs. It's one of Minnesota's oldest towns, but still has just over 900 residents. If you adore small towns and nostalgia, visit on a summer Tuesday night, when classic cars rumble along Main Street.

getting there

Head south on US 169 to Belle Plaine, exiting at Walnut Street (MN 25), which crosses the Minnesota River. Turn south on CR 6 to follow the Minnesota River Valley Scenic Byway as it curves and ambles for about 10 miles before reaching Henderson. Along the way, watch for Jessenland, the state's earliest Irish settlement, marked with a country church and hillside cemetery.

where to go

Kerfoot Canopy Tours. 30200 Scenic Byway Rd.; (952) 873-3900; kerfootcanopytour.com. Put the southern Minnesota scenery on fast-forward with this 14-line zip line tour that runs more than a mile and eventually rises 175 feet above the Minnesota River Valley. Allow at least 2.5 hours for the tour, which is open to participants age 10 and older (from $95 per person). You can also test your endurance with a self-paced high ropes challenge course. Kerfoot's aerial adventure park has three stories (up to 50 feet high) and 60 obstacles that can take about 2 hours to complete. It's open to participants 7 years old and up (from $45/person).

Ney Nature Center. 28238 Nature Center Ln.; (507) 357-8580; neycenter.org. This 446-acre former homestead east of Henderson is now threaded with trails that follow former oxcart and stagecoach routes, loop around ponds, through Big Woods remnants and natural prairie, and past historic farm buildings. There are also great overlooks for viewing the Minnesota River Valley. It's open for winter skiing too.

where to eat

Henderson RoadHaus. 514 Main St.; (507) 248-3691; facebook.com/hendersonroad haus. Look for wings, burgers, sandwiches, hot beef commercials, and a few vegetarian choices. Watch for live music too. Open Tuesday through Sunday. $.

Toody's. 417 Main St.; (507) 248-3326. Tiny but welcoming, this soda fountain serves up ice cream and hot coffee and a daily lunch special or sandwiches. The storefront also contains a pharmacy and art center displaying local paintings, pottery, and photography. Open Tuesday through Sunday. $.

st. peter, mn

St. Peter was a gathering place long before settlers started moving into Minnesota. It was here at the Traverse des Sioux crossing that Native Americans, traders, oxcarts, and explorers would ford a shallow part of the Minnesota River. It connected the Big Woods to the east to the prairies in the west.

This is also where one of Minnesota's most momentous documents—the 1851 Traverse des Sioux Treaty—was signed with the Dakota. It opened 24 million acres for White settlement. The city of St. Peter was founded two years later. It was even considered a candidate for the state capital, which explains the extra-wide main street. While that didn't pan out, it's still impressive to drive through downtown.

There are 40 St. Peter buildings on the National Register of Historic Places. Brick and sturdy, they rise beautifully against a blue fall sky. Gustavus Adolphus College, built in 1862 on the bluff above downtown, keeps the city youthful and thoughtful and tied to its Lutheran Swedish roots. Among the key events is an annual Nobel Conference that brings together global leaders in science to discuss ethics and cutting-edge issues, from genetics and the energy crisis to the impact of globalization.

getting there

You can get there the speedy way down US 169 or take the Minnesota Valley Scenic Byway from Henderson to Le Sueur (land of the Jolly Green Giant), across an iron bridge and past St. Peter's symbolic pearly gates.

where to go

Linnaeus Arboretum. 800 College Ave.; (507) 933-8000; gustavus.edu. Named for a Swedish botanist, this 125-acre arboretum includes a dozen formal gardens, such as a white garden, a Swedish garden, and a rose garden. Two miles of trails wind through its restored natural areas that represent Minnesota's various biomes: tallgrass prairie, wetlands, coniferous forest, and deciduous woods. The arboretum also contains the Melva Lind Interpretive Center and an 1866 cabin that was built by Swedish settlers in the nearby community of Norseland. Visitors can take a self-guided arboretum tour with 21 interpretive stops or check for guided tours on the events calendar. It's open for skiing in the winter. Also worth a stop: the Hillstrom Museum of Art, with rotating exhibitions and free admission. Open daily when school is in session.

Seven Mile Creek Park. Six miles south of St. Peter on US 169; (507) 931-1760; dnr.state. mn.us. You can park near the Minnesota River and a boat landing and then take a tunnel under the highway and into the ravines carved by Seven Mile Creek. There are 8 miles of trails in this 628-acre park. They wind past the creek's clear pools stocked with brown trout each spring. You can also see exposed sections of Jordan Sandstone, which is older than the creamy yellow Kasota Sandstone mined on the other side of the Minnesota River.

Swedish Kontur. 310 S. Minnesota St.; (507) 931-1198; swedishkontur.com. If you want to fit in with St. Peter's Swedish heritage or stay stylishly warm in the middle of winter, you can find a large selection of Scandinavian sweaters here, along with glassware and dinnerware, table linens, cookbooks, silver jewelry, folk art decor, and gifts. Opened in 1962, it's one of the oldest continuously operated Swedish import retailers in the United States.

Treaty Site History Center. 1851 N. Minnesota Ave.; (507) 934-2160; nchsmn.org. As home to the Nicollet County Historical Society, this center was built to recognize the importance of the nearby centuries-old Traverse des Sioux, a safe crossing place along the Minnesota River. It was used by indigenous peoples, early traders, and then European settlers for travel or meetings. A public television documentary explains the 1851 treaty that was signed here, ceding 24 million acres of Dakota land to the US government, which opened it to westward expansion. Failure to honor the treaty, which promised to provide payments and food for Dakota families who vacated land needed for sustenance, led to the US-Dakota War of 1862. The effect and tragedies of the war reverberated up and down the Minnesota River Valley. In addition to Native American and early European stories, the museum includes rotating exhibits plus outdoor trails leading to the river, interpretive signs about the oxcart trails converging here, and examples of native prairie plantings. Admission: $7, adults; $6, seniors age 65 and up; free for children under 18. Open Tuesday through Saturday. History enthusiasts can also book a tour of St. Peter's 1871 Italianate-style Julian Cox House at 500 N. Washington Ave. for an additional fee.

where to eat

Blaschko's Embassy Bar. 325 S. Minnesota Ave.; (507) 934-3903. Head here for half-pound burgers heaped with plenty of sauces and fixings, fish-and-chips, and a variety of wraps, salads, and appetizers. Open daily. $.

Diamond Dust Bakery and Coffee Shop. 320 Sunrise Dr.; (507) 934-9898; facebook .com/diamonddustbakery. While you can find a case full of sweet temptations and stylish cupcakes here, you can also find rotating lunch specials such as chicken shawarma wraps, chicken salad on cranberry wild rice bread, pasta salads, and creamy Italian sausage soup with fresh-baked breads. $$

River Rock Coffee & Tea. 301 S. Minnesota St.; (507) 931-1540; rrcoffee.com. Catch up over a steaming espresso and scones, a slice of quiche, daily soups, salads, or sandwiches at this rustic modern coffee shop. $

St. Peter Food Co-op & Deli. 228 Mulberry St.; (507) 934-4880; stpeterfood.coop. You can grab cold sandwiches and salads for warm-weather picnics or dine at the hot bar at this impressively large co-op. You can get shawarma, falafel, and Cuban sandwiches; build your own burrito; or try out specials such as chicken and andouille gumbo and savory vegetarian soups. Open daily. $.

Third Street Tavern. 408 S. Third St.; (507) 934-3314; 3rdstreettavern.com. Known for its smoky wings and appetizers like its queso dip with pulled smoked chicken, this eatery inside the Konsbruck Hotel leans on smoked favorites such as brisket and ribs and Southern comfort classics like cheesy potatoes, corn bread, mac-and-cheese, and pit-baked beans. $–$$.

where to stay

Konsbruck Hotel. 408 S. Third St.; (507) 381-1089; konsbruckhotel.com. A block off St. Peter's main street, the historic Konsbruck Hotel stands sturdy and welcoming with five swank and spacious rooms. Each has its own character, with exposed brick walls plus colorful and luxurious decor and bedding. A few rooms have balconies and fireplaces near soaking tubs, and all have access to a cozy central gathering room. $$.

Riverside Park Campground. (507) 934-0070; saintpetermn.gov. There are 11 campsites along an oxbow of the river in this 120-acre park that includes a playground, picnic areas, and access to hiking, biking, and ski trails. There is a 2-acre fishing pond for children, but no swimming is allowed there or in the river. Reservations are first come, first served only, and campers must register at the police department at 207 S. Front St. $.

day trip 02

southwest

>>> **waterfalls, bison & bike trails:**
mankato, mn

mankato, mn

Mankato, the biggest city in southwest Minnesota's patchwork of farms and former prairies, tucks into the valley and sandstone ravines carved out by both the Blue Earth and Minnesota rivers. It's an especially idyllic getaway for families with Sibley Farm and the Children's Museum of Southern Minnesota. It also appeals to nature lovers, who come to pedal its many trails, paddle the rivers that wind past mossy ravines, and see the waterfalls and resident bison herd at Minneopa State Park.

You can find free summertime concerts along the riverfront at Vetter Stone Amphitheater or join the city's annual Ribfest in August for even more music. While strolling downtown, which is rich in dining and nightlife as a college community (home to Minnesota State University–Mankato and South-Central Technical College), look for 30 art sculptures that are installed each April as part of the CityArt Walking Sculpture Tour.

Permanent public art ranges from a playful 10-foot Godzilla built from steel scraps to a mural dedicated to Maud Hart Lovelace, author of Betsy-Tacy books, and the fictional town of Deep Valley that was modeled after Mankato. The most impressive work of art goes to Australian artist Guido Van Helten's mural of a Dakota girl at the Mahkato Wacipi (Mankato Pow Wow) teaching other children to dance. Looking like a black-and-white photograph, it spans across eight connected 135-foot-tall grain silos that tower above the Minnesota River.

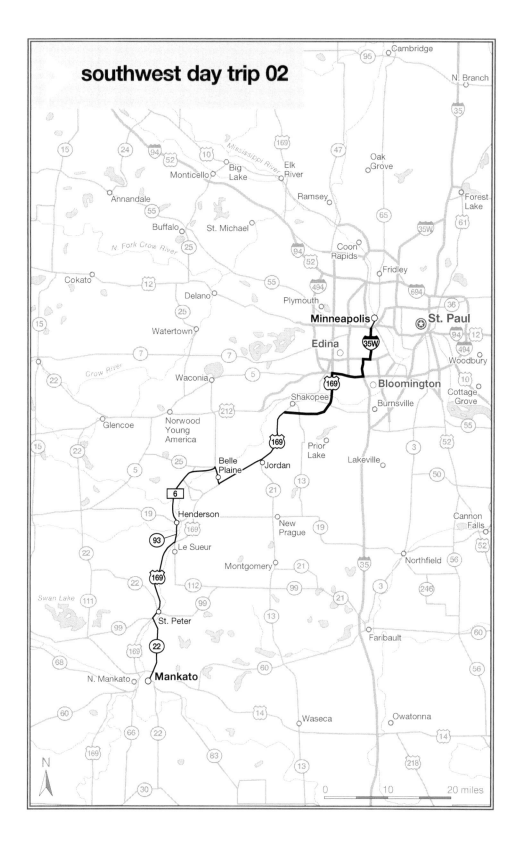

southwest day trip 02

Nearby, a 67-ton block of local Kasota stone carved into a bison at Reconciliation Park marks the site where 38 Dakota were killed in the country's largest mass hanging, which followed the U.S.-Dakota War of 1862. The annual Mahkato Wacipi at Dakota Wokiksuye Makoce (Land of Memories Park) continues the effort of reconciliation, healing, and understanding while sharing and honoring the heritage of Mdewakanton Dakota who had been exiled from Minnesota after the war.

For more information on the area's history, Native American heritage, events such as Old Town Mankato Day of the Dead (Dia de los Muertos), artwork, and trail maps, contact Visit Mankato, 3 Civic Center Plaza, Ste. 100; (800) 657-4733; visitmankatomn.com.

getting there

Take US 169, which follows the Minnesota River from Shakopee on the southwestern edge of the Twin Cities. From Shakopee, the drive is about 56 miles.

what to do

Bent River Outfitters. 530 N. Riverfront Dr.; (507) 388-2368; bentriveroutfitter.com. Join a guided trip or rent a kayak, paddleboard, or canoe for a DIY paddle along the Blue Earth River with a stop at Devil's Gulch, a narrow, lush ravine; Triple Falls, which trickle into another ravine; and Big Moe, a giant river boulder popular for hanging out or having a picnic. Shuttle services are available. Paddlers can also follow the Minnesota River State Water Trail. Open Thursday to Sunday.

Children's Museum of Southern Minnesota. 224 Lamm St.; (507) 386-0279; cm southernmn.org. Taking inspiration from the region with theme and industries, this spacious hands-on learning museum replicates an interactive stone quarry, an area dedicated to farming and growing food, a supersized tree house with bridges and tunnels connecting multiple forts, scientific and engineering labs, outdoor play areas, costumes, and a stage. Open Tuesday to Sunday. Admission: $13.

Land of Memories Park. 100 Amos Owen Ln. (just off US 169), Mankato; mahkatowacipi .org. Mahkato Mdewakanton Association hosts a public powwow here on the third full weekend in September. The Mahkato Wacipi website includes etiquette tips for attending powwows and being respectful during sacred parts of the ceremonies. Land of Memories Park welcomes campers and offers a canoe launch on the river throughout the warm months.

Minneopa State Park. Southwest of Mankato at 54497 Gadwall Rd.; (507) 389-5464; dnr.state.mn.us. Southern Minnesota's largest waterfall flows across sandstone ledges and drops into a lush, wooded gorge. It's especially popular in the spring and after storms, when the falls are the most dramatic, and in September and October, when colorful maple and basswood leaves drift across the creek. Spring and early summer are also good times to possibly see the cinnamon-colored calves in the park's resident bison herd.

The falls are along a tributary away from the Minnesota River, but the park covers 1,145 acres and offers 61 campsites along a bluff overlooking the Minnesota, plus 1 camper cabin. On the opposite side of the river (40923 Judson Bottom Rd.), you can stop at Minnemishinona Falls, a gentle flow that drops 45 feet into a gorge below a footbridge. Park permit: $7.

Minnesota River Valley Scenic Byway. mnrivervalley.com. This rich-in-history byway hugs the Minnesota River from Belle Plain near the Twin Cities all the way to the South Dakota border. The Mankato-area stretch follows the south side of the Minnesota River, which is ideal for heading to Minneopa State Park. If you have the chance, though, drive along the northern side of the river as well, following Judson Bottom Road, with a stop at Minnemishinona Falls, before continuing to New Ulm.

Mount Kato Ski Area. 20461 MN 66; (507) 625-3363; mountkato.com. Mount Kato drops 240 vertical feet, and the 55-acre attraction is popular in winter, with 19 trails for skiers and snowboarders plus a tubing park. Open Thursday to Tuesday. Lift tickets range from $28 for kids 12 and under after 4 p.m. to $50 for adults on weekend days. In summer it opens for mountain biking.

Old Town. 300 to 800 blocks of North Riverfront Dr.; oldtownmankatomn.com. Stroll through this historic neighborhood for stops such as River Valley Makers, Lakota Made herbal remedies, River City Quilts, Sunny and Dot boutique, Tune Town, and home decor at Salvage Sisters. Take a break at the Coffee Hag, a longtime favorite where you can often find live music, steaming cups of herbal blends at CuriosiTea, or creative ice cream and sorbet flavors at Mom and Pop's.

Sibley Park and Petting Zoo. 900 Mound Ave.; (507) 387-8600; mankatomn.gov. With spacious acreage, vistas from its hilltop, an impressive playground, and a charming petting zoo with pigs, goats, alpacas, and peacocks, this is a don't-miss if you have kids. It's worth a return trip in December too, when the Kiwanis Holiday Lights spectacle turns the park into a winter wonderland with 1.5 million lights strung through trees and displays. The sledding hill is legendary.

where to eat

Chankaska Creek Ranch, Winery and Distillery. 1179 E. Pearl St., Kasota; (507) 931-0089; chankaskawines.com. This scenic vineyard 10 miles north of Mankato started in 2008 on 25 acres. It has grown to be the second-largest winery in Minnesota, producing reds, whites, and rosés before expanding into spirits with its distillery for whiskey, gin, vodka, rum, bourbon, and brandy. You can order wine or spirits and enjoy locally sourced pizzas, a seasonal bison–wild rice soup, charcuterie, or desserts such as truffles. Watch for frequent special events and live music. $$.

trail town

The League of American Bicyclists named Mankato a bronze-level bike-friendly community. The community claims more than 50 miles of easy paved trails, but it's also a favorite of road cyclists for the many rural loops with wide shoulders and mellow traffic. Mountain bikers and fat-tire bikers can find bluff and ravine trails for lively rides. If you want to rent a bike or join casual and weekly group rides, contact **Nicollet Bike & Ski Shop,** *(507) 388-8390; nicolletbike.com. Bikers converge for the River Valley 100 in late August and the Mankato River Ramble in early October to coincide with fall colors. For more information, go to bikemn.org.*

Kiwanis Mountain Bike Trail and Skills Park. *Northeast intersection of US 169 and US 14. Ideal for beginning mountain bikers with a skills park, this spot also pumps up the adrenaline with 5 miles of wooded trails along the west shore of the Minnesota River. The site includes a dog park, archery range, and access to the river for kayakers and canoers.*

Minnesota River Trail. *This trail hugs the river levees from Riverfront Park, through the city center to Sibley Park, providing a connection between the Sakatah Singing Hills State Trail and the Minneopa Cut-off Trail to the state park.*

Red Jacket Bike Trail. *This 13-mile paved and crushed-stone path starts at the downtown YMCA, heads through countryside and over an 80-foot-high trestle bridge on the way to Rapidan Dam for the best reward ever: homemade pies (and more) at the delightfully vintage Rapidan Dam Store.*

Sakatah Singing Hills State Trail. *This 39-mile trail follows the former railroad grade from Mankato east to Faribault, passing farmlands, lakes with beaches (Cannon and Madison) and Sakatah State Park.*

Mankato Brewery. 1119 Center St., North Mankato; (507) 386-2337; mankatobrewery.com. You can grab a flight of beer and sample choices such as Kato lager, Rhuby Rhubarb Sour, or a Russian stout with Minnesota maple syrup in this lively tasting room with pinball and arcade games, frequent live music, and a seasonal patio. $.

Nolabelle Kitchen and Bar. 520 S. Front St.; (507) 720-0841; nolabellekitchen.com. This farm-to-table restaurant delivers creative, eclectic dishes such as vegan twists on a charcuterie plate, short-rib egg rolls, a grilled cheese sandwich with peach preserves and bacon, lamb burgers with tzatziki, butter-baked walleye with risotto, and pork chops with pomegranate-molasses reduction. Desserts include beignets with berries. Reservations recommended. $$.

Number 4 Steakhouse. 124 E. Walnut St.; (507) 344-1444; number4mankato.com. This gastropub serves up meals such as a vegetarian burrata cheese, tomato, and avocado sandwich with hand-cut fries; lobster bisque soup; lemon basil spaghetti with shrimp; chicken potpie; tender steaks with add-on scallops or bourbon-glazed shrimp; and a "mile-high" 1-pound slice of chocolate cream cake. $$–$$$.

where to stay

Arch + Cable. 201 N. Riverfront Dr. Suite 105; (507) 479-1015; archandcable.com. This locally owned modern boutique hotel opened in late 2023 with 20 guest suites downtown. Many windows face the Minnesota River and North Mankato or frame up the city's mural painted across eight silos. $$$.

Moulin Rouge B&B. 811 S. Second St.; (507) 519-3400; moulinrougehouse.com. This colorfully restored turreted 1886 Victorian on the National Register of Historic Places has three rooms for one to two guests with modern amenities and two suites that sleep two to four guests in The Laven House, which is 3 blocks away. Rates include continental breakfast, but guests can add on a four-course breakfast on weekends and the option to rent e-bikes for area trails. $$.

day trip 03

southwest

a taste of germany:
new ulm, mn

new ulm, mn

New Ulm (pop. 14,000) wears its German heritage proudly. You might hear oompah-pah polka piped into the street or the bells of the glockenspiel that spins to life three times a day. Settled as a utopian town in the 1850s, with businesses and homes strategically built into the hillsides overlooking the Minnesota River Valley, it features some of Minnesota's most ornate and distinctive buildings and some of its best festivals. You'll also find a legacy of bohemian artists and extensive exhibits on the US-Dakota War of 1862.

August Schell Brewing, arguably the town's most famous business, survived the war and even Prohibition, when it sold root beer and soda. Today, when every town seems to have a brewery, Schell's can claim itself the nation's second-oldest family-run brewery—and Minnesota's largest brewery after acquiring the Grain Belt label.

The family's property along the Cottonwood River retains its historic charm with brick brewery buildings, its ornate 1885 mansion, gardens, a deer park, and a few free-roaming peacocks.

Another essential stop? Driving uphill on Center Street and climbing the stairs of the "Hermann the German" monument for a breathtaking view of the valley with picturesque steeples and the town below.

You can reward yourself with a cold beer afterward. When you arrive in town, get oriented at the New Ulm Visitor Center, 1 Minnesota St.; (507) 233-4300; newulm.com.

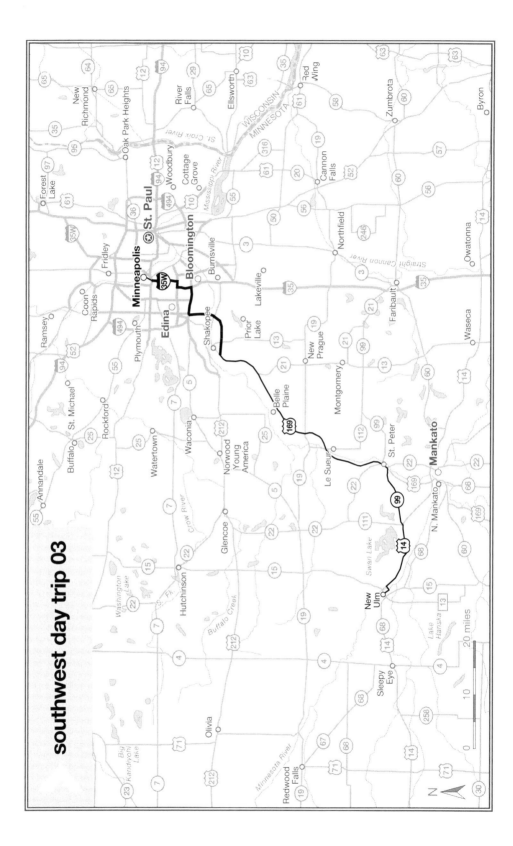

southwest day trip 03

getting there

Take US 169 southwest out of the Twin Cities until you reach St. Peter. Take a right onto MN 99 and follow it southwest to US 14. Go west on US 14 until it reaches New Ulm. It's a 95-mile drive from the Twin Cities.

where to go

Domeier's German Store. 1020 S. Minnesota St.; (507) 354-4231. It can feel like Christmas year-round with this shop's large selection of German imports—especially holiday ornaments, nutcrackers, and fine chocolates. The shelves and aisles are also filled with glassware and steins, clocks ticking away on pillars and walls, gummi candies and chocolates, glittering glass-blown ornaments, spaetzle and dumpling mixes, and European condiments and seasonings. Don't forget to look up. Postcards are plastered across the ceiling. Call for seasonal hours.

Flandrau State Park. 1300 Summit Ave.; (507) 233-1260; dnr.state.mn.us. It takes four days to fill the only man-made, sand-bottom pool in the state park system. It's a unique place to cool off, with clear well water, views of the Cottonwood River, and a historic stone bathhouse. Book early for camping spots here—especially if you want one of the two camper cabins. Visitors can follow 8 miles of hiking trails that wind through woods, prairie, and along the river or try them in the winter with cross-country skis or snowshoes; both are available to rent, first come, first served. The staff stokes up a nice fire in its stone warming house. Entrance fee: $7/day; skis: $10; snowshoes: $6.

Glockenspiel. 327 N. Minnesota St.; (888) 463-9856; newulm.com. A Native American, pioneers, a polka band, and a barrel maker are among the dozen figurines that twirl from this 45-foot-tall chiming clock at 12, 3, and 5 p.m. At Christmas, some figurines are replaced with a Nativity scene. You can see another German icon, a heritage tree, at 101 S. Minnesota St. The sculpture includes town events on each branch, including a riverboat and the railroad, the New Ulm Battery, and a beer wagon.

The Grand Center for Arts & Culture. 210 N. Minnesota St.; (507) 359-9222; thegrand newulm.org. New Ulm's 150-year-old Grand Hotel comes to life for live entertainment and a simple menu on weekends or special events. You can shop for gifts from local artists, browse art exhibits, or sign up for art workshops on the hotel's second floor.

Hermann Monument. 14 Monument St.; hermannmonument.com. Climb the 99 steps and a short ladder to the top of the 102-foot-tall monument nicknamed "Hermann the German." Hermann, who defended Germanic tribes against a Roman imperial army in 9 CE, became a national symbol of the contributions German Americans have made. There's a small museum in the monument's lower level.

river of history

The Minnesota River was a highway for the area's indigenous peoples for thousands of years before European pioneers arrived with high hopes for new lives. When the starving Dakota rebelled against the failed promises of the Traverse de Sioux treaty, the US-Dakota War broke out. While that war was overshadowed by the US Civil War, it remains one of Minnesota's darkest chapters and America's bloodiest battles. You can learn much about its history around the New Ulm area, but there are more stories, commemorative sites, and opportunities to learn about Dakota culture throughout the 287-mile Minnesota River Valley Scenic Byway from St. Paul to Ortonville. Go to mnrivervalley.com.

Brown County Historical Society. 2 N. Broadway; (507) 233-2620; browncounty historymn.org. New Ulm's former post office impresses visitors with its ornate German Renaissance architecture and three floors of historical exhibits about New Ulm's history, agricultural roots, and artistic legacies. The top floor includes a birchbark canoe, a buggy, Native American regalia, a buffalo robe, uniforms, paintings, and artifacts from the US-Dakota War of 1862. The Brown County Historical Society also hosts seasonal activities at the Kiesling House, the only wood-framed home to survive the war. Open Tuesday through Saturday. Admission: $7, adults; $5, seniors; $4, children 5 to 18.

Fort Ridgely State Park and Historic Site. 72404 CR 30, Fairfax; (507) 628-5591; mnhs.org/fortridgely. The visitor center 20 miles from New Ulm tells how White settlers fled here to safety and how the fort—thinly guarded during the Civil War—fended off 1862 attacks. The fort ruins are part of Fort Ridgely State Park (72158 CR 30, Fairfax; dnr.state.mn.us), which has 33 sites at its campground. $7 park permit required.

Harkin General Store. 66250 CR 21; mnhs.org/harkinstore. This seasonal store introduces visitors to the goods early pioneers would need for their homesteads, from nails and buckets to coffee grinders and bonnets. The store's location of West Newton was one of the area's earliest settlements along the Minnesota River, but it faded away after the arrival of trains in 1873 replaced the river for transporting goods to farming communities. Admission: Free.

Lower Sioux Agency Historic Site. 32469 CR 2, Morton; (507) 697-8674; mnhs .org/lowersioux. About 15 miles from Fort Ridgely, this site tells how The Bdewakantunwan and Wahpekute Bands of the Dakota were forced to abandon traditions and culture and were restricted to reservations, colonizing as farmers, and not provided essential provisions promised through treaties. Open Friday through Sunday, late April through mid-October. Admission: $4 to $6.

Minnesota Music Hall of Fame. 27 Broadway St. North; (507) 354-7305; mnmusichallof fame.org. Minnesota's music legends such as Bob Dylan, Bobby Vee, Judy Garland, and Prince are all recognized in this museum, but polka is king. Exhibits pay homage to home-grown old-time bands influenced by their European roots. It can be a fun walk down memory lane for visitors who remember the heyday of Minnesota's ballrooms and polka legends such as Whoopee John. Open Thursday to Saturday, April through October. Admission: $7.

Schell's Brewing Co. 1860 Schell Rd.; (507) 354-5528; schellsbrewery.com. Riding up a winding, wooded road, you wouldn't expect a brewery at the end of it. Then again, that's part of the charm. You can take a tour to see the huge copper kettle and loud bottling machines and taste some of the brews, such as Firebrick, a Vienna-style amber lager; the pilsner; and seasonal brews such as Maifest, a blond double bock; or Zommerfest, a honey ale, at the Bierhalle. It's free to roam the grounds, the museum, and shop its extensive store—a great place to get vintage Schell's or Grain Belt souvenirs. Tours ($10 per person, ages 12 and up) do sell out, so call for reservations.

Wanda Gag House. 226 N. Washington; (507) 359-2632; wandagaghouse.org. Even if you've never read the children's book *Millions of Cats* (in print since 1928), this tour of Wanda Gag's childhood home sparks an appreciation for her career as an author and lithographer. It also offers a colorful glimpse into the struggles and triumphs of freethinking, unconventional bohemian artists, including her father and sister, in the early 1900s. Open weekends late May through early October. Admission: $5.

quilt shop hopping

Quilters wait all year for the statewide Quilt Minnesota Shop Hop, but you can hit a trio of quilt shops within 1.5 miles in New Ulm, making it a quilters' destination. The Prairie Piecemakers Quilt Guild displays more than 400 quilts for the New Ulm Quilt Show every two years, while the Quiltistry event in odd years installs quilts at historic sites throughout New Ulm. Quilt shops include Sewing Seeds Quilt Co. (1417 S. State); Spinning Spools Quilt Shop (106 S. Minnesota); and The Thimble Box (2 S. Minnesota).

where to eat

George's Fine Steaks and Spirits. 301 N. Minnesota St.; (507) 354-7440; georgessteaks .biz. This classic downtown steak house opens for dinner with New York strip steaks and T-bones, stuffed portobello mushrooms, kebabs, lamb chops, lobster tail, roast duck, spitini with pasta, and sandwiches with soup. Open Monday through Saturday. $$.

Lola—An American Bistro. 16 N. Minnesota St.; (507) 359-2500; lolaamericanbistro.com. This spacious yet cozy brick-walled restaurant downtown displays local artwork and a great array of breakfast and lunches, from drunk apple French toast and Mexican skillet hash to bulgogi bibimbap, potpie, and a shawarma bowl. Open daily until 3 p.m. $$.

MN EIS. 10 N. Minnesota St.; (507) 354-0660; mneisnewulm.com. A play on Minnesota Nice and *Eis*, the German word for "ice cream," this seasonal ice-cream shop has home-made waffle cones, candy, and German specialties, including *Spaghettieis*, vanilla ice cream that looks like noodles topped with strawberry sauce and cookie-dough shaped like meat-balls. $.

Morgan Creek Vineyards and Winery. 23707 478th Ave.; (507) 947-3547; morgan creekvineyards.com. They've been making 14 different wines since 2003 with Minnesota-developed, winter-hardy varieties. "Winedown for the Weekend" Friday nights, Saturday Toast brunch, and Saturday Jazz Nites make the most of the charming location and local musical talents in a valley about 8 miles southeast of New Ulm. They serve gourmet brunches and appetizers from a brick oven, plus wines and mimosas on the patio. Reservations recommended. Open April through December. $$.

The Starkeller 2215 Garden St.; (507) 359-7827; schellsbrewery.com. Located across town so the specialized beer yeasts don't mingle, this brewery specializes in Berliner Weisse sours aged in floor-to-ceiling cypress tanks. The taproom opens on Friday and Saturday and features creatively repurposed industrial parts and barn boards. You can also order tradi-tional beers on tap or in cans, along with Grain Belt N'icebreakers hard seltzers or cocktails crafted with seltzers and locally made Sweethaven tonics. Food includes bar pizzas, pret-zels, and charcuterie or Redhead Creamery cheese curds. $.

Veigel's Kaiserhoff. 221 N. Minnesota St.; (507) 359-2071; kaiserhoff.org. The 70-plus-year-old restaurant reflects its heritage, serving schnitzel, smoked chops, and sausage—and having castles painted on the walls—but it's best known for its tangy sweet ribs with a creamy mayonnaise-enhanced barbecue sauce. The throwback feel can be endearing—especially if you sit at one of eight booths with little free jukeboxes. $$.

where to stay

Bingham Hall B&B. 500 S. German St.; (507) 276-5070; bingham-hall.com. Look for a lot of extras with the four spacious, stylish rooms in this historic home: chocolates, light snacks, wine or beverages, down comforters, and chenille robes. The Elijah room even includes a full-body massage chair. Start the day with filling breakfasts such as raspberry stuffed French toast or waffles. $$$.

west

day trip 01

west

> ## water skis & glacial lakes:
> spicer, mn; new london, mn

If you want to avoid the flood of traffic heading "up north" each weekend, go west. The Little Crow Lakes region, anchored by New London and Spicer, offers an old-fashioned lake getaway with great beaches, camping, mom-and-pop resorts, and a weekly waterskiing show.

These are the kinds of small towns where a kid can bike up to the ice-cream stand, ask for the "usual," and know he'll get it. These towns east of Willmar are each barely over 1,000 residents and surrounded by even smaller farming communities, many with Nordic heritage. You can still find white country churches with pioneer cemeteries and Swedish meatball dinners advertised on the bulletin boards.

If you're good at following maps, join the 245-mile Glacial Lakes Scenic Byway as it zigs and zags north and west toward Alexandria.

You can find more places to stay and eat in nearby Willmar (willmarlakesareas.com).

spicer, mn

This town has long been a favorite summer destination thanks to 5,000-acre Green Lake, the area's largest body of water. If you visit in winter when Glacial Lakes State Trail opens to snowmobilers and the lake fills with fish houses, you might also catch sight of Spicer's Ice Castle on Green Lake.

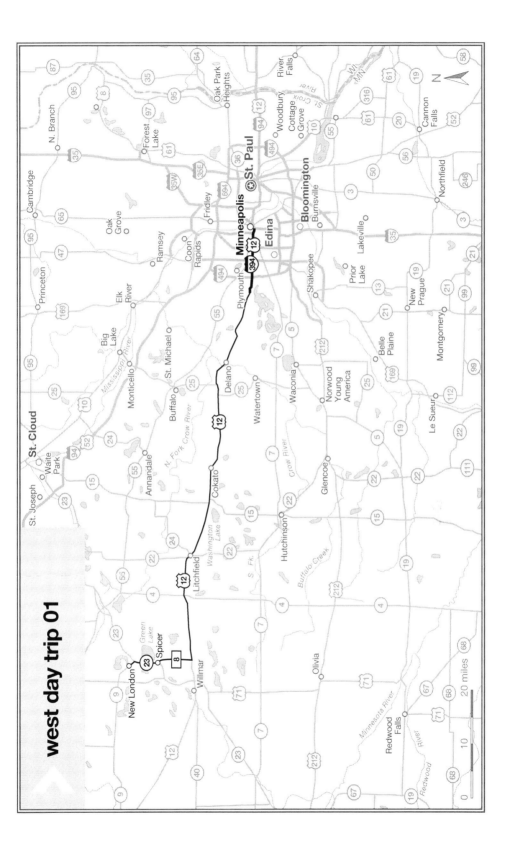

getting there

Follow US 12 west out of the Twin Cities about 50 miles. Go north on Kandiyohi CR 8 for 7 miles to reach Spicer.

where to go

Big Kahuna Fun Park. 190 Progress Way; (320) 796-2445; spicerfunpark.com. If you've got kids in tow, this place brings together minigolf, go-karts, bumper boats with squirt guns, and games. There's a Powerwheels course for kids too young for go-karts. Open daily Memorial Day through Labor Day with game or go-kart tickets starting at $7. Call for spring and fall weekend hours and price packages.

Glacial Lakes State Trail. dnr.state.mn.us. This 22-mile paved trail follows a former rail corridor to link the northeast edge of Willmar, New London, Spicer, and Hawick, with a connection to Sibley State Park. Another paved section, from Roscoe to Cold Spring, adds 7.5 miles to Willmar. In winter, parts of the trail are open to snowmobiling.

Green Lake Cruises. 159 Lake Ave. S.; (320) 894-5774; greenlakecruises.com. Themed 2-hour cruises around the lake on the 55-passenger double-decker *Danny Boy* may include fajitas and margaritas, acoustic musicians, Sunday brunch, Bloody Marys, or light-lunch cruises. Check online for schedules and costs. Pontoon rentals are also available.

Saulsbury Beach. 151 Lake Ave. S., on Green Lake; willmarlakesarea.com/listings/kandiyohi-county-park-4. This is a favorite gathering spot and considered one of Minnesota's great beaches. Lifeguards help supervise the action. You also can bike around the 12-mile perimeter of the lake.

where to eat

O'Neil's Restaurant and Bar. 152 Lake Ave. N.; (320) 796-6524; oneilsbar.com. You can warm up inside on a cold day with a bourbon burger, salmon BLT, and pork and pickles pizza or grab a coveted spot on the nicely shaded patio for views of Green Lake on warm days. Watch for live music on weekends and prime rib specials on Saturdays. $$.

Westwood Café. 142 Lake Ave. N.; (320) 796-5355; westwoodcafe.com. For a homey breakfast or lunch with your family, this spot ranks as a favorite with daily sweet rolls, griddled French bread with wild rice sausage, a kitchen sink omelet, hand-cut homestyle french fries, zingy popper burgers, and malts. $

Zorbaz on the Lake. 159 Lake Ave. S.; (320) 796-2195; zorbaz.com. With close to a dozen lakeside locations in Minnesota, this place on the Green Lake shoreline draws visitors with pizzas like Zorba the Greek and Thai pie, taco Tuesdays, drink specials, and Saturday night DJ dance parties. $$.

where to stay

Dickerson's Lake Florida Resort. 13194 Second St. NE; (320) 354-4272; dickersons resort.com. Thirteen cabins—almost all right along the water—make it easy to hop in a boat, splash in the water, or build sandcastles on 674-acre spring-fed Lake Florida. Cabins range from one to five bedrooms and include kitchens and the use of kayaks, hydro-bikes, rowboats, and bicycles. $$.

new london, mn

With a pretty millpond as its centerpiece, New London's Main Street offers a refreshing assortment of shops and local artwork. Most shops are open Monday through Saturday. You can find a full listing at experiencenewlondon.com.

The town's most popular event is the Friday-night waterskiing shows. The Little Crow Ski Team has been performing for three decades, earning 2 national championships and 16 regional championships along the way. It's a unique outing for families and a nice way to kick off a summer weekend.

getting there

From Spicer, travel north 6 miles on MN 23/9. Exit at MN 9 to enter downtown New London.

where to go

Little Crow Ski Team. 311 Second Ave. SE; littlecrow.com. Settle into the bleachers along the Crow River to see the acrobatic athletes build four-tiered pyramids, soar across jumps, and inspire applause while zipping across the water at Neer Park. Shows start at 7:30 p.m. in June and July and 7 p.m. in August. Be sure to double-check the schedule. The team sometimes hits the road for competitions or may offer additional home shows. Reserved seating: $8. Regular admission: $5. If the bleachers fill up, you can grab a spot on the hill to watch.

The Lucky Duck. 24 Main St. North; (320) 347-1137; luckyduckmn.com. Expect to linger in this shop with gourmet popcorn, ice cream, candy, puppets, Lego sets, toy trucks, kids' books, puzzles for cold and rainy days, and games from classic Monopoly to Settlers of Catan. You can continue the vacation vibe with cabin-comfy but stylish clothes and accessories next door at Happy Sol.

Sibley State Park. 800 Sibley Park Rd.; (320) 354-2055; dnr.state.mn.us. This state park makes the most of its location with a popular beach on Lake Andrew, an interpretive center featuring the area's wildlife and fauna, and 18 miles of trails. The top trail—quite literally—is the one to Mount Tom. The hill, a long-ago lookout and spiritual place for the Dakota, features a historic stone tower where you can look across its 2,510 acres. Other trails head through the woods and along ponds. In winter, visitors can cross-country ski or snowshoe. The park includes 132 campsites, half of which are near the beach and convenient for families with young children. There also are four camper cabins.

Three Sisters. 2550 MN 9 NE; (320) 354-4480; threesistersfurnishings.com. This spacious collection of clothing, Amish furniture, colorful Adirondack chairs, gourmet eats, bath and body products, and children's toys makes it a favorite. Take a cooler for the local meats, artisanal cheeses, and drink mixes that give you a head start on happy hour.

where to eat

The Deep Freeze. 10 Fourth St. SE; (320) 354-0093; facebook.com/DeepFreezeMN. Two blocks from the Glacial Lakes State Trail you can get summer favorites such as sundaes, malts, freezes, hot dogs, barbecue sandwiches, chips, and ice-cream cones swirled with flavors like cotton candy, bubble gum, and mocha cappuccino. Open seasonally. $.

Goat Ridge Brewing Company. 17 Central Ave. W.; (320) 345-2383; goatridgebrewing. com. Order up a pizza with names like Burning Pig Party and The Taco Man Cometh, grab something on tap like The Wolf amber IPA, Girl Trouble fruited sour, or a Krampus doppelbock and enjoy a spot on the patio as the Middle Fork Crow River ripples by. Even better: Join a game or trivia night, or catch a concert and warm up by the fires. $$.

Sweet River Cafe. 34 Main St. N.; (320) 354-2124; facebook.com/SweetRiverCafe. You can fill up with a slice of cowboy quiche, scones, chicken wild rice salad, and homemade soups in a fresh bread bowl, but the gooey caramel rolls, sumptuously layer cakes, or dessert bars may be the hardest to choose. $.

where to stay

Bug-Bee Hive Resort. 29659 Queen Bee Ln., Paynesville; (320) 243-4448; bugbee hiveresort.com. Fourteen miles northeast of New London, this third-generation year-round family resort rents 32 vacation homes with one to six bedrooms along Lake Koronis. You'll also find a beach along the 3,014-acre lake, water toys, a playground, boat rentals, summer kids' programs, family activities, an indoor pool, and ice house rentals. $$$.

northwest

day trip 01

northwest

>>> **rocking in the granite city**
st. cloud, mn

st. cloud, mn

Plan a hike through Quarry Park and Nature Preserve to experience what makes St. Cloud ("The Granite City") and its neighboring Waite Park unique. This 680-plus-acre county park encompasses more than 20 water-filled granite quarries. Nature has reclaimed this former industrial area where you can still see historic derricks reaching toward the sky and a few industrial remnants, but wooded trails lead to serene quarries where you can find picnic tables, trout-stocked fishing quarries, a scenic overlook high on a former slag pile, and two designated swim quarries where you can cannonball off docks or rocky ledges into the chilly depths.

Need more adventure? It's also popular for mountain biking, scuba diving, and rock climbing.

Locally quarried granite was used to build its imposing 1860s state prison along US 10, but you can also see its telltale speckled gray-and-white and red granite polished or rough-hewn throughout downtown's historic buildings. You can find a fountain built of granite columns at Eastman Park's Lake George and rent a paddleboat, SUP, or canoe and enjoy the backdrop of downtown, St. Mary's Cathedral, and the former 1917 school converted to City Hall. The biggest draw? Free Summertime by George concerts on Wednesday nights from late June through August. Bands, such as the Fabulous Armadillos and Killer Vees, draw crowds of close to 19,000.

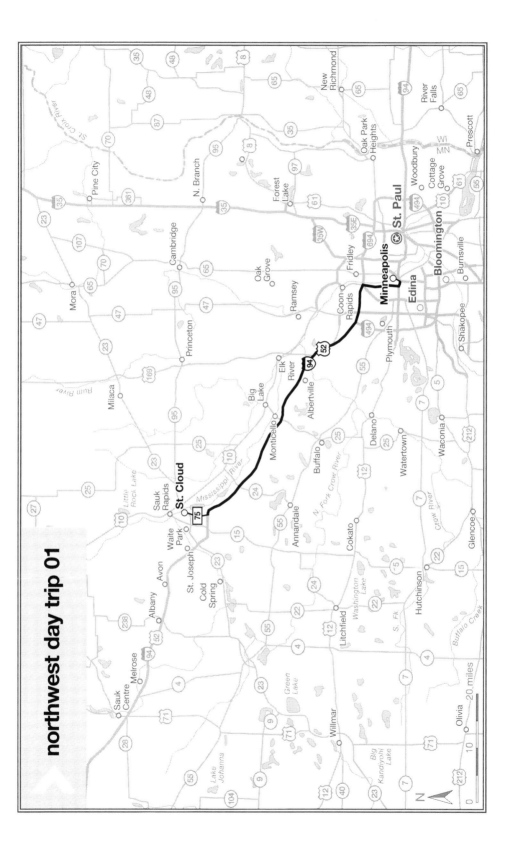

northwest day trip 01

If you visit on a Thursday or prefer smaller crowds, head across the Mississippi River to Sauk Rapids' Rock the Riverside summertime concerts at The Clearing. They're also free and overlook the river.

Music fans can also watch for concerts at The Ledge Amphitheater, which has hosted the Doobie Brothers and Bonnie Raitt at the stage built between former granite quarries in 2021. It gives new meaning to *rock* concerts and offers another groovy way to savor a perfect summer night in central Minnesota. For upcoming concerts and events, check with Visit Greater St. Cloud, 1411 W. St. Germain St.; (320) 251-4170; visitstcloud.com.

getting there

Take I-94 northwest to St. Cloud. It's about 70 miles from the Twin Cities.

where to go

Back Shed Brewing. 624 Sundial Dr., Waite Park; (320) 371-0636; backshedbrewing .com. You could make a day out of hitting the breweries in the St. Cloud area, from Beaver Island Brewing Company downtown to Pantown Brewing, but this one stands out, even with its unexpected location in Sundial Industrial Park. Why? It happens to be next to another popular destination: **Crafts Direct,** the Midwest's largest independently owned craft store. Try a glass of pink guava pineapple seltzer, Cranky Man blonde ale, Accordion Slip Kölsch, and pretzels. Grab a spot on the patio for lawn games, or check the schedule for live music and food trucks.

Beaver Island Trail. West bank of the Mississippi; visitstcloud.com. Access this paved path at the trailhead south of St. Cloud State University's Halenbeck Hall. It heads south to River Bluffs Regional Park or north through campus to downtown, where it connects to the River Walk behind the River's Edge Convention Center. Keep an eye out for eagles, herons, and swans.

Clear Waters Outfitting. 100 Pine St., Clearwater; (320) 558-8123; cwoutfitting.com. The Mississippi River stretch from St. Cloud to Clearwater has been designated as Wild and Scenic by the Minnesota Department of Natural Resources since 1976. While it looks pretty from the trails, it's even better on the water. It takes about 2 hours to float or paddle the 15 miles between the two communities. Clear Waters offers shuttles for paddlers and rents kayaks, wood-strip canoes, paddleboards, and fishing kayaks, which are popular for anglers looking to try some of the country's best smallmouth bass fishing. Guides can also provide lessons for beginners or deliver watercraft to area lakes.

The Grande Depot. 8318 MN 23, St. Cloud; (320) 257-5500; thegrandedepot.com. This 1912 Soo Line depot was relocated from Eden Valley to this spot along the interstate, where it houses two upscale stores one exit south of St. Joseph. This depot offers seasonal and home decor, fragrant bath and body products, and gourmet foods such as sauces, dressings, jams, and jellies. Cork and Cask is the place to grab wine or beer, imported cheeses, and crackers for a picnic.

Great River Children's Museum. 111 Seventh Ave. S.; greatrivercm.org. Expected to open in the heart of downtown by late 2024, the state's newest children's museum will explore the role of weather and water, the Mississippi River and the importance of the outdoors through multi-level and interactive play areas. Check the website for updates and admission.

Paramount Center for the Arts Gallery & Gifts. 913 W. St. Germain St.; (320) 259-5463; paramountarts.org. The vertical marquee blazes brightly on this 1921 theater, which was restored to its original grandeur for concerts, musicals and plays, comedians, and dance. The lobby includes monthly art exhibits, while workshops and open art nights (Thursdays October to May) are offered in the basement studios, which include pottery kilns and glass fusing. More than 50 regional artists sell paintings, handblown glass, stained glass, wood-turning, art cards, jewelry, and more at the Paramount Gift Shop.

Pioneer Place on Fifth. 22 Fifth Ave. South; (320) 203-0331; ppfive.com. This imposing granite-pillared building offers a modern, intimate venue for performances such as Granite City Radio Theatre, the Fabulous Armadillos, tribute concerts, theater, and comedy nights. Grab a drink, including local brews such as Beaver Island Brewing, at **The Veranda Lounge** (ppfive.com/veranda-lounge), a wine bar with seating indoors or on the granite veranda over-looking historic Fifth Avenue. On Wednesday through Saturday nights look for clues to get into the intimate and hidden **Blue Goose Speakeasy** (ppfive.com/blue-goose).

Quarry Park & Nature Preserve. 1802 CR 137, Waite Park; (320) 255-6172; co.stearns .mn.us. At 116 feet deep, Quarry 2 (also known as Melrose Deep 7) ranks as the hottest way to cool off with super-chilled spring-fed water. Quarry 11 draws more families with its sandy beach. While summer is popular, autumn also ranks as a showy time to visit and view the colorful oak, aspen, and maple leaves reflected in the 20 different quarries. During winter there's an illuminated trail for cross-country skiers. Daily parking pass: $5 (offseason); $10 (Labor Day through Memorial Day).

Stearns History Museum. 235 S. 33rd Ave.; (320) 253-8424; stearnshistorymuseum.org. As one of the state's best history museums, it takes visitors into a virtual quarry, shows off the Pan automobile, and offers additional exhibits, either local or touring, about topics such as immigrants or author Sinclair Lewis. Watch for events such as Hops and History tours, a World War II weekend, and cemetery walks. Open Wednesday through Sunday. Admission: $7, adults; $3, children 5 and older; or $17 per family. Swing into the gift shop for a wide selection of local books and gifts.

where to eat

Anton's Restaurant. 2001 Frontage Rd. N., Waite Park; (320) 253-3611; antonsrestaurant .com. On St. Cloud's far western edge, this used to be far enough out of town that it ran as

a tale of two gardens

*It may be hard to pick a favorite: the saturated colors, fragrant roses, and elegant fountains of **Clemens Gardens** or the shady **Munsinger Gardens** beneath a tall canopy of pines and nestled along a serene stretch of the Mississippi River.*

While different in character, these two gardens cover several city blocks and rank among Minnesota's best free attractions. Munsinger Gardens were first planted in the 1930s with hosta-lined paths that meander and curve past swaths of lush begonias and coleus, granite urns overflowing with sweet potato vines, a gazebo, a vintage log tourist cabin, a wishing well and stream, an ox-head fountain that's a nod to the area's location along historic oxcart trade routes, and sweet fairy gardens that kids love to find.

A path leads up the riverfront hillside to Clemens Gardens, which have full sunshine, geometric designs, an impressive iron treillage, and several fountains as focal points. The six themed gardens planted in the 1990s include a rose garden and a white garden that was modeled after Sissinghurst Castle in Kent, England. You can park along the streets or drive to a lot beneath the University Bridge. The parking lot connects to the sprawling, shady-oaked Riverside Park, where there's a splash pad, playground, disc golf course, and viewing area for the dam and Beaver Islands.

Find the gardens and Riverside Park where Michigan Avenue meets Kilian Boulevard, just across the Mississippi from St. Cloud State's campus (320-258-0381; munsingerclemens.com).

a Prohibition speakeasy and distributor of Stearns County's infamous Minnesota 13 moonshine. Expanded many times, it still has some original log walls and a focus on seafood, steaks, and giant popovers with honey butter. You can dine inside or out; it's wise to make a reservation if you want a seat overlooking the Sauk River or in one of the booths designed like a covered wagon. $$.

Backwards Bread Company. 3360 Southway Dr.; (320) 493-8254; backwardsbreadco .us. Tucked into a south St. Cloud industrial park 2 miles from the CR 75 exit, this place bakes croissants with seasonal fruits, savory stuffed croissants, olive and other artisan breads, handmade granola, and stellar ginger cookies. Use it as a reward for a ride or run along the Beaver Island Trail. $.

Bravo Burrito. 66 33rd Ave. S.; (320) 252-5441; bravoburritos.com. Don't let the strip mall location underwhelm you. This St. Cloud favorite has been cooking tender, savory meats for fist-size burritos since 1985—long before the Chipotle chain was born. Order a combo burrito with three meats, such as zippy cubes of beef Colorado, spiced chorizo, carnitas pulled pork, pork verde stewed with tomatillos, chocolate-brown chicken mole, and tangy chicken verde. $.

Granite City Food & Brewery. 3945 Second St. S.; (320) 203-9000; gcfb.com. This popular chain with American fare, their own line of beer, and Sunday brunch is worth mentioning because this is the original location. A long-ago entrance arch to St. Cloud welcomed visitors to "the Granite City," which inspired the name. $$.

Jules' Bistro. 921 W. St. Germain St.; (320) 252-7125; julesbistrostcloud.com. This small but classy cafe next to the Paramount Center for the Arts rotates local artwork and welcomes diners with espresso and rise & shine pizza and chilaquiles, followed by creative soups, appetizers such as bruschetta with creamy goat cheese and a sweet dried fruit tapenade, plus sandwiches such as a caprese grill, an avocado portobello Reuben panini, wood-fired pizzas, homemade layer cakes and pastries, wines, and rotating kombuchas, such as cherry basil, on tap. $.

Val's Rapid Serv. 628 E. St. Germain St.; (320) 251-5775; valshamburgers.com. With this tiny but beloved 50-year-old institution 2 blocks from US 10, you order and pay for your burgers, toppings, malts, etc., with automated machines, then wait for a deliciously grease-splotched bag with a mountain of fries. $.

White Horse Restaurant & Bar. 809 W. St. Germain St.; (320) 257-7775; whitehorsemn .com. This comfortable downtown eatery always features globally diverse and creative fare with items such as chimichurri steak sandwich, Thai steak salad, Indian vegetarian curry, gyro burger, swordfish, and Rogan Josh. $$.

Worth more time

*If you enjoy wild places, take a drive about 30 miles east of St. Cloud to **Sherburne National Wildlife Refuge.** The 30,700-acre swath of woods, prairie, and St. Francis River watershed has long been a favorite with birders, who take the Prairie's Edge Wildlife Drive to look for songbirds in the woods, an eagle's nest, trumpeter swans, sandhill cranes, and more along the many ponds and pools. Keep an eye out for deer and beaver and wildflowers, such as meadows thick with purple lupine and rich yellow hoary puccoon in early June. By October you can hear and see large groups of cranes flying overhead as they return from farm fields to roost at night and prepare for fall migration (17076 293rd Ave. NW; 763-389-3323; fws.gov/ refuge/sherburne).*

where to stay

Best Western Plus Kelly Inn. 100 Fourth Ave. South; (320) 253-0606; bestwestern.com. St. Cloud has many chain hotels and newer properties, but this one has a choice location next to the Mississippi River and within walking distance to downtown restaurants, shopping, and the River's Edge Convention Center. $$.

Hilton Garden Inn. 550 Division St., Waite Park; (320) 640-7990; hilton.com. One of the area's newest hotels, it's also convenient for visitors focused on Waite Park attractions on the western side of St. Cloud, such as The Ledge, Quarry Park, or exploring the Lake Wobegon Trail. $$.

day trip 02

northwest

>>> **saints, scribes & lake wobegon:**
st. joseph-collegeville, mn

st. joseph-collegeville, mn

St. Joseph—or Joetown as it's often called—hums with the chill vibe of a small town (pop. 6,930) enhanced by the arts, activities, and ideas of a college town. The College of St. Benedict stretches alongside downtown with its smattering of boutiques, coffee shops, brewery, and eateries, including the addition of Krewe, a destination New Orleans–themed restaurant that's been featured in the *New York Times*, and Rockhouse Productions, a recording studio started by the late rock legend Bobby Vee and his sons in a renovated bank.

Five miles away, St. John's University was founded in 1857 in Collegeville on 2,700 wooded and rolling acres, making it an idyllic place to catch a fall football game or take a hike. Church bells reverberate across St. John's Lake Sagatagan as falling maple leaves swirl above the wooded path curving around the shore until it reaches the picturesque Stella Maris chapel.

The surrounding woods and prairie played a role in inspiring some of the artwork when St. John's commissioned a global team of experts to painstakingly illustrate and write out the Bible by hand in 1998—an undertaking that hadn't been done in the 500 years since the printing press was invented. A video at the university explains how they created the intricate, vibrant illustrations on vellum using feather quills, hand-ground minerals for color, and gold leaf to richly illuminate the pages. Completed passages have been featured in the

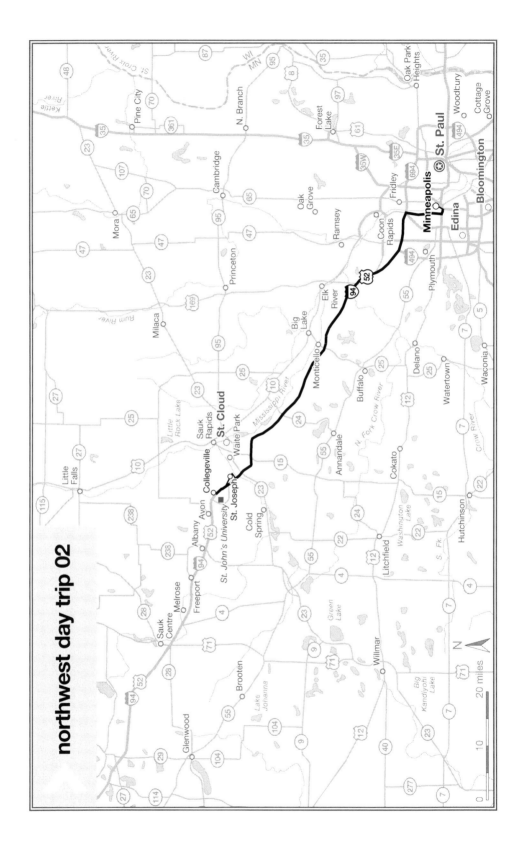

northwest day trip 02

Smithsonian, at the Minneapolis Institute of Arts, and alongside touring exhibits of the Dead Sea Scrolls. You can see pages on permanent exhibit at the Hill Manuscript Library.

Work up an appetite and leave time for another meal before leaving town. For more information, go to joetown.org.

getting there

Follow I-94 about 72 miles to Stearns CR 2, the St. Joseph exit. Collegeville is the next exit, 3 miles to the northwest. You'll go through one of I-94's prettiest and most wooded passages in Minnesota as you drive under the pedestrian and biking bridge that connects the campuses.

where to go

Art and Heritage Place. St. Benedict's Monastery, 104 Chapel Ln., St. Joseph; (320) 363-7113; sbm.osb.org. Some of the best shopping and artwork can be found in this combination of Haehn Museum and Whitby Gift Shop and Gallery. The Benedictine sisters sell delicate hand-painted scarves, handmade cards, jewelry, pottery, and candy and cracked wheat bread mixes from the monastery kitchens. Closed from Christmas through early February.

Bad Habit Brewing Company. 25 College Ave. North, St. Joseph; (320) 271-3108; bad habitbeer.com. With its taproom and a sweet patio in the heart of St. Joe and across from Krewe Restaurant, it's a groovy place to be on a summer night or when there are yard games or events, such as art projects or puzzle nights, going on as you sip a Beach Bum lemon lime seltzer, Bennie light ale, or a Friendship Picnic cherry pineapple milkshake.

Collegeville Orchards. 15517 Fruit Farm Rd., St. Joseph; (320) 356-7609; collegeville orchardsmn.com. Near the St. John's campus, these orchards draw families for the 20 varieties of apples, pumpkins, harvest crafts, honey and jams, and a petting zoo with alpacas, rabbits, potbelly pigs, goats, miniature horses, and ducklings. Open daily, 10 a.m. to 6 p.m. Labor Day weekend through October.

Hill Museum and Manuscript Library. 2835 Abbey Plaza, Collegeville; (320) 363-3514; hmml.org. The main attraction here is the St. John's Bible (saintjohnsbible.org), but it's also home to the world's largest collection of images from ancient handwritten manuscripts—more than 115,000 of them from Europe, Ethiopia, the Middle East, and India. Check for seasonal hours.

Milk and Honey Ciders. 11738 CR 51; (320) 271-3111; milkandhoneyciders.com. The rolling country setting feels charming and fitting for folks who take heirloom hard ciders seriously. Ask for samples to find your perfect taste, including the Flora cider with floral notes; a Chaga Chai with chicory and licorice among its aromatics, and Alchemy, an ice cider aged seven months in a bourbon barrel. Open Thursday through Sunday. Check online for the summer concert series.

St. John's Abbey Arboretum. 32011 St. John's Road, Collegeville; (320) 363-3163; csbsju.edu/outdooru/abbeyarboretum. Get oriented at the prairie kiosk as you drive toward campus. Trails loop across native prairie, through maple and basswood forest, and across wetland boardwalks that are part of the 2,830-acre arboretum. Natural history lectures are offered fall through spring, along with special events such as the maple syrup festival, spring birding, and a moonlight winter hike to call for owls.

explore Lake Wobegon–inspired towns

The small towns of Stearns County inspired a young Garrison Keillor, who went on to create the wildly popular A Prairie Home Companion *radio show. Each episode included "News from Lake Wobegon," with humorous stories about a fictional Minnesota town "where all the women are strong, all the men are good-looking, and the children are above average." The show ran from the mid-1970s to the 2010s with up to 2.6 million listeners on close to 600 public radio stations.*

Travelers can explore the towns that inspired Keillor's stories throughout the county, but the 65-mile paved **Lake Wobegon Trail** *conveniently strings many of them together and keeps bicyclists happy. Visitors can start the trail at River's Edge Park (1300 Great Oak Drive) in Waite Park on the western edge of St. Cloud or at the St. Joseph trailhead (600 College Ave. N). These locations may have bike share rentals via the Movatic app if you don't have your own set of wheels (ci.waitepark.mn.us/549/Bike-Share-Program).*

Heading northwest, you'll find the towns of Avon, Albany, Freeport, Melrose, Sauk Centre, West Union, and Osakis. Each offers trailheads with shelters, and most have water and restrooms or are near a local city hall or café.

A spur trail heads to Holdingford and connects to the Soo Line Trail, which heads east to Little Falls. Lake Wobegon Trail also connects to the Central Lakes Trail in Osakis.

If you want to sweeten your cruise, there's an annual Caramel Roll Ride the second weekend in June, followed by the Lady Slipper Nature Ride the third Saturday in June to see the state flower in bloom, and a Caramel Apple Ride the first Saturday after Labor Day. For more information, go to lakewobegontrail.com.

If you are driving through Lake Wobegon territory, here are a few other stops worth the drive:

St. Joseph Meat Market. 26 First Ave. NW; (320) 363-4913; stjosephmeatmarket.com. This area's German and Polish heritage shines with more than 60 kinds of homemade sausages from savory (kielbasa, *Landjaeger*, wild rice brats) to bizarre (sour gummy bratwurst, funeral hot-dish brats, and macaroni cheese brats). The choices liven up grilled dinners, whether you're camping or taking some home. BYOC (Bring Your Own Cooler).

where to eat

Bella Cucina. 15 E. Minnesota St.; (320) 363-4534; bellacucina.com. Enjoy Italian-inspired meals here, such as vodka meatballs, lobster au gratin, avocado bruschetta, hand-tossed

- *Hemker Park Zoo.* 26715 CR 39, Freeport; (320) 836-2426; hemkerzoo.com. This family-run zoo opened to the public in 1994 and offers a surprising array of animals from around the world, including penguins, lemurs, zebras, spider monkeys, wildebeest, a camel, macaws, flamingos, and cranes. Open May 1 to October 31.
- *The Palmer House Hotel & Restaurant.* 500 Sinclair Lewis Ave., Sauk Centre; (320) 351-9100; thepalmerhousehotel.com. Even if you're not spending the night at this hotel 16 minutes north of Freeport, you can soak up the atmosphere at this century-old main street hotel with original tin ceilings and stained glass. If you spend the night, be prepared for things that go bump in the night. The site's original hotel, built in 1863, burned down around 1900, but it apparently left a few spirits behind. Guests have reported doors slamming, the sound of knocking, abrupt temperature changes, the voices of children, and lights going on and off—especially in Rooms 11 and 17. $$.
- *Red Head Creamery.* 31535 463rd Ave., Brooten; (320) 346-2246; redhead creamery.com. More than 16 miles south of Sauk Centre and deep into Stearns County, people find their way to this farmstead that has made artisanal cheese since 2013 and scored awards at international competitions. Visitors can greet the cows, take a farm tour that explains the creamery and cheese-making process, and sample their cheddars, Havarti, and Brie cheeses and fresh curds. Their next venture includes an expansion and launching Redhead Creamery Spirits, a whey-based distillery in 2024. Farm tours: $10.
- *Tutti Fruitti Restaurant and Market Farm.* 38914 CR 186, Sauk Centre; (320) 352-2059; tuttifruittimarketfarm.com. With an on-site produce market and from-scratch menu, this off-the-beaten-path gem has built a steady following with fall-apart roast beef, tater tot hotdish, bacon-stuffed potato pancakes, soups, and pie. You can also get a frozen pie and cookies to go or buy garden produce from May through November. Open daily for breakfast and lunch. $.

flatbread pizzas, chicken Marsala risotto, Italian sausage cannelloni, and lobster tossed with butternut squash ravioli. Eat inside or on the patio. $$.

Jupiter Moon. 15 E. Minnesota St.; (320) 557-0141; jupitermoonicecream.com. Artisan ice cream and nondairy variations continually rotate with the seasons and may include flavors such as lemon poppy seed, ginger peach, mango fire, matcha, strawberry rhubarb pie, lavender honey, cheddar apple (with cheddar from Redhead Creamery), Kinder coffee, and vanilla cardamom with blueberries. $.

Kay's Kitchen. 303 College Ave. N.; (320) 557-0030; facebook.com/bestbreakfastmn. As homey as its classic neon sign with an ice-cream cone, this has been a gathering place since 1972. Eggs, caramel rolls, and hash browns give way to burgers and pulled pork sandwiches, hamburger steak, pie, and apple strudel. Open daily breakfast through midafternoon. $.

Krewe. 24 College Ave. N.; (320) 557-0083; krewemn.com. This buzzworthy restaurant leans heavily on New Orleans, Cajun, and Creole heritage to inspire a seasonal menu featuring crab cakes, hush puppies, beignets, po'boys, jambalaya, and gumbo. You can also find cocktails such as Thai basil sangria, spirit-free basil-strawberry limeade, and desserts from its next-door business: **Flour and Flower**, which sells fresh bouquets and fresh-baked croissants, pastries, pies, and artisan breads (26 College Ave. N.; flourand flowerbakery.com). Krewe opens Wednesday to Saturday and on Sunday for a Jazz brunch. $$-$$$.

The Local Blend, 19 W. Minnesota St.; (320) 363-1011; thelocalblend.net. If you need a pick-me-up or a meal, this locally roasted coffee cafe across from campus features almond croissants, pancakes, sandwiches, a variety of pizzas, plenty of vegetarian choices, and a full case of sweets and treats. $.

where to stay

Abbey Guest House. 2380 Water Tower Rd., Collegeville; (320) 363-2573; abbeyguest-house.org. There are 29 modest rooms in this guesthouse run by the Benedictine monks of Saint John's Abbey. Most face the lake or the Abbey Church and were designed to be part of a quiet getaway. Meals can be included. $$.

El Rancho Manana Campground. 27302 Ranch Rd., Richmond; (320) 597-2740; campelrancho.com. There are 120 sites at this popular campground, recreation area, and riding stables about 14 miles from St. Joseph or 12 miles from Avon on Long Lake. You don't have to be a campground guest to take a trail ride. The 1,208-acre property includes horse trails, family programs, a playground, biking trails, boats, canoes, and hydro-bikes for fun along the beach. $.

The Estates Bed and Breakfast. 29 E. Minnesota St.; (320) 557-0300; estatesbedand breakfast.com. This 1909 home with three suites is right downtown near restaurants, shopping, and College of St. Benedict. $–$$.

The Pillar Inn. 419 Main St., Cold Spring; (320) 685-3828; thepillarinn.com. About 15 minutes from St. Joseph, this B&B in one of Cold Spring's 1905 homes has three guest rooms, including one with a *Casablanca* theme featuring tropical Art Deco decor. Breakfast main courses may include their fruit-filled puff pancakes, sausage crepes, or wild rice quiche. Packages are offered for horseback riding, birding, and massage. $$–$$$.

day trip 03

northwest

land of vikings & lakes:
alexandria, mn

alexandria, mn

All hail Big Ole. This Minnesota Viking has nothing to do with football. But he does stand 28 feet tall in the middle of downtown with the bold claim on his shield: "Alexandria: Birthplace of America."

He's one of Minnesota's best-known characters when it comes to roadside attractions and funny photo ops. (Where else can you look up a giant man's skirt?) But he also represents one of the state's greatest mysteries: Does the Kensington Runestone found in 1898 prove Vikings were in Minnesota in 1362—long before Christopher Columbus took credit for "discovering" America?

You can draw your own conclusions at the local museum or make a beeline for the lakes. More than a dozen of them ring Alexandria, giving it the easy-breezy feel of a vacation town with a dose of Viking spirit. You'll also find plenty of arts in the area, from live music at Bold North Cellars and musical comedies at Theatre L'Homme Dieu to free Thursday-night concerts at the Douglas County Courthouse Lawn throughout the summer.

For more information on events, contact Explore Alexandria Tourism, 324 Broadway St.; (320) 763-0102; explorealex.com.

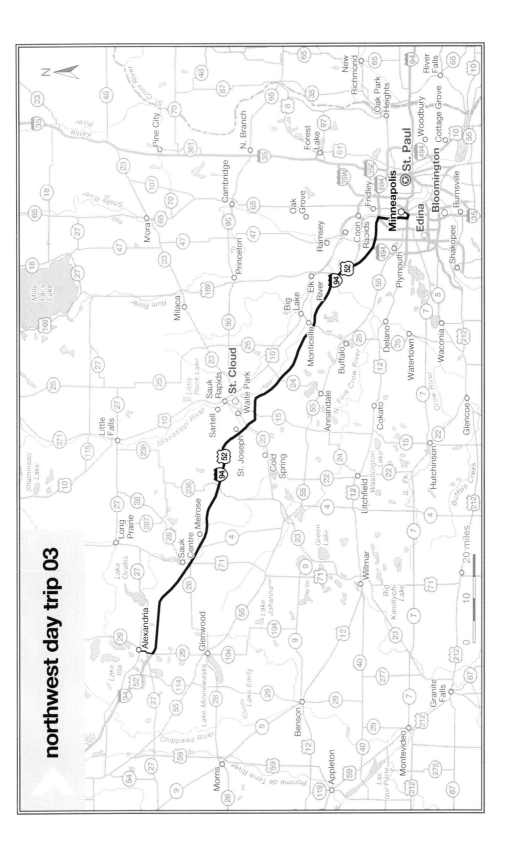

northwest day trip 03

getting there

Follow I-94 about 135 miles to Alexandria. It takes about 2 hours and 15 minutes to get here. Give yourself extra time if you're heading north on a Friday or returning on a Sunday with cabin traffic.

where to go

Bold North Cellars. 6693 CR 34 NW; (320) 846-5443; carloscreekwinery.com. This sprawling venture comprises **Carlos Creek Winery**, **22 Northmen brewery**, **Stoke Wood-Fire Pizza**, and **Sizzle** seasonal food truck with gourmet burgers, live music, and grounds to roam. Winter visitors can cross-country ski along their trails and warm up with the extra heat of a Northmen pizza, carnitas calzone, or salted caramel s'more. Fall brings the popular annual Grape Stomp Fall Festival. Year-round tastings include their many wines, such as Minnescato, Hot Dish Red, Wobegon White, and You Betcha Blush, along with hard ciders. Vineyard tours run spring through fall. Brews include a cave series aged in red wine or whiskey barrels, an oak-smoked wheat lager, and other adventurous beers for those who prefer grains to grapes.

Central Lakes Trail. 206 N. Broadway; (320) 763-0102; centrallakestrail.com. This 55-mile paved bike trail runs along a former Burlington Northern railroad route between Fergus Falls to the west and Osakis to the east, where it connects to the Lake Wobegon Trail, which runs south toward St. Cloud. Grab the trail near the Big Ole statue.

Lake Carlos State Park. 2601 CR 38 NE, Carlos; (320) 852-7200; dnr.state.mn.us. Campers can get close to the northern shore of Lake Carlos with many of these 121 campsites. The 1,230-acre state park is also popular for its shallow beach and crystal-clear water that's ideal for young swimmers and toddlers. Winter visitors can ski 6 miles of rolling terrain or snowmobile along 9 miles of park trails before connecting to the 500-mile Douglas Area Trail Association network. Summer hikers have 14 miles of trails. Four camper cabins are also available. Fee: $7.

Legacy of the Lakes Museum. 205 Third Ave. West; (320) 759-1114; legacyofthelakes .org. You can find historic displays on resorts and fishing at this museum, but the focus is on Minnesota's boat manufacturers, including Alexandria Boat Works, Larson Boat works, and Chris-Craft. It's a great place to admire the skillfully built curves of vintage wooden boats and appreciate how they've evolved over the decades. Open seasonally. Admission: $10, adults; $8, seniors; $5, students.

Runestone Museum. 206 Broadway St.; (320) 763-3160; runestonemuseum.org. While the Runestone anchors this museum with Viking lore, you'll also find other Middle-Age Nordic artifacts, interactive areas to dress like a Viking or learn the Rune alphabet, wildlife and pioneer-era displays, and Native American artwork. At the replicated 1860s Fort Alexandria and open-air section of the museum (open April 1 to Oct. 31), you can visit a one-room schoolhouse and check out a 40-foot Viking trading ship. Admission: $10, adults; $9, seniors; $7, children/students.

Theatre L'Homme Dieu. 1875 CR 120 NE; (320) 846-3150; tlhd.org. This beloved theater has presented a strong lineup of summer productions—often comedies, musicals, and light fare—since 1961. You can settle in for everything from a touring Minnesota comedy to a Prince tribute concert. Tickets start at $30.

where to eat

Depot Smokehouse & Tavern. 104 Broadway St.; (320) 763-7712; depotmn.com. This historic Burlington Northern depot with a patio overlooking Lake Agnes and the Central Lakes Trail serves smokehouse brisket, burnt ends, chicken-and-wild-rice pizza, burgers, pulled pork sandwich with pineapple coleslaw, strawberry salad with a popover, and barbecue ribs. $$–$$$.

Eddy's Interlachen Inn. 4960 CR 42 NE; (320) 846-1051; interlacheninn.com. Located near the thin strip of land separating Lake L'Homme Dieu and Lake Carlos, this restaurant which began in the 1940s serves homey meals such as meat loaf, along with green-olive cheeseburgers with homemade potato chips, salmon Oscar served over baked barley, and pasta L'Homme Dieu with chicken, Italian sausage, and sun-dried tomatoes in a cream sauce. $$.

The Garden Bar on 6th. 115 Sixth Ave. E.; (320) 759-2277; thegardenbaronsixth.com. At this brick-walled downtown restaurant, global flavors mix with such menu items as with falafel and lamb gyros, harvest or Thai bowls, ahi tuna sandwich, citrus and herb pheasant, and star anise scallops. $$.

La Ferme. 613 Broadway St.; (320) 846-0777; lafermemn.com. With a contemporary vibe and elevated comfort foods, this farm-to-table bistro updates its short-and-sweet menu every few days to fit the seasons and incorporate farm-to-table ingredients. Look for choices such as a pizza of the week, shrimp jambalaya, classic fried chicken, and blends of meats and cheeses or wings to share while you wait for your food. You can also reserve a seat at the chef's table. $$.

Lure Lakebar. 2800 N. Nokomis NE; (320) 219-7755; luremn.com. You'll want to linger at this Lake L'Homme Dieu location with great lake views, outdoor seating, and a modern design including cozy private booths, natural light, and after-dark ambience. Craft cocktails complement fare such as a queso fondue with baguette, peel-and-eat shrimp, shrimp scampi flatbread, lobster roll, and pan-fried walleye. $$.

where to stay

Arrowwood Resort & Conference Center. 2100 Arrowwood Ln.; (320) 762-1124; arrow woodresort.com. This ranks among Minnesota's largest resorts, with 200 guest rooms along the shore of Lake Darling, including hotel-style rooms, suites, apartments, and newly built log townhomes. The 450-acre resort also is home to Minnesota's first big indoor water park, a spacious indoor pool, a beach and boats, trail rides, a golf course, and tennis and basketball courts. Winter amenities include snowmobiles, sleigh rides, and a skating pond. $$.

Cedar Rose Inn Bed and Breakfast. 422 Seventh Ave. W.; (651) 303-4466; cedarrose inn.com. There are four rooms in this 1903 gabled Tudor mansion, nicely situated within a block of Lake Winona and 3 blocks from downtown. Once considered part of Alexandria's well-to-do "silk-stocking district," it still feels gracious and luxurious, with stained-glass windows, vintage furnishings, and fancy chandeliers. Breakfast includes egg bakes, pancakes or French toast, and extras such as caramel rolls. $$.

Peters Sunset Beach Resort. 20000 S. Lakeshore Dr., Glenwood; (320) 634-4501; petersresort.com. This classic family resort has welcomed folks to the shores of Lake Minnewaska (the state's 13th largest lake) since 1915. It's about 20 miles south of Alexandria and includes 24 rooms and suites, plus 10 luxury townhomes and a variety of cottages— some large enough for reunions. Amenities include a beach packed with water toys, basketball and tennis courts, a playground, saunas, and packages for their Pezhekee Golf Course. Meal packages are also available, with food served in the historic dining room. Open May through October. $$.

day trip 04

northwest

>>>> **lindbergh and the mississippi:**
little falls, mn

little falls, mn

One of the world's first mega-celebrities, Charles Lindbergh, grew up in modest Little Falls, a town of about 9,000 along the Mississippi River. He watched the skies, took apart engines, and fearlessly explored the land long before making the world's first solo flight across the Atlantic Ocean in 1927. With his wife, Anne Morrow Lindbergh, often exploring the skies with him, they forever shaped the aviation industry to come. You can tour his home and hear about his unusual boyhood just south of downtown. An adjacent museum looks at Lindbergh's complexities, tragedies such as the kidnapping of their infant son, and forgotten accomplishments (such as lifesaving medical inventions) and the legacies he and his wife left behind.

But there's much more than Lindbergh in Little Falls. This classic small town boasts several family-friendly attractions, especially fun for those who wants to climb into a replica cockpit of Lindbergh's *Spirit of St. Louis* plane, follow their curiosity through Pine Grove Zoo or the Minnesota Fishing Museum, watch trains rumble by a historic depot, bike the Soo Line Trail, camp at the state park, or fish in the Mississippi River.

The river played a key role in helping the town flourish as logging boomed and logs were floated downriver. That early success left a legacy of Victorian homes on picturesque streets. Today the river thunders across a hydroelectric dam with enough power to light up Duluth.

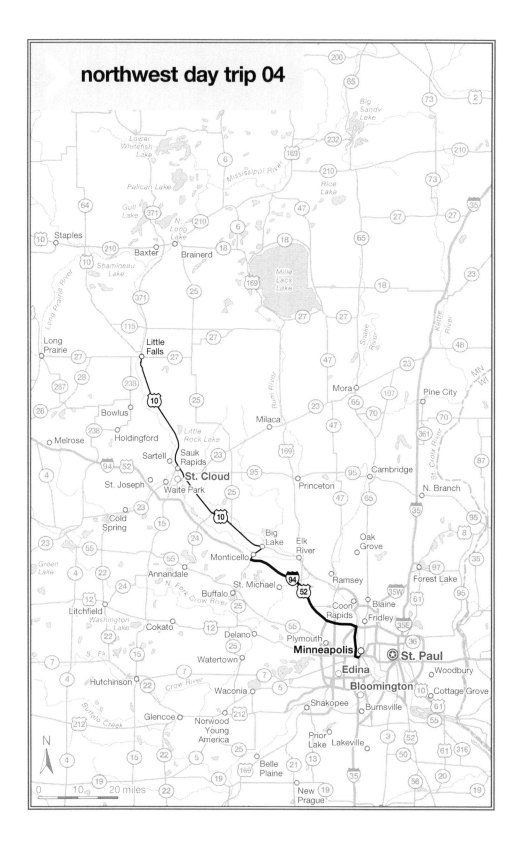

northwest day trip 04

getting there

Take I-94 about 38 miles from Minneapolis to Monticello. Exit at MN 25. Go right (northeast) into town for about 3.5 miles, crossing the Mississippi River and heading to Big Lake. Go left (northwest) on US 10 for 57 miles until you reach Little Falls. Exit at MN 27/First Avenue Northeast and turn left to reach downtown. Total trip: About 95 miles (1 hour and 50 minutes).

where to go

Little Falls Convention and Visitors Bureau. 606 SE First St.; (320) 616-4959; littlefallsmn.com. Grab a community guide here and get a glimpse of historic elegance at the 1903 Burton/Rosenmeier House, built in the Classical Revival style. Guests are welcome to walk upstairs and peek into a few rooms furnished with period furniture and art. You can also grab a guide to the town's murals and public art, including imaginative bike racks.

Charles Lindbergh House and Museum. 1620 Lindbergh Dr. South; (320) 616-5421; mnhs.org/lindbergh. Walk in the footsteps of Charles Lindbergh at his boyhood home 1.4 miles south of Little Falls. Minnesota Historical Society interpreters lead seasonal tours of his home, pointing out what fueled his thirst for adventure. Even his habit of sleeping on the cold screen porch most of the year helped acclimate him to freezing altitudes when flying.

The adjacent visitor center includes exhibits on Lindbergh's marriage to author Anne Morrow, the "Crime of the Century" kidnapping and murder of their infant son, their joint role in mapping Pan Am routes, his controversial stance against the US entering World War II, his medical inventions to aid surgeries, and his later work for environmental groups. These facilities are open Memorial Day weekend through Labor Day. Special events and prearranged group tours may be available at other times. Admission: $10, adults; $8, seniors/students/children 5–17.

Charles A. Lindbergh State Park. 1615 Lindbergh Dr. South; (320) 616-2525; dnr.state.mn.us. Charles Lindbergh used to roam these woods and build bridges across Pike Creek, which flows through this 436-acre park and empties into the Mississippi River. He donated the land to the state in 1931 in memory of his father, Charles A. Lindbergh Sr. You can hike along the creek, watch for spring wildflowers, listen for songbirds among the oak and pines, camp at 38 sites, enjoy the WPA picnic grounds and a playground, or seek geocaching boxes stashed throughout the park. $7 for daily permit.

Crane Meadows National Wildlife Refuge. 19502 Iris Road; (320) 632-1575; fws.gov/refuge/crane-meadows. For another hiking option, check out 3.5 miles of looped trails through sedge meadows and grasslands along the Platte River to the edge of Rice Lake. The 2,000-acre property, 8 miles southeast of Little Falls, contains one of the state's most intact wetland complexes and harbors more than 200 species of birds (including nesting eagles), making it an Audubon-designated Important Bird Area.

Downtown Little Falls. Broadway Avenue and First Street; (320) 616-4959. Ask for a history guide at the visitor center and then explore downtown, much of which was built in the late 1800s. The brick buildings house a vintage movie theater, dining venues, and boutiques such as Baby's on Broadway (47 Broadway E.), Rustic Diamond Boutique (108 First St. SW), and the Shoppes of Little Falls, which includes home goods, clothing, accessories, and repurposed furniture from 80 artisans at 102 First St. SE. Don't miss a stroll through Maple Island Park alongside the Mississippi.

Great River Arts. 122 First St. SE; (320) 632-0960; greatart.org. Look for locally written and performed plays, comedy acts, concerts, and music nights at Little Falls' arts hub. You can also find handmade gifts from local artisans, including mobiles, glass sculpture, pottery, paintings, and photography by more than 50 regional artists.

Little Falls Arts and Crafts Fair. Throughout downtown; (218) 632-5155; littlefallsmn chamber.com. Close to 100,000 people flood Little Falls during the second weekend in September for one of the largest craft fairs in the Midwest. Watch for shuttles to get visitors from fairgrounds parking to two days of artsy fun.

Minnesota Fishing Museum and Hall of Fame. 304 W. Broadway; (320) 616-2011; mnfishingmuseum.com. The wooden dock-like walkway and boat for a counter provide just a hint of the Minnesota fishing history packed into this museum. Little Falls was once home to Larson boat manufacturing and sits only 30 miles south of the famed fishing waters of the Brainerd Lakes. The museum blends all aspects of Minnesota's favorite sport with exhibits on motors and boats, spearfishing, ice fishing, fly fishing in southern Minnesota's trout rivers, and even the best catch from Lake Superior. Among the quirkier items: "Old Fish," a massive muskie that weighed more than 40 pounds. As a legendary catch along the Mississippi, locals would keep tossing him back until his fatal encounter with the dam. Check out the O-Fish-L gift shop too. Open Wednesday through Sunday. Admission: $25 per family or $10, adults; $8, seniors; $5, students and kids ages 6–17.

Minnesota Military Museum. 15000 MN 115, Camp Ripley; (320) 616-6050; facebook .com/MinnesotaMilitaryMuseum. The 53,000-acre Fort Ripley has been a hub for training Minnesota's soldiers since it began as a frontier outpost in 1849. The museum offers a glimpse into soldiers' lives from those early years to the National Guard's key role at home and abroad today. Outside exhibits include tanks and Jeeps. Open daily May through September; Thursday through Saturday, October through April. Admission: $12 per family; $2–$5 per person; free to active military. Adults must show photo identification to enter Camp Ripley.

Pine Grove Zoo. 1200 W. Broadway; (320) 616-5595; pinegrovezoo.com. This little zoo about 10 blocks west of the Mississippi River began with owls and deer in 1913 and today features tigers, wolves, elk, bobcats, and bears. You can add on Animal Encounter programs for up-close 20-minute interactions with the sloth, river otters, red kangaroos, and more. Open daily May 1 through Labor Day; Thursday through Sunday through mid-October. Admission: $14, adults; $13 for age 62 and older; $12 for ages 3–9.

Shirley Mae's Outfitters. 61 First Ave NE, (320) 414-0382; shirleymaesoutfitters.com. Rent Kevlar Wenonah or handmade cedar-strip canoes, along with kayaks and standup paddleboards for Mississippi River treks, exploring area lakes, or getting outfitted for a Boundary Waters adventure. Staff will drop off customers at six different landings for river trips ranging from 2 hours to 2 days.

Touright Bicycle Shop. 124 Second St. NE, (320) 639-2453; tourightbicycleshop.com. Whether you need a patch kit or a quick tune-up or want to rent a bike for hitting the Soo Line State Trail or national Mississippi River Trail, you can find it here. The shop sells and rents electric and touring bikes, mountain bikes, and scooters and skis and snowshoes in winter.

Two Rivers Campground and Tubing. 5116 145th St. NW, Royalton; (320) 584-5125; tworiverscampground.net. You don't have to camp at this popular resort with pools, minigolf, and scenic river sites to enjoy tubing the Platte River. The campground rents tubes and shuttles people to a private launch site near Royalton (15 minutes south of Little Falls). From there, it's a leisurely family-friendly float back to the campground, where the Mississippi and Platte Rivers meet.

where to eat

A.T. The Black and White. 116 SE First St.; (320) 632-5374; attheblacknwhite.com. This downtown institution built a reputation on great burgers for more than 75 years, but also adds tasty twists, such as an olive burger on a pretzel bun, blackened walleye tacos, Korean pork lettuce wraps, and a smoky beet vegetarian alternative to the Reuben sandwich. Desserts may include carrot cake or sticky toffee pudding cake. Decor incorporates a rescued Rexall drugstore sign, a massive "Airport" sign from the town's former drive-in movie theater, and vintage photos galore. $$.

Caffè Strolaga. 500 E. Broadway E; (320) 414-0400; facebook.com/caffestrolaga. Start the day with local Reality Roasters coffee, drinks such as the Sicilian Mocha (chocolate pistachio flavoring and whipped cream), breakfast sandwiches, scones, and pastries. For lunch, look for specials such as Thai chicken peanut wrap, pierogi hot dish, beef Stroganoff, and homemade soups. Open Monday through Friday. $.

Little Falls Bakery and Deli. 121 E. Broadway; (320) 632-6388. Little Falls' sweetest destination would be worth a stop as a bakery alone, but it ups the ante with a homey, affordable cafe serving burgers, sandwiches, soups, and homey hot dishes Tuesday through Friday and breakfast Tuesday through Saturday. Glass cases fill with brownies; homemade fudge; fish-shaped cookies; dense bread made with cranberries, wild rice, and walnuts; sizable fritters; and sticky orange blossoms. $.

Sanchez Burrito. 110 11th St. SE; (320) 414-0800; sanchezburrito320.com. Find a blend of burritos with beans and barbacoa, vegetarian fillings, nacho bowls, and tacos.

Starry Eyed Brewing Company. 16757 11th St. NE; (320) 232-0382; starryeyedbrewing .com. Customers can sit among 250 strings of hops at this brewery while sampling 40 brews on tap, plus seltzers and ciders. Check the Tapfoolery board for rotating small-batch variations of their standard brews, such as pale ale with pistachio, Moscow Mule, blueberry wheat, or chocolate caramel apple.

Thielen Meats. 300 NE 13th St.; (320) 632-2821; thielenmeatslf.com. If you're heading to lake country or home with a cooler, swing into this bustling meat market for their popular bacon. Other enticements include double-smoked picnic ham, Amish chickens, summer sausage and steaks, chorizo, smoked fish, turkey jerky, kraut brats, grilling glazes, and hamburger premixed with Vidalia onions, blue cheese, or wild rice.

where to stay

AmericInn by Wyndham Little Falls. 306 LeMieur St.; (320) 632-1964; wyndhamhotels .com. Hotel rooms range from queen doubles to suites with whirlpools, all with in-room minifridges and microwaves. Also included: free hot breakfast, a pool, and a hot tub. $–$$.

Campfire Bay Resort. 31504 Azure Road, Cushing; (218) 575-2432; campfirebayresort .com. If you're craving a classic Minnesota lakeside resort experience, this resort on Fish Trap Lake offers one- to four-bedroom cabin units, along with fishing, water toys, an on-site spa for massage and pampering, a gym and recreation area, and a coffee and ice-cream shop. $$.

Country Inn and Suites. 209 16th St. NE; (320) 632-1000; choicehotels.com. These hotel rooms range from double queens to whirlpool suites and one-bedroom king rooms with a sleeper sofa. Amenities include cookies at check-in, in-room microwave and minifridge, hot breakfast with waffles, and pet-friendly rooms. $$.

worth more time

Grab a stretch of the Soo Line Trail southwest of Little Falls for a couple of sweet small-town stops along the way. You can find the well-marked trailhead parking lot on the east side of US 10 just north of Royalton. Take the trail 2.3 miles southwest to the Mississippi River for a memorable trestle bridge ride above the 46-foot-high 1925 Blanchard Dam. The views are lovely, especially in the fall.

If you want a shorter ride or to drive to the dam, there are a few parking spots on either side of the river, but they can be rugged and aren't well marked. If you take an old strainer to the bank below the dam, you may get lucky and sift a staurolite (also known as fairy stones or cross rocks) from the silt.

From Blanchard Dam, continue 3.6 miles to Bowlus, where **Jordie's Trail Side Café** (320-584-8193; jordiestrailside.com) offers outdoor seating in its artsy gardens, homey antiques inside the cafe and a menu with breakfast omelets, hot sandwiches, burgers, salads, and homemade pies.

The trail continues 6.8 miles to Holdingford's **Art in Motion** (1400 Fourth St.; 320-746-0680; artinmotiononthelakewobegontrail.com). This surprising destination combines The Boho Café (a coffee shop and deli) with a beautifully designed spacious venue with murals and gallery art on exhibit. Outdoors, you can stroll through the gardens, catch live music on the weekends, and enjoy wood-fired pizzas. Keep rolling into Holdingford to reach the covered bridge across the South Two River with cows and farms as the backdrop and a funky sculpture telling the tale of the county. Serious cyclists can catch another 56 miles on the Lake Wobegon Trail, or you can return to Little Falls.

appendix a: regional information

north

day trip 01

Brainerd Lakes Area Welcome Center
7393 MN 371 South, Brainerd, MN
(218) 829-2838
explorebrainerdlakes.com

day trip 02

Nisswa Chamber of Commerce
25532 Main St., Nisswa, MN
(218) 963-2620
nisswa.com

Pequot Lakes Welcome Center
31095 Government Dr.
Pequot Lakes, MN
(218) 568-8911
pequotlakes.com

day trip 03

Cuyuna Lakes Chamber of Commerce
21236 Archibald Rd., Ironton, MN
(218) 546-8131
cuyunalakes.com

day trip 04

Mille Lacs Area Tourism Council
42099 MN 47, Isle, MN
(320) 676-9972
millelacs.com

day trip 05

Cloquet Area Tourism Office
225 Sunnyside Dr., Cloquet, MN
(218) 879-1551
visitcloquet.com

Hinckley Area Convention & Visitors Bureau
111 Main St. East, Hinckley, MN
(320) 384-0126
hinckleymn.com

Moose Lake Chamber of Commerce
4524 Arrowhead Ln., Moose Lake, MN
(218) 485-4145
mooselakechamber.com

Visit Sandstone
511 Main St., Sandstone, MN
(320) 245-2271
visitsandstonemn.com

day trip 06

Visit Duluth
345 S. Lake Ave., Duluth, MN
(218) 722-4011
visitduluth.com

northeast

day trip 01

Chisago Lakes Visitors Bureau
30525 Linden St., Lindstrom, MN
(651) 257-1177
chisagolakes.org

Falls Chamber of Commerce
106 S. Washington St., St. Croix Falls, WI
(715) 483-3580
fallschamber.org

day trip 02

Cable Area Chamber of Commerce
13380 CR M, Cable, WI
(715) 798-3833
cable4fun.com

Hayward Area Chamber of Commerce
15805 US 63, Hayward, WI
(715) 634-8662
haywardareachamber.com

east

day trip 01

Discover Stillwater
333 Main St. North, Stillwater, MN
(651) 351-1717
discoverstillwater.com

day trip 02

Go Chippewa County
1 N. Bridge St., Chippewa Falls, WI
(715) 723-0331
visitchippewafallswi.com

Menomonie Area Chamber & Visitor Center
1125 N. Broadway St., Ste. 3,
Menomonie, WI
(715) 235-9087
menomoniechamber.org

Visit Eau Claire
128 Graham Ave., Ste. 234, Eau Claire, WI
(715) 831-2345
visiteauclaire.com

southeast

day trip 01

Alma Area Chamber of Commerce
110 N. Main St., Alma, WI
(608) 685-3303
almawisconsin.com

Visit Pepin County
740 Seventh Ave. West, Durand, WI
(715) 672-7242
visitpepincounty.com

day trip 02

Red Wing Visitors and Convention Bureau
439 Main St., Red Wing, MN
(651) 385-5934
redwing.org

day trip 03

Visit Lake City
100 E. Lyon Ave., Lake City, MN
(877) 525-3248
visitlakecity.org

Wabasha-Kellogg Area Chamber of Commerce
257 Main St. West, Wabasha, MN
(651) 565-4158
wabashamn.org

day trip 04

Winona Visitor Center
924 Huff St., Winona, MN
(507) 452-2278
visitwinona.com

day trip 05

Lanesboro Area Chamber of Commerce
100 Milwaukee Rd., Lanesboro, MN
(507) 467-2696
lanesboro.com

south

day trip 01

Minnesota's Rochester
30 Civic Center Dr. SE., Rochester, MN
(507) 288-4331
experiencerochestermn.com

day trip 02

Northfield Convention and Visitor's Bureau
19 Bridge Square, Northfield, MN
(507) 645-5604
visitnorthfield.com

day trip 03

Faribault Area Chamber of Commerce and Tourism
530 Wilson Ave., Faribault, MN
(507) 334-4381
visitfaribault.com

Owatonna Area Chamber of Commerce and Tourism
320 Hoffman Dr., Owatonna, MN
(800) 423-6466
visitowatonna.org

southwest

day trip 01

Jordan City Hall
210 E. First St., Jordan, MN
(952) 492-2355
jordanmn.gov

St. Peter Tourism and Visitors Bureau
101 S. Front St., St. Peter, MN
(507) 934-3400
stpeterchamber.com

day trip 02

New Ulm Chamber of Commerce and Visitor Center
1 Minnesota St., New Ulm, MN
(507) 233-4300
newulm.com

west

day trip 01

Willmar Lakes Area Convention & Visitors Bureau
2104 US 12, Willmar, MN
(320) 235-3552
willmarlakesarea.com

northwest

day trip 01

Visit Greater St. Cloud
1411 W. St. Germain St., St. Cloud, MN
(320) 251-4170
visitstcloud.com

day trip 02

Visit Greater St. Cloud
1411 W. St. Germain St., St. Cloud, MN
(320) 251-4170
visitstcloud.com

Visit Joetown
Joetown.org

day trip 03

Explore Alexandria Tourism
324 Broadway St., Alexandria, MN
(320) 763-0102
explorealex.com

day trip 04

Visit Little Falls
606 SE First St., Little Falls, MN
(320) 616-4959
littlefallsmn.com

appendix b: festivals & celebrations

Sometimes events are so big, they become part of a town's identity. Think Grandma's Marathon on the North Shore; the Birkebeiner in Cable, WI. These are the events that bring people from around the state and around the world. You can celebrate everything from bald eagles and rhubarb to Shakespeare and the defeat of outlaws. This list is by no means complete, but it's a good seasonal sampling to get you started.

For more details and additional festivals, go to exploreminnesota.com or travelwisconsin.com.

january

Brainerd Jaycees Ice-Fishing Extravaganza. Brainerd, MN; icefishing.org. About 7,000 participants come from several states away to grab one or more of the 10,000 holes drilled into Hole in the Day Bay on Gull Lake. Winners can drive home a new truck or ATV or score ice-fishing gear and other big prizes that make this one of the world's largest charitable ice-fishing contests.

John Beargrease Sled Dog Marathon. Duluth, MN; (218) 461-1834; beargrease.com. This famed late-January race includes a 390-Mile Marathon and a 150-Mile Mid-Distance Race that run along the North Shore of Lake Superior. Onlookers can become volunteers or visit the Cutest Puppy Contest, attend opening ceremonies, and meet mushers in Duluth before it kicks off. Winners can qualify for the Iditarod.

Sandstone Ice Festival. Sandstone, MN; sandstoneicefest.com. This event in Robinson Park includes ice climbing, winter camping, skijoring, snowshoeing, cross-country skiing, and dogsledding.

february

American Birkebeiner. Cable, WI; (715) 634-5025; birkie.com. More than 9,000 cross-country skiers from around the world meet in Wisconsin's north woods for North America's largest cross-country ski marathon. The 50-kilometer (32-mile) race runs from Cable to the finish line in downtown Hayward. The "Birkie" is part of the Worldloppet, a circuit of 15 Nordic ski races held on four continents. It's the largest cross-country ski marathon in the nation.

Grumpy Old Men Festival. Wabasha, MN; (651) 565-4158, wabashamn.org. The town that inspired *Grumpy Old Men* celebrates winter with an ice-shack contest, Frisbee games, golf tournaments on snow, birdwatching, and a spaghetti dinner and dance.

march

International Festival of Owls. Houston. (507) 896-6957; festivalofowls.com. The Home of the International Owl Center brings owl lovers together in early March to meet resident owls and learn more about these unique birds.

april

Bluff Country Studio Art Tour. Southeastern Minnesota; (507) 452-0735; bluffcountry studioarttour.com. More than two dozen artist studios and galleries stay open for this three-day event the last weekend of the month in the Lanesboro, Harmony, and Winona areas. Artwork includes paintings, pottery, jewelry, weaving, quilting, beads, wood carving, and multimedia projects.

may

Kettle River Paddle Festival. Sandstone, MN; kettleriverpaddlefest.com. With spring waters rushing, this festival includes the Kettle River Run with a kayak, canoe, and raft race; a whitewater rodeo; paddling films; and fireworks in downtown Sandstone.

100-Mile Garage Sale. Hastings to Winona; (507) 452-0735; facebook.com/official100 milegaragesale. You can mix a scenic road trip with bargain hunting the first weekend in May when 15 Mississippi River towns host citywide garage sales. They range from Hastings south to Winona on the Minnesota side and across to Wisconsin from Fountain City to Prescott.

june

Grandma's Marathon. Duluth, MN; (218) 727-0947; grandmasmarathon.com. Usually the second weekend in June, the Grandma's Marathon 26.2-mile route from Two Harbors to Canal Park ranks among the largest marathons in the country and one of its largest multi-race festivals. The 2022 races drew more than 21,000 participants from every state and 60 different countries.

Granite City Days. St. Cloud, MN; (320) 255-7201; granitecitydays.com. This four-day event kicks off with a concert and art show and includes a downtown parade, community block party, canoe paddle down the Sauk River, music, and an outdoor expo at Lake George.

Great River Shakespeare Festival. Winona, MN; (507) 474-7900; grsf.org. Starting in late June and running for about six weeks, this festival includes professional productions of Shakespeare's plays. They change from year to year and usually include a mix of tragedy and more lighthearted productions performed at Winona State University.

Nisswa-Stämman Scandinavian Folk Music Festival. Nisswa, MN; (218) 764-2994; nisswastamman.org. The Pioneer Village comes to life with three stages filled with Swedish,

Finnish, Danish, and Norwegian music, dancing, and singing. About 150 folk musicians participate.

Rhubarb Festival. Lanesboro, MN; (507) 467-2696; facebook.com/people/Lanesboro -Rhubarb-Festival/100093228128911. The first Saturday in June belongs to the sweet-tart plant that made this the Rhubarb Capital of Minnesota. Events at Sylvan Park include rhubarb golf, a rhubarb stalk throw, and cooking contests with soups, chutneys, sauces, jams, and chili.

Rochesterfest. Rochester, MN; (507) 285-8769; rochesterfest.com. This weeklong city-wide celebration includes dances, concerts, plays and musicals, special tours of Mayowood, a kennel club carnival, Frisbee dogs in action, a treasure hunt, a grand parade, and a moon-light launch of hot air balloons.

july

Bavarian Blast. New Ulm, MN; (507) 359-2222; bavarianblast.com. Grab the lederhosen for New Ulm's biggest German celebration of the year. This mid-July weekend includes a grand parade, sauerkraut-eating contest, plus musicians from Germany, regional musicians, beer tents, craft shows, and children's games. Look for appearances by the town's gnomes and Narren, characters that wear traditional carved wooden masks.

Bean Hole Days. Pequot Lakes, MN; pequotlakes.com. More than 3,000 people line up for free bowls of the town's prized beans, which are cooked in giant cast-iron pots under-ground for 18 hours at Trailside Park. The tradition (and secret recipe) goes back more than 70 years and anchors a weekend of events that include a coronation, music, and a hunt for a hidden paddle.

Fourth Fest. Duluth, MN; (218) 722-5573; visitduluth.com. This daylong music and food fest at Bayfront Park ends with the largest fireworks show in the Upper Midwest. About 40,000 pounds of pyrotechnics explode and shower across Duluth Harbor, synchronized to music.

Honor the Earth Pow-wow. Hayward, WI; (715) 634-8934; haywardlakes.com. One of the largest powwows in North America takes place the third weekend in July and brings in 10,000 participants and spectators from across the country, Canada, and beyond. The gath-ering honors Mother Earth and the Creator with traditional drumming, dancing, and singing, plus crafts and food, a coronation, and a traditional arts cooking contest.

Lumberjack World Olympics. Hayward, WI; (715) 634-2484; lumberjackworldchampion ships.com. Lumberjacks and lumberjills from the United States, Canada, Australia, and New Zealand compete and show off their strength, agility, and speed with events such as sawing, logrolling, axe-throwing, and pole climbing.

Moose Lake Agate Days. Moose Lake, MN; (218) 485-4145; mooselakechamber.com. You'll find traditional elements of a celebration such as music, a car show, and an art show, but there's also a gem and mineral show throughout the weekend and a hunt for agates in downtown.

august

Bayfront Blues Festival. Duluth, MN; (715) 817-6933; bayfrontblues.com. One of the largest outdoor music festivals in the Midwest brings together 30 national performances on two concert stages with Lake Superior in the background. Additional weekend events include a Moonlight Mardi Gras Cruise and live blues at nearly 20 Duluth nightclubs.

Lucas Oil NHRA Nationals. Brainerd, MN; (218) 824-7223; brainerdraceway.com. More than 100,000 fans pack the stands at Brainerd International Raceway for Minnesota's biggest car-racing event. The full-throttle rumble of engines can be heard from miles away.

september

Carlos Creek Winery Grape Stomp. Alexandria, MN; (320) 846-5443; ccwgrapestomp .com. Huge and sprawling, this winery hosts one of the state's biggest events with its annual September Grape Stomp with multiple live bands, artists, and even an *I Love Lucy* look-alike contest. The dress division in the Grape Stomp contest could be one of Minnesota's most creative ways to trash a wedding dress—or at least give it a new color.

Chequamegon Fat Tire Festival. Cable, WI; (952) 229-7330; cheqmtb.com. This weekend of mountain biking events is anchored by a 40-mile race with about 1,850 competitors, with another 900 riders in The Short & Fat, a 16-mile race through the forest.

Defeat of Jesse James Days. Northfield, MN; (507) 645-5604; djjd.org. About 150,000 people come to this event the weekend after Labor Day to see townspeople reenact the James Gang's notorious 1876 bank raid. There's also a PRCA rodeo, old-time tractor pull, midway, parade, and arts and crafts show.

Little Falls Arts & Crafts Fair. Little Falls, MN; (320) 632-5155; littlefallsmnchamber.com. The weekend after Labor Day, more than 600 juried arts and craft exhibitors sell pottery, paintings, jewelry, clothing, rugs, furniture, and more at Minnesota's most legendary art show.

Rock Bend Folk Festival. St. Peter, MN; rockbend.org. Thousands of people gather along the Minnesota River each September for this free two-day festival. There are two stages going all weekend with a variety of music, along with family activities at Minnesota Square Park.

october

Duluth Haunted Ship. Duluth, MN; (218) 722-7876; duluthhauntedship.com. This retired ore ship offers an extra dose of eerie and puts a different spin on a typical walk through a Halloween haunted house. The event runs throughout the month until Halloween.

Harvest Fest and Giant Pumpkin Weigh-Off. Stillwater, MN; harvestfeststillwater.com. The biggest pumpkins in the Midwest are brought to the shores of the St. Croix River for a weigh-off. The world record of 1,810.5 pounds was set here in 2010. The event includes vendors, a street dance, a pumpkin drop, carving demonstrations, a chili feed, beer and wine tasting, gondola and trolley rides, and even a regatta for folks game enough to paddle a carved-out pumpkin down the river.

november

Bentleyville. Duluth, MN; bentleyvilleusa.org. The free Bentleyville Tour of Lights, Thanksgiving through Christmas, transforms Bayfront Park into an illuminated wonderland with a castle, replicas of the lift bridge and ore boats, and lights that synchronize with music. Bonfires are kept blazing for warmth and roasting marshmallows.

Kiwanis Holiday Lights. Mankato, MN; (507) 385-9129; kiwanisholidaylights.com. This free wonderland of lights transforms Sibley Park's trees and many acres into a holiday wonderland that's free to visit by foot or a drive-through route. Watch for live reindeer too.

december

Lucia Dagen. Scandia, MN; (651) 433-5053; gammelgardenofscandia.org. Lucia with her wreath of candles appears for this traditional Lucia Day service in the Gammelgården Museum's historic Gammel Krykan, the oldest surviving Lutheran sanctuary in Minnesota. The Swedish celebration includes a Swedish breakfast buffet and Lucia program by the Svenskarnasdag Choir in the community center across the street.

index

14 Lakes Brewery, 20
22 Northmen brewery, 200
100-Mile Garage Sale, 215

A

Aamodt's Apple Farm, 79
Aamodt's Hot Air Balloons, 81
Abbey Guest House, 196
Acoustic Café, The, 126
Action City, 92
Adventure to Go, 10
Agate and Geological Interpretive
    Center, 41
Agate Days, 41, 217
agates, 41, 53, 217
Albany, MN, 194
Alec's Nine, 32
Alexander Mansion B&B, 127
Alexandria Boat Works, 200
Alexandria Lakes Area Chamber of
    Commerce, 213
Alexandria, MN, 198, 213, 217
Allen, Rick, 53
Alma Chamber of Commerce, 211
Alma, WI, 97, 102, 103, 211
America's Dairyland, 84
AmericInn, 208
AmericInn by Wyndham Little Falls, 208
AmericInn Wabasha, 120
Amish Backroads Tour by R&M, 130
Angel Hill, 62
Angry Minnow Restaurant & Brewery,
    The, 72
Ann Bean Mansion, 82
antiques, 37, 54, 77, 80, 111
Antiques America, 37

Anton's Restaurant, 188
A-Pine Family Restaurant, 17
Appeldoorn's Sunset Bay Resort, 27
Arch + Cable, 171
Aroma Pie Shoppe, 132
Arrowwood Lodge at Brainerd Lakes, 9
Arrowwood Resort & Conference
    Center, 202
Art and Heritage Place, 193
Art Dock, 53
Art in Motion, 209
Artisan Forge Studios, 92
AtoZ Bakery—The Pizza Farm, 104
At Sara's Table Chester Creek Café, 58
A.T. The Black and White, 207
Audubon Cooperative Sanctuary, 147
Audubon Signature Sanctuary, 12
Avon, MN, 194

B

Back Alley, The, 48
Back Shed Brewing, 186
Backus, MN, 7
Backwards Bread Company, 188
Bad Habit Brewing Company, 193
Banning State Park, 39
Bar Harbor Supper Club, 7
Barnum, MN, 39
Bass Lake, 32
Bavarian Blast, 216
Baxter, MN, 6, 9
Bayfront Blues Festival, 217
Bayfront Park, 216, 218
Bayview Bar and Grill, 26
Bean Hole Days, 17, 216
Beaver Islands, 188

Beaver Island Trail, 186
Bella Cucina, 196
Bentleyville, 218
Bentleyville Tour of Lights, 50
Bent Paddle Brewing, 48
Bent River Outfitters, 167
Berwood Hill Inn, 133
Best Western Plus Kelly Inn, 190
Big Axe Brewing, 13
Big Fish Golf Club (golf course), 71
Big Fun Tuesdays (Crosslake, MN), 19
Big Kahuna Fun Park, 180
Big Ole, 198
Big Woods, 146, 162
Bingham Hall B&B, 176
Birke, 74
Birkebeiner, 69, 214
Birke Trail, 74
Black Bear Casino Resort, 42, 43
Black Brook (golf course), 24
Black Pine Beach Resort, 20
Blaschko's Embassy Bar, 164
Bleu Duck Kitchen, 141
Bloedow Bakery, 126
The Blue Door Inn, 104
Blue Heron Coffeehouse, 126
Blue Heron Trading Company, 53
Bluff Country Studio Art Tour, 215
Bluffscape Amish Tours, 130
Bobby's Legacy, 12
Bold North Cellars, 200
Boyd Lodge, 21
Brainerd, MN, 12, 210, 214, 217
Brainerd International Raceway, 4, 217
Brainerd Jaycees $150,000 Ice-Fishing
    Extravaganza, 9, 214
Brainerd Lakes, 12, 34, 210
Brainerd Lakes Area Welcome Center,
    6, 210
Brainerd Zip Line Tour, 5
Bravo Burritos, 189
Breezy Belle Cruise, 18
Breezy Point, MN, 17

Breezy Point Resort, 19
The Brewing Projekt, 93
Brick House Café, 75
Bridge Street Art & Gifts Cooperative, 88
Broken Paddle Guiding, 117
Brown County Historical Society, 174
Brunet Island State Park, 90
Buena Vista Park, 102
Bug-Bee Hive Resort, 182
Bunyan, Paul, 4, 7, 10, 17
Burlington Hotel & Bar, 105
Burton/Rosenmeier House, 205

C

Cabela's, 155
Cable Area Chamber of Commerce, 211
Cable Area Fall Color Tour, 74
Cable Natural History Museum, 74
Cable, WI, 69, 74, 211, 214, 217
Caddie Woodlawn Historical Park and
    State Wayside, 86
Caffè Strolaga, 207
Campfire Bay Resort, 208
Canadian Honker, The, 141
Canal Park, 44, 55
Canal Park Brewing Company, 53
Canal Park Lodge, 55
Cannon Falls, MN, 109
Cannon River, 144, 146, 147, 155
Cannon Valley Trail, 109
Caramel Roll Ride, 194
Carleton College, 144
Carleton College Cowling Arboretum, 146
Carlos, MN, 200
Carlos Creek Winery, 200
Carlos Creek Winery Grape Stomp, 217
Carlton, MN, 42, 43
Carlton County, 41
Carlton County Gem and Mineral Club, 41
Carriage House B&B, 127
Carson Park, 92, 93
Castlerock Museum, 103
caves, 131, 139

Cedar Rose Inn Bed and Breakfast, 202
Cedars Grille, 164
Cedar Valley Resort, 133
Cedarwood Family Restaurant, 26
Centerstone Plaza Hotel Soldiers
    Field, 142
Central Lakes Trail, 200
Chankaska Creek Ranch, Winery and
    Distillery, 169
Charles A. Lindbergh Historic Site, 205
Charles A. Lindbergh State Park, 205
Charlie's Irish Pub, 84
Chateau St. Croix Winery, 64
Chequamegon Area Mountain Bike
    Association, 75
Chequamegon Fat Tire Festival, 217
Chequamegon National Forest, 69
Chester's Kitchen and Bar, 141
Chickadee Cottage Café, 116
Children's Museum of Eau Claire, 92
Children's Museum of Southern
    Minnesota, 167
Chippewa Falls, WI, 84, 88, 211
Chippewa Falls Visitor Center, 211
Chippewa Flowage, 74
Chippewa River, 84, 97
Chippewa River Distillery & Brewster Bros.
    Brewing, 89
Chippewa River State Trail, 87, 92
Chippewa Valley Museum, 92
Chippewa Valley Railroad, 93
Chippewa Valley Trails, 93
Chisago City, MN, 68
Chisago Lakes Visitors Bureau, 211
Chocolate Escape, 119
Chocolate Ox, The, 11
Chocolaterie Stam, 142
Chris-Craft, 200
Clamshell Beach Resort, 22
Classic, The (golf course), 10, 12
Clear Waters Outfitting, 186
Clemens Gardens, 188
Cloquet, MN, 41, 210

Cloquet Area Chamber of
    Commerce, 210
Cloquet-Carlton, MN, 35, 42
Cloquet/Duluth KOA Journey, 43
Club XIX, 26
Clyde Ironworks, 49
Cochrane, WI, 104
Coffee Mill Golf, 118
Coffee Mill Ski Area, 118
Cold Spring, MN, 198
Collective Charm, 88
Collegeville, MN, 191
Collegeville Orchards, 193
Colvill Park, 109
Commonweal Theatre Company, 130
Contented Cottage Bed and
    Breakfast, 150
Contented Cow, The, 148
Cork and Cask, 187
Costa's Candies, 156
Cottonwood River, 173
Counterpoint II and Counterpoint
    Home, 140
Country Fest, 88
Country Inn and Suites, 208
Cragun's Resort, 6, 9, 12
Crane Meadows National Wildlife
    Refuge, 205
Cray Computers, 88
Crosby, MN, 28
Crosby Memorial Park, 32
cross-country skiing, 6, 25, 27, 35, 38,
    42, 69, 84, 87, 109, 124, 146, 154,
    173, 182, 187, 200, 214
Crosslake, MN, 17, 19
Cross Lake Recreation Area, 20
Crosslake Welcome Center, 19
Crow River, 181
Crow Wing State Park, 5
Crystal Cave, 86
Cuyuna Brewing Company, 33
Cuyuna Country State Recreation
    Area, 30

Cuyuna Cove, 34
Cuyuna Lakes Chamber of
    Commerce, 210
Cuyuna Meets the World Murals, 32
Cuyuna Outfitters, 31
Cuyuna Range, 28
Cykel, 31

D
Da Boathouse Restaurant and Bar, 27
Dakota, 162, 164, 174, 182
Dalles House Restaurant and Lounge, 66
Dalles of the St. Croix, 62, 63
Damage Boardshop, 48
Danbury, WI, 37
Dancing Dragonfly Winery, 64
Danzinger Vineyards & Winery, 103
Darn Knit Anyway, 80
Deacon's Lodge Golf Course, 19
Deep Freeze, The, 182
Deerwood, MN, 32, 33, 34
Defeat of Jesse James Days, 217
Depot Bar and Grill, 154
Depot Smokehouse & Tavern, 201
Devil's Punchbowl, 86
DeWitt-Seitz Building, 53
Diamond Dust Bakery and Coffee
    Shop, 164
Dickerson's Lake Florida Resort, 181
Dixon's Autumn Harvest Winery, 89
Dock Café, 81
Domacín Restaurant and Wine Bar, 81
Domeier's German Store, 173
Donahue's Greenhouse, 153
Douglas Area Trail Association
    network, 200
downhill skiing, 6, 47
Downtown Little Falls, 206
Driftless Fly Fishing Company, 134
Drive In, The, 64
driving, xiv
Duluth, MN, 28, 39, 46, 47, 56, 211, 214,
    215, 216, 217, 218

Duluth Children's Museum, 48
Duluth Convention & Visitors Bureau, 211
Duluth Entertainment Convention
    Center, 51
Duluth Folk School, 48
Duluth Grill, 49
Duluth Pack, 53
Dunmire's on the Lake, 8
Dutch Legacy, 12
Dylan, Bob, 175

E
eagles, 97, 103, 109, 112, 114, 119,
    158, 214
East Gull Lake, MN, 8, 9
East Gull Lake Trail, 5
Eau Claire, WI, 84, 91, 211
Eau Claire Area Convention and Visitors
    Bureau, 211
Eau Claire Cheese and Deli, 94
Eau Claire River, 93
Eau Claire Sculpture Tour, 93
Eddy's, 26
Eddy's Interlachen Inn, 201
Edgewater Hotel & Waterpark, 58
Ellsworth Cooperative Creamery, 87
El Rancho Manana Campground, 197
Empire Builder, 109, 124
Enger Park, 46
Enger Park Golf Course, 46
Enger Tower, 46
Ernie's on Gull, 8
The Estates Bed and Breakfast, 197
Express Suites Riverport Inn, 127

F
Fairfax, MN, 174
Fairfield Inn and Suites, 150
Falconer Vineyards, 109
Falls Chamber of Commerce, 211
Faribault, MN, 151, 212
Faribault Chamber of Commerce, 212
Faribault Woolen Mill Co., The, 153

Father Hennepin State Park, 27
Fawn-Doe-Rosa Wildlife Educational
    Park, 65
Feed Mill Restaurant, 160
Fergus Falls, MN, 200
Ferguson's Minnesota Harvest, 160
Fielders Choice Tap & Table, 148
Filmore County, 131
Fine Line Salon and Spa, 34
Finlayson, MN, 40
Fires of 1918 Museum, 41
fishing, 9, 11, 24, 27, 38, 71, 103, 155,
    165, 206
fishing guides, 11
Fitger's, 51, 53
Fitger's Inn, 56
Flandrau State Park, 173
Flour and Flower, 196
Folsom House, 62
Fond du Lac Band of Ojibwe, 43
Forager Brewery, 142
Forestville/Mystery Cave State Park, 135
Fort Alexandria, 201
Fort Ridgely State Park and Historic
    Site, 174
Fort Ripley, 206
Fountain City, WI, 97, 105, 106, 215
Four Daughters Vineyard and Winery, 135
Fourth Fest, 216
Franconia, MN, 63
Franconia Sculpture Park, 63
Freeport, MN, 194
Freshwater Fishing Hall of Fame and
    Museum, 71
Frontenac, MN, 116
Frontenac State Park, 116
Frost River, 48

G
Gag, Wanda, 175
gambling, 25, 26, 37, 42, 43
Gammelgården Museum, 67, 218
Gandy Dancer Trail, 37

Ganley's Restaurant, 13
Garden Bar In 6th, The, 201
Garland, Judy, 175
Garmisch USA Resort, 75
Garrison, MN, 24
Garvin Heights, 121
Garvin Heights Vineyards, 124
General Andrews State Forest, 40
George's Fine Steaks and Spirits, 175
George's Vineyards, 148
Getaway Kettle River, 40
Glacial Lake Duluth, 41
Glacial Lakes Scenic Byway, 178
Glacial Lakes State Trail, 180, 182
Glacial Pothole Trail, 63
Glacial Waters Spa, 11
Glädje, 67
Glensheen Mansion, 56
Glenwood, MN, 203
Glockenspiel, 173
Goat Ridge Brewing Company, 182
Goldstrand, Joel, 32, 37
golfing, 9, 10, 12, 14, 26, 34, 37, 46, 71,
    118, 147, 202, 203, 215
Gonda Building, 140
Gondola Romantica, 81
Good Ol' Days Resort, 14
Gordy's Hi-Hat, 43
Gordy's Warming House, 43
Govin's Farm, 86
Grand Casino Hinckley, 37, 39
Grand Casino Mille Lacs, 25, 26
Grand Casino Mille Lacs Buffet, 27
Grand Center for Arts & Culture, The, 173
Grande Depot, The, 187
Grand Hotel, 173
Grandma's Marathon, 54, 214, 215
Grandma's Saloon & Grill, 54
Grand National Golf Course, 37
Grand View Lodge, 14, 19
Granite City Days, 215
Granite City Food & Brewery, 189
Great Alma Fishing Float, 103

Greater Menomonie Area Chamber of Commerce & Visitor Center, 211
Great Hinckley Fire, 41
Great Lakes Aquarium, 50
Great River Arts Association, 206
Great River Bluff State Park, 124
Great River Children's Museum, 187
Great River Road, 97, 114
Great River Shakespeare Festival, 121, 124, 215
Green Lake, 180
Green Lake Cruises, 180
Grindstone Lake, 40
Grumpy Old Men, 117, 119, 153, 214
Grumpy Old Men Festival, 117, 214
Gull Lake, 6, 9, 13, 14, 214
Gull Lake Cruises, 5
Gull Lake Recreational Area, 5
Gustaf's on Main Eatery, 68
Gustavus Adolphus College, 162

H

Hackensack, MN, 7
Hager City, MN, 111
Hairy Mosquito Trading Post, 25
Half Moon Lake, 92, 93
Hallett Antique Mall, 32
Hanabi Japanese Cuisine, 54
Hanisch Bakery and Coffee Shop, 111
Happy's Drive-In, 26
Harbor 360, 53
Harbor Hill Inn, 102
Harbor Restaurant, Bar & Marina, 111
Harborview Café, 102
Harkin General Store, 174
Harmony, MN, 131, 215
Harmony-Preston Trail, 132
Harmony-Preston Valley State Trail, 134
Harvest Fest and Giant Pumpkin Weigh-Off, 218
Hawk Ridge Bird Observatory, 56
Hawk's View Lodges & Cottages, 106
Hayward, WI, 69, 211, 214, 216, 217
Hayward KOA Holiday, 73
Hayward Lakes, 69, 75
Hayward Lakes Visitors and Convention Bureau, 71, 211
Heartland Kitchen, 33
Heartland Trail, 7
Heirloom Seasonal Bistro, 126
Hemker Park Zoo, 195
He Mni Can (Barn Bluff), 109
Henderson, MN, 158, 161
Henderson RoadHaus, 162
heritage tree, 173
Hermann Monument, 173
Hermann the German, 171
HideAway Coffeehouse and Wine Bar, The, 148
High Court Pub, 132
Hill Museum and Manuscript Library, 193
Hilton Garden Inn, 190
Hinckley, MN, 35, 47, 210
Hinckley Convention & Visitors Bureau, 210
Hinckley Fire Museum, 37
Historic Anderson Hotel House, 120
Historic Forestville, 135
Historic Hutchinson House, 154
Historic Scanlan House B&B Inn, 133
Hobgoblin Music and Stoney End Harps, 109
Hoffman Hills State Recreation Area, 86
Hok-Si-La Municipal Park, 116
Hole in the Day Bay, 9, 214
Honor the Earth Pow-wow, 216
Hotel Crosby, 82
The Hudson, 33

I

Ice Age Interpretive Center, 65
Ice Age National Scenic Trail, 65
Ice Festival, 214
ice fishing, 9, 22, 206, 214
Imminent Brewing, 148
Indigenous First Art & Gifts, 53

Indigo Swan Jewelry and Fine Art, 99
Inn on Lake Superior, The, 56
International Paralympic, 69
Interstate State Park—Minnesota, 63
Interstate State Park—Wisconsin, 65
Iron Range Eatery, 33
Ironton, MN, 28, 210
Irvine Park & Zoo, 88
Irvin Haunted Ship, 218
Isle Bakery, 27
Isle, MN, 24, 27, 210
Izaty's golf courses, 24
Izatys Resort, 26

J

Jack's 18, 32
Jacob Leinenkugel Brewing Company, 90
James, Jesse, 146, 217
James Krom Natural Images Art Museum
    Gallery, 141
Jay Cooke State Park, 35, 39, 42, 43
Jenkins, MN, 7, 17
John Beargrease Sled Dog Marathon, 214
John Hall's Alaska Lodge, 117
Jordan Chamber of Commerce, 212
Jordan, MN, 158, 212
Jordie's Trail Side Café, 209
Journey Inn, 100
Jules' Bistro, 189
Juneberry Cafe, 64
Juniper's Restaurant, 132
Jupiter Moon, 196

K

Kahler Grand Hotel, 142
Kashubian Cultural Institute and Polish
    Museum, 125
Käthe Wohlfarht of America, 80
Kavanaugh's Sylvan Lake Resort, 9
Kay's Kitchen, 196
Keepsake Cidery, 149
Kellogg, MN, 118
Kensington Runestone, 198, 201

Kerfoot Canopy Tours, 161
Kettle River, 38, 39, 40, 215
Kettle River Paddle Festival, 215
Kettle River Run, 215
Kinstone, 105
Kiwanis Mountain Bike Trail and Skills
    Park, 169
Knotty Pine Bakery, 8
Konsbruck Hotel, 164
Krewe, 196

L

La Ferme, 201
Lake Agnes, 201
Lake Andrew, 182
Lake Avenue Restaurant and Bar, 54
Lake Byllesby Campground, 150
Lake Byllesby Campground" . 7650, 151
Lake Carlos, 200, 201
Lake Carlos State Park, 200
Lake City, MN, 114, 212
Lake City Tourism Bureau, 212
Lake Country Craft and Cones, 20
Lake Darling, 202
Lake Florida, 181
Lake George, 215
Lake Koronis, 182
Lake L'Homme Dieu, 201, 202
Lake Minnewaska, 203
Lake O' the Dalles, 65
Lake Owen, 75
Lake Park, 123
Lake Pepin, 97, 101, 114, 116, 119, 215
Lake Pepin Pearl Button Company, 116
Lakers, 52
Lakeside Antiques, 116
Lake Superior, 51, 52, 56, 206, 214, 217
Lake Superior Art Glass, 53
Lake Superior & Mississippi Railroad, 46
Lake Superior Railroad Museum, 50
Lake Superior Tug, 51
Lake Superior Zoo, 46
Lakeview Drive Inn, 126

Lakewalk, 51, 55, 56
Lake Winona, 202
Lake Wissota, 88, 90, 91
Lake Wissota State Park, 90
Lake Wobegon Trail, 194, 200
Land of Memories Park, 167
Lanesboro Area Chamber of
    Commerce, 212
Lanesboro Art Gallery, 131
Lanesboro Farmers' Market, 131
Lanesboro, MN, 212, 215, 216
Lanesboro Pastry Shoppe, 133
LARK Toys, 117, 118
Larson Boatworks, 200, 206
Laura Ingalls Wilder Historic Highway, 101
Laura Ingalls Wilder Museum, 101
Lazy Moose Grill, 41
Legacy of the Lakes Museum, 200
Legacy, The (golf course), 9
Leif Erickson Rose Garden, 51
Lenora Stone Church, 130
Leo's Grill and Malt Shop, 81
Lindbergh, Charles, 203, 205
Lindström Bakery, 68
Lindstrom Historical Walking Tour, 67
Lindstrom, MN, 60
Links Lodge Hotel, 26
Linnaeus Arboretum, 163
Lismore Hotel, 94
Little Angie's Cantina and Grill, 55
Little Crow Lakes, 178
Little Crow Ski Team, 181
Little Falls Arts and Crafts Fair, 206
Little Falls Arts & Crafts Fair, 217
Little Falls Bakery and Deli, 207
Little Falls Convention and Visitors
    Bureau, 205, 213
Little Falls, MN, 203, 213, 217
Little House Wayside, 101
Little Larke Bakery, 100
Little River General Store, 132
The Livery Restaurant and Saloon, 94
Local 218, The, 8

The Local Blend, 196
Lola—An American Bistro, 176
Lolo American Kitchen and Craft Bar, 82
Long Lake, 197
Loon Liquors, 149
Loopy's Saloon & Grill, 90
Loopy's Tube & Canoe Rentals, 90
Lora Hotel, 82
Love Creamery, 49
Lowell Inn, The, 83
Lower Cullen Lake, 14
Lower Sioux Agency Historic Site, 174
Lucas Oil NHRA Nationals, 4, 217
Lucia Dagen, 218
The Lucky Duck, 181
Lucky's Tavern, 18
Lumberjack World Olympics, 71, 217
Lundrigans, 11
Lure Lakebar, 202

M

Mabel Tainter Center for the Arts, 87
MacDaddy's Donut Garage, 33
Madden's, 12
Madden's on Gull Lake, 10
Maiden Rock, WI, 100, 101
Maiden Rock Bluff State Natural Area, 99
Maiden Rock Inn, 101
Maiden Rock Winery and Cidery, 100
Main Street Alehouse, 13
Makeshift Accessories Gallery &
    Studio, 147
Malt-O-Meal Company, 144
Mango Thai, 142
Manhattan Beach, MN, 17
Mankato Brewery, 169
Mankato, MN, 167, 168
Maritime Museum, 50
Martin's Sports Shop, 12
Mason Shoe Outlet Store, 90
MatchStick Restaurant and Spirits, 82
Maucieri's Italian Bistro & Deli, 20
Mayo, Charlie, 139, 140

Mayo Clinic, 140
Mayo Clinic Heritage Hall, 140
Mayo Historical Suite, 140
Mayowood Mansion, 139, 216
McCormick House Inn, 73
McQuoid's Inn, 28
Mdewakanton Dakota, 25
Melrose, MN, 194
Melva Lind Interpretive Center, 163
Mennonites, 84
Menomonie, WI, 84, 211
Merchant's Bank, 123
Merrick State Park, 106
Merrifield, MN, 7, 10, 11
Midtown Antique Mall, 80
Milk and Honey Ciders, 193
Mille Lacs Area Tourism Council, 210
Mille Lacs Band of Ojibwe, 24, 25, 37
Mille Lacs Indian Museum and Trading
    Post, 25
Mille Lacs Kathio State Park, 25
Mille Lacs Lake, MN, 22, 24, 27, 210
Mille Lacs Soo Line Trail, 25
Mineral Springs Brewery, 156
minigolf, 4, 7, 47, 58, 64, 92, 118, 180
Minnemishinona Falls, 168
Minneopa State Park, 168
Minnesota Department of Natural
    Resources, xv, 38
Minnesota Fishing Museum and Hall of
    Fame, 206
Minnesota Historical Society, xvi, 24, 205
Minnesota Marine Art Museum, 125
Minnesota Military Museum, 206
Minnesota Music Hall of Fame, 175
Minnesota Office of Tourism, xv
Minnesota River, 158, 174, 218
Minnesota River State Recreation
    Area, 161
Minnesota River Trail, 169
Minnesota River Valley Scenic Byway, 168
Minnesota School of Diving, 31
Minnesota Ski Pass, 6

Minnesota's Largest Candy Store, 160
Minnesota Square Park, 218
Minnesota State Academy for the
    Deaf, 151
Minnesota Whitewater Rafting, 42
Miracle at Big Rock, 65
Mississippi River, 97, 102, 109, 114, 116,
    121, 124, 186, 188, 215
MN EIS, 176
MN Soulstice Boutique, 147
MN Traders Co, 18
Moccasin Bar, 71
Mona Lisa's, 94
Monarch Gift Shop, 147
Mont Du Lac Resort, 42
Moondance Inn, 112
Moonlite Bay Family Restaurant and
    Bar, 20
Moose Lake Brewing Company, 41
Moose Lake Chamber of Commerce,
    41, 210
Moose Lake City Campground, 41
Moose Lake Depot, 41
Moose Lake, MN, 35, 40, 210, 217
Moose Lake State Park, 41
Morgan Creek Vineyards and Winery, 176
Moulin Rouge B&B, 170
Mountain Villas, 47
Mount Kato Ski Area, 168
Mount Tom, 182
Munsinger Gardens, 188
Museum of Red Wing, 110
Music Loft, 110
muskies, 72
muskie, world's largest, 71
Mystery Cave, 131

N
Namekagon River, 69, 73
Namekagon River Visitor Center, 72
National Audubon Sanctuary, 24
National Eagle Center, 114, 117, 119
National Farmers' Bank, 155, 156

National Freshwater Fishing Museum Hall of Fame, 71
National Loon Center, 20
Neer Park, 181
Nelson Cheese Factory, 102
Nelson, WI, 104
Nemadji State Forest, 37
Nerstrand Big Wood State Park, 146
New London, MN, 178, 180, 181
New Ulm, MN, 171, 174, 213, 216
New Ulm Visitor Center, 213
Ney Nature Center, 161
Niagara Cave, 131
Nicolin Inn B&B, 161
Nicollet Bike & Ski Shop, 169
Nisswa Chamber of Commerce, 210
Nisswa Family Fun Waterpark, 11
Nisswa, MN, 6, 7, 9, 10, 11, 210, 216
Nisswa-Stämman Scandinavian Folk Music Festival, 216
Nisswa Totem Pole Boutique Marketplace, 12
Nobel Conference, 162
Nolabelle Kitchen and Bar, 170
Nordic Shop, The, 141
North Country Café, 33
Northern Lake Tavern and Grill, 68
Northern Pacific Center, 5
Northern Waters Smokehaus, 55
Northfield Arts Guild, 146
Northfield Convention and Visitors Bureau, 212
Northfield Historical Society Museum and Historic Bank Site, 146
Northfield, MN, 144, 212, 217
Northfield Yarn, 147
North Isle, MN, 28
North, John Wesley, 144
Northland Arboretum, 6
Northland Kart Kountry, 5
North Long Lake, 10
North Long Lake Beach, 10
North Shore Scenic Railroad, 51

Northwoods Pub at Grand View Lodge, 13
Norway Ridge Supper Club, 18
Nosh, 126
Notch 8, 8

O

Ohara, Japan, 46
Ojibwe, 24, 25, 37, 43, 93
Old Abe Trail, 90
Old Barn Resort, 135
Oldenburg House, 43
Oldenburg Point, 42
Old Fish, 206
Old Town, 168
Ole Store Restaurant, 149
Olson's Ice Cream, 90
OMC Smokehouse, 49
Onamia, MN, 24, 25
O'Neil Creek Winery, 89
O'Neil's Restaurant and Bar, 180
Osakis, MN, 194, 200
Osceola, WI, 66, 67
Osprey Wilds Environmental Learning Center, 40
Outlaw Trail, 146
Owatonna Area Chamber of Commerce and Tourism, 212
Owatonna, MN, 151, 155, 212
The Oxbow, 94

P

Pablo Center at the Confluence, 93
Palate, The, 100
Palmer House Hotel & Restaurant, The, 195
Panola Valley Gardens Tea, 69
Paradise Center for the Arts, 153
Paramount Arts Gallery & Gifts, 187
Park Point, 51, 56
Pasquale's Neighborhood Pizzeria, 142
Paul Bunyan Bike Trails, 10
Paul Bunyan Land, 5

Paul Bunyan Scenic Byway, 17, 19
Paul Bunyan Trail, 6, 7, 14
Paynesville, MN, 182
Peace Plaza, 144
Pedal Pusher's Café, 133
Pelican Lake, 19
Pepin Heights, 116
Pepin Visitor Information Center, 211
Pepin, WI, 97, 101, 211
Pequot Lakes, MN, 7, 11, 15, 18, 19,
    210, 216
Pequot Lakes Welcome Center, 210
Peterson, MN, 132
Peters Sunset Beach Resort, 202
Pezhekee Golf Course, 203
Pier B Resort Hotel, 56
Pillar Inn, The, 198
Pillsbury State Forest, 6
Pine Beach cross-country ski trails, 6
Pine Beach East, 12
Pine Beach Peninsula, 10
Pine Grove Zoo, 206
Pine Lake, 40
Pine River, MN, 7, 17
Pines Golf Course, The, 12
Pioneer Place on Fifth, 187
Pioneer Village, 216
Pirate's Cove, 7
pizza farms, 104
Pleasant Valley Orchard, 63
Pleasantview Bed and Breakfast, 91
Portage Trail, 41
Portsmouth Mine, 30
Pottery Place, 110
Pottery Place Antiques, 110
Prairie Island Campground, 127
Prairie Moon Museum & Sculpture
    Garden, 105
Pratt-Taber Inn, 112
Prescott, WI, 215
Preserve, The (golf course), 17
Preston, MN, 131, 135
Prince, 175

Q
Quarry Campground, 161
Quarry Hill Nature Center, 139
Quarry Park & Nature Preserve, 187
Quarterdeck Resort, 14

R
Ramone's Ice Cream Parlor, 94
Rare Pair, The, 147
Raw Deal, The, 87
Ray's Place, 94
Reads Landing Brewing Company, 119
Red Barn Pizza Farm, 149
Red Cedar River, 84
Red Cedar Trail, 87
Redemption Kitchen and Cocktails, 154
Red Head Creamery, 195
Red Jacket Bike Trail, 169
Red Jacket Trail, 86
Red Raven Bike and Coffee Shop, 31, 33
Red Rider Resort, 34
Red Wing Arts, 111
Red Wing Brewery, 111
Red Wing, MN, 107, 212
Red Wing pottery, 107, 110
Red Wing Shoe Store & Museum, 110
Red Wing Visitors and Convention
    Bureau, 211
Reptile and Amphibian Discovery (RAD)
    Zoo, 156
Reunion, 149
Revival Records, 93
Rhubarb Capital of Minnesota, 216
Rhubarb Festival, 216
Richard Dorer State Forest, 130
Richard J. Dorer Memorial Hardwood
    Forest, 132
Richmond, MN, 197
Rieck's Lake Park & Observation
    Deck, 103
River Bend Nature Center, 154
River Bend Winery & Distillery, 89
River Jams, 90

River Rock Coffee & Tea, 164
The Rivers Eatery at Ideal Market, 75
Riverside Bike & Skate, 93
Riverside Park, 188
Riverside Park Campground, 164
Rivertown Inn, 83
River Valley Folk School, 65
River View Campground, 156
Riverwalk Market Fair, 147
Riverwood Canoe Rental, 65
Robinson Park, 214
Robinson Quarry Park, 40
Rochester Art Center, 139
Rochester Convention and Visitors
    Bureau, 212
Rochesterfest, 216
Rochester, MN, 137, 212, 216
Rochester Trolley & Tour Company, 139
Rock Bend Folk Art Festival, 218
Rocque Ridge Guide and Outfitting
    Service, 90
Rolling Hills Arabians and Farm Tours, 25
Root River, 130, 132
Root River Inn & Suites, 133
Root River Outfitters, 132
Root River Valley Trail, 132
Round Barn Farm B&B, 112
Roundhouse Brewery, 13
Ruby's Dining Room at Ruttger's Bay
    Lake Lodge, 33
Rum River, 25
Runestone Museum, 201
Rusche, Herman, 106
Rushford, MN, 132
Rushing Rapids Scenic Byway, 43
Rush River Produce, 100
Russell J. Rassbach Heritage
    Museum, 87
Rustic Roots Winery, 67
Ruttger's Bay Lake Lodge, 32, 34
R.W. Lindholm Service Station, 43
Rølvaag, O. E., 146

S
Safari North Wildlife Park, 7
Saint John's Abbey, 196
Sakatah Lake State Park, 155
Sakatah Singing Hills State Trail, 153,
    154, 169
sales tax, xiii
Salties, 52
Sanchez Burrito, 208
SandBar and Grill, 91
Sandstone, MN, 35, 39, 210, 214, 215
Sapori di Sicilia, 127
Sauk Centre, MN, 194
Sauk River, 188, 215
Saulsbury Beach, 180
Scandia, MN, 218
Scarlet Kitchen and Bar, 111
Scheers Lumberjack Village, 72
Schell's Brewing Co., 175
Schlosstein, Fred, 106
SEMVA Art Gallery, 141
September Grape Stomp, 217
Seven Fires Steakhouse, 43
Seven Hawks Vineyards, 106
Seven Mile Creek, 163
Seven Mile Creek Park, 163
Shafer, MN, 63
Shattuck St. Mary's, 151
Sheldon Theatre, 110
Sherwood Forest North, 13
Shift Cyclery and Coffee Bar, 94
Shirley Mae's Outfitters, 207
Sibley Park and Petting Zoo, 168
Sibley State Park, 180, 181
Siiviis and Sivertson Gallery, 53
Silver Lake Park, 139
Simple Sports, 87
Sivertson, Liz, 53
Sketchy Artist, The, 148
Ski Gull, 6
Slippery's Bar & Restaurant, 117, 119
The Smokin' Oak Rotisserie and Grill, 112

snowmobiling, 7, 25, 35, 38, 87, 146, 154, 180, 200
Soar with the Eagles, 119
Solglimt Bed & Breakfast, 56
Soo Line South Trail, 41
Southeastern Minnesota Visual Artists, 141
South Pier Inn on the Canal, 56
Spicer, MN, 178
Spicer's Ice Castle, 180
Spider Lake Lodge, 73
Spirit Mountain, 47
Spring Street Sports, 90
S.S. William A. Irvin, 50, 51
stained glass, 123
Staples Mill Antiques, 80
The Starkeller, 176
State Forest Campgrounds, 34
State School for Dependent and Neglected Children, 153
State School Orphanage Museum, 156
St. Cloud Convention and Visitors Bureau, 213
St. Cloud, MN, 184, 200, 213, 215
St. Croix ArtBarn, 65
St. Croix Boat and Packet Company, 81
St. Croix Falls, WI, 60, 64, 211
St. Croix National Riverway Visitor Center, 66
St Croix River, 38
St. Croix River, 38, 64, 69, 77, 81, 218
St. Croix River Inn, 66
St. Croix Scenic Byway, 40
St. Croix State Forest, 37
St. Croix State Park, 35, 37, 38
St. Croix Vineyards, 79
Stearns History Museum, 187
Stillwater Art Guild Gallery, 80
Stillwater, MN, 77, 211, 218
Stillwater/Oak Park Heights Convention and Visitors Bureau, 211
Stillwater Olive Oil Company, 81
Stillwater Trolley, 79

St. James Hotel, 112
St. John's Abbey Arboretum, 194
St. John's Bible project, 193
St. Joseph, MN, 191
St. Joseph Meat Market, 195
St. Louis River, 35, 42, 44, 46, 47
St. Mary's Hospital, main lobby, 140
St. Mary's University, 121
Stockholm, WI, 97, 99, 104
Stockholm Gardens, 100
Stockholm Pie General Store, 100
St. Olaf, 144
St. Olaf Christmas Festival, 144
St. Olaf College, 147
Stone Barn, The, 104
Stonehouse Coffee & Roastery, 14
Stone Mill Hotel & Suites, 133
Stoneware Cafe, 112
Stoney End harps, 110
Stout, 84
St. Peter Food Co-op & Deli, 164
St. Peter, MN, 158, 162, 165, 213, 218
St. Peter Tourism and Visitors Bureau, 212
Straight River, 154
Sugar Loaf, 125
Suncrest Gardens, 104
Superior, WI, 41
Superior Hiking Trail, 47
Suzette's Restaurant, 160
Swedish Gift Store, 67
Swedish Kontur, 163
Sweet River Cafe, 182
Swiftwater Adventures, 43
Sylvan Brewing, 133
Sylvan Park, 216

T
Tangled Up in Blue Restaurant, 64
Tanzenwald Brewing Company, 150
Tasty Pizza North, 18
Tavern on the Hill, 58
Taylors Falls, MN, 60

Taylors Falls Canoe and Kayak Rental, 63
Taylors Falls Recreation, 63
Teddy Bear Park, 79
Thaines River, 28
Theatre L'Homme Dieu, 201
Thielen Meats, 208
Third Street Tavern, 164
This Old Farm, 7
Thompson Hill, 44
Thompson Hill Welcome Center, 46
Three Sisters, 182
The Tilted Tiki Tropical Bar and
    Restaurant, 82
Tobies, 39
Toody's, 162
Touright Bicycle Shop, 207
Trailside Park, 216
Trail Town USA, 74
Train Bell Resort, 10
Traverse des Sioux, 162
Treasure Island Resort and Casino, 112
Treaty Site History Center, 163
Treelands on Chippewa Flowage, 74
Trego, WI, 72
Tremblay's Sweet Shop, 72
True North Basecamp, 34
Turning Waters Bed, Breakfast, and
    Brewery, 120
turtle races, 10
Turtle Town Books & Gifts, 12
Tutti Fruitti Restaurant and Market
    Farm, 195
Twigs Tavern and Grille, 142
Two Harbors, 51
Two Loons Gallery and Boutique, 49
Two Rivers Campground and Tubing, 207

U

Uff-Da Shop, 111
Unbound Adventures, 31
University of Wisconsin, 84
Up North Bike Rentals, 11
US-Dakota War, 164, 174

V

Va Bene Berarducci's Caffé, 55
Val's Rapid Serv, 189
Vee, Bobby, 175
Veigel's Kaiserhoff, 176
Veranda, The, 187
Veterans Evergreen Scenic Byway, 43
Vikre Distillery, 55
Villa Bellezza Winery, 101
Vino in the Valley, 100
Vintage, etc., 148
Vista Fleet Sightseeing & Dining
    Cruises, 52

W

Wabasha, MN, 114, 117, 153, 212, 215
Wabasha-Kellogg Area Chamber of
    Commerce, 117, 212
Wagner Apple Farm and Bakery, 160
Waldheim Resort, 40
Walker, MN, 7
Walleye Dan Guide Service, 11
Wanda Gag House, 175
Warden's House Museum, 80
Waterfront Bar and Grill, 87
waterskiing shows, 181
Water Street Inn, 83
Waterville, MN, 155
Watkins Administration Building, 123
Watkins Heritage Museum, 125
Welch Village Ski and Snowboard
    Area, 110
West's Hayward Dairy, 73
West Union, MN, 194
Westwood Café, 180
Whalan, MN, 132
Wheel Fun Rentals, 52
Whistle Stop Café, 39
Whitefish Chain of Lakes, 17, 22
Whitefish Golf Club, 17
White Horse Restaurant & Bar, 189
Whitewater State Park, 140
Whoopee John, 175

Wilder, Laura Ingalls, 101
Wilderness Walk Zoo, 72
Wild Mountain, 63
Wild Mountain Winery and Pizza, 63
Willard Munger Inn, 47
Willard Munger Trail, 38, 41, 47
William O'Brien State Park, 67
Willingers Golf Club, 147
Willmar Lakes Area Convention & Visitors
   Bureau, 213
Willmar, MN, 180
Willow River Campground, 40
Willow River Flowage, 40
Willows on the River, 117
Winds Steakhouse, 39
wine, 68, 79, 89, 124, 200, 217
Winehaven Winery and Vineyard, 68
Wings Over Alma Nature and Art
   Center, 103
Winona, MN, 121, 212, 215
Winona County History Center, 123
Winona State University, 121, 125, 215
Winona Visitor Center, 124, 212
Wisconsin Department of Natural
   Resources, xvi
Wisconsin Department of Tourism, xvi
Wisconsin Historical Society, xvi
Wisconsin Logging Museum, 93
Wissota High Shores Supper Club, 91
WNB Financial, 123
Woodhouse, Caroline, 86
Woodland Culture, 5
Worldloppet, 214
Wright, Frank Lloyd, 43

Y

Yellowstone Cheese, 90

Z

Zaiser's, 12
Zalesky Lake, 40
Zorbaz, 8, 14
Zorbaz on the Lake, 181
Zumbro River, 139, 140